Risk Quantification

For other titles in the Wiley Finance Series
please see www.wiley.com/finance

The authors would like to thank Bruno Bajard, David Breden, Gilles Deleuze
and Philippe Garnier for their contributions to chapters 3, 4 and 5.

Risk Quantification

Management, Diagnosis and Hedging

Laurent Condamin

Jean-Paul Louisot

Patrick Naïm

John Wiley & Sons, Ltd

Other Wiley Editorial Offices

John Wiley & Sons Inc., 111 River Street, Hoboken, NJ 07030, USA

Jossey-Bass, 989 Market Street, San Francisco, CA 94103-1741, USA

Wiley-VCH Verlag GmbH, Boschstr. 12, D-69469 Weinheim, Germany

John Wiley & Sons Australia Ltd, 42 McDougall Street, Milton, Queensland 4064, Australia

John Wiley & Sons (Asia) Pte Ltd, 2 Clementi Loop #02-01, Jin Xing Distripark, Singapore 129809

John Wiley & Sons Canada Ltd, 6045 Freemont Blvd, Mississauga, ONT, L5R 4J3, Canada

Wiley also publishes its books in a variety of electronic formats. Some content that appears
in print may not be available in electronic books.

Library of Congress Cataloging-in-Publication Data

Condamin, Laurent.
   Risk quantification : management, diagnosis & hedging / Laurent Condamin,
Jean-Paul Louisot, and Patrick Naïm.
        p.   cm.—(Wiley series in financial engineering)
      Includes bibliographical references and index.
      ISBN-13: 978-0-470-01907-8 (HB: alk. paper)
      ISBN-10: 0-470-01907-7 (HB : alk. paper)
      1. Risk management—Mathematical models.   I. Louisot, Jean-Paul.
   II. Naïm, Patrick.   III. Title.
   HD61.C65 2007
   658.15′5—dc22   2006033489

British Library Cataloguing in Publication Data

A catalogue record for this book is available from the British Library

ISBN 13 978-0-470-01907-8 (HB)
ISBN 10 0-470-01907-7 (HB)

Typeset in 10/12pt Times by TechBooks, New Delhi, India
Printed and bound in Great Britain by Antony Rowe Ltd, Chippenham, Wiltshire
This book is printed on acid-free paper responsibly manufactured from sustainable forestry
in which at least two trees are planted for each one used for paper production.

Contents

Foreword

This book offers a much needed contribution to the practice of risk management, more specifically the quantification.

Whereas more and more governance and ethics issues are brought to the forefront of any human activity, the reduction of uncertainties takes the front seat in their pursuit. Therefore, managing risks is the cornerstone to success in delivering the expected objective, uncertainties can be under control to the extent that all types of exposures are identified, quantified and mitigated. Seeking to measure risks evermore precisely, specifically those with dire consequences, is the path of development for this field the management science.

Starting from the current state of the art, the authors propose a new tool box combining qualitative and quantitative approaches, descriptive of the causes and conditional, formalising not only data but also knowledge. They lead the reader like a tutorial through an original path paved with the fundamentals of risk management and cindynics. Beyond the traditional elements of statistics, they incorporate in their models behavioural and systemic components. This allows to better determine the range of possible outcomes and to test extreme scenarios of different natures.

Thanks to their trainings, professional tracks, researches and international exposures, they offer a practical as well as prospective insight into risk quantification. They have integrated international compliance considerations, including what control authorities are currently designing for financial institutions, banks as well as insurance companies. They rest their expertise on practical situations, inspired by huge projects in existing institutions.

Even when it uses sophisticated concepts, their approach remains always operational, practical and understandable even by line managers with scant mathematical background. Furthermore, with proper parameters, it can be used in any field of human activity.

It would not surprise me if this approach was to become rapidly the reference for all those risk managers challenged by the measure and mitigation of risks in a rapidly evolving international economic environment in the beginning of this 21st century.

As a matter of fact, a better understanding of one's risks, a sound mitigation designed with this improved knowledge, and the development and placement of risk financing mechanisms and insurance covers all contribute to a reduction of the residual uncertainties. Even though risk cannot, and may be should not, be completely eliminated, all the tools that lead to some mitigation constitute a source of Sound Practice for risk management.

Let the authors be thanked by all those who wish to gain a better understanding of risk assessment!

Catherine Veret
Corporate Risk and Insurance Director – CM-CIC
Chair of RMSF-Risk Manager Sans Frontière

Introduction

"Without risk there is no advance" and *"The higher the risk the greater the reward"* are well established truisms. Both however can only succeed if the risk is *managed* and to do this effectively the risk must be quantified. This is relatively easy with respect to traditional insurable risks but presents significant challenges with respect to uninsurable exposures.

Risk management has been a significant part of the insurance industry for some fifty years, but in recent times it has developed a wider currency as an emerging management philosophy across the globe. It is a common sense methodology that allows a clear direction and pathway for decision making within an enterprise. Inherently culture and acceptance of risk varies from location to location.

Risk management practitioners are often their own worst enemy when it comes to championing the cultural change required in an organisation if it is to effectively manage its risks. Sadly, this is not a recent phenomenon as this quote from Felix Kloman, a long time commentator, prophet and philosopher on risk management and the management of risk. His comment in "The Revolt of the Risk Manager" published in Bests Review of October 1971 is as fresh and applicable today as when first published 35 years ago:

"Until the Risk Manager can be completely free of his real and psychological ties to insurance and the insurance industry, he will not be able to perform the risk management function."

The challenge facing the risk management practitioner of the 21st Century is not just breaking free of the mantra that risk management is all about insurance, and if we have insurance, then we have managed our risks, but rather being accepted as a provider of advice and service to the risk makers and the risk takers at all levels within the enterprise. It is the risk makers and the risk takers who must be the owners of risk and accountable for its effective management.

Professor Jean-Paul Louisot and his colleagues Laurent Condamin and Patrick Naim have clearly identified this challenge and this work takes the management of risk into the 21st Century by recognising that quantification is necessary to enable the most efficient risk control measures to be used at all levels within the organisation so as to ensure both optimum return on capital and reliable protection against bankruptcy. They address the challenge of balancing the level of operational loss control that must be implemented, as part of an overall risk control policy, with the corporate level that risk financing instruments must be selected and implemented as part of the overall financial strategy so as to best integrate all components of the portfolio of organizational risks, both threats and opportunities, systematic and non systematic risks.

Today's most vibrant industries and organisations understand that doing business in this dynamic marketplace demands highly trained and well-rounded workers equipped to handle the challenges of an ever-changing, fast-paced, business environment. This has encouraged the development and expansion of the skills that are needed to survive the complexity and uncertainty which is faced in an increasingly competitive world. The risk management practitioner of the future must facilitate the knowledge needs of directors, officers of companies, and government entities to ensure survival and sustainability.

Management of risk is an integral part of good management. It is an iterative process of continuous improvement that is best embedded into existing practices or business processes.

An effective risk management regime is a combination of the culture, processes and structures that are directed towards realising potential opportunities whilst managing adverse effects.

An organisations culture is the sum of its people, symbols, stories, business experiences, power structures, control systems, organisational structures, rituals and routines that when combined makes it unique.

Professor Jean-Paul Louisot and his colleagues Laurent Condamin and Patrick Naim are to be congratulated for this excellent work that equips the reader with a sound understanding of the tools available for the quantification of risk. They provide risk management practitioners with a most stimulating resource that will enable them to enter constructive discussions with management as well as consultants so as to ensure the decision maker is presented with soundly based options from which to choose.

Kevin W. Knight CPRM; Hon FRMIA; FIRM (UK)
Chairman ISO Working Group on Risk Management

1

Foundations

This chapter demonstrates the need for quantification in the definition of a risk management programme. In the first section, we introduce the foundations of risk management, based on the definition of an exposure: object of risk, peril, and consequences. We present the structure of the risk management decision process: (1) diagnosis of exposures, (2) risk treatment, and (3) audit and corrective actions. The design of a risk management program is the most significant part of step 2. Recent progresses in risk management show that this design should be addressed in a strategic, enterprise-wide manner, and therefore account for conflicting objectives and trade-offs. This means that risk cannot be limited any more to the downside effect but takes into account also the upside effect. The central objective of global risk management is enhancing opportunities while mitigating threats, i.e. driving up stockholders' value. *Therefore, risk quantification has become the cornerstone of effective strategic risk management.* In the second section, we propose a general approach for risk quantification: exposure quantifies the objects exposed, peril is quantified by a probability of occurrence, and consequences are quantified by a severity or impact, all these quantities being of course variable, and, most importantly, partially controllable.

RISK MANAGEMENT: PRINCIPLES AND PRACTICE

At a time when the world was fairly stable and the economy was based on scarce physical goods, purchasing insurance cover seemed the right answer to risk management: most of the perils were insurable, and the insurers acted as guardians of the mutualization process – eager to keep their costs down, they had even developed sophisticated ways to control those perils. Part of the deal in any insurance contract was to help the insured mitigate their risks so as to protect the overall mutuality. Furthermore, physical assets – plant and equipment – were essentials as customers were queuing to gobble up the production as soon as it was flowing again. Therefore, the insurer providing the capital necessary for rebuilding the production capacity was enough to pull the insured through a difficult time. However, even then, a more structured approach to risk management might have saved lives unduly wasted as they were altogether "cheap" for those liable for the deaths! Then in the 1960s and 1970s the pace started to accelerate, and in most of the developed world markets became mature. Marketing techniques became more sophisticated, creating differences and niches, while the offers among which customers could choose became increasingly differentiated. At the same time, services grew in importance, and producers became more and more intertwined. Other perils – economic (such as changes in customers' taste), natural (such as earthquake or flood), human (such as industrial intelligence or terrorism) – started to make evident the limitations of the "all insurance" approach. It was then that risk management started to emerge as a separate management field.

Furthermore, so many catastrophic events have taken place since the beginning of this century that it may seems frivolous to go back to 1 January, 2000 when the feared "Year 2000 bug" did not strike, or at least did not create the chaos that some predicted. However, in the developed world, whose economy is heavily dependent on computer energy, all the entities involved, both public and private, had invested heavily to amend their information systems to stand off any problems. In addition, crisis teams had been set up to correct any last minute incident.

We know now that a number of "small" incidents did occur but have been fended off thanks to the experience gained through the preparation process. On the other hand, at the same time, metropolitan France lived through one of its worst recorded natural disasters during the last week of 1999. Mother Nature reminded French executives and elected officials that risk always occurs with dire consequences where it is not expected, where it has not been identified and analyzed beforehand. The immediate reaction is to call upon insurers or the state authorities for remedies!

However, the final lesson came when it was learned that in most public utilities, providing electricity and railways travel in France, for example, the "2000 readiness crisis management team" was on hand to make immediate decisions that helped reduce the impact on the economic life of the two consecutive tornadoes that destroyed many electrical lines and stopped trains in the middle of nowhere!

In spite of the current evolution, the risk management responsibility is still limited to insurance administration in too many private as well as public entities. This limited view of the function is even further restricted when the talents are spent on long bidding processes or hard annual bargaining with the insurance carriers, with the help of an intermediary, in order to limit premium budget increase for the next period, or, even better, to obtain significant cuts with improved cover. Of course, many risk managers are in charge of claims management. This means they can, on a day-to-day basis, contribute to the speedy conclusion of substantial loss compensations from the insurer.

On the other hand, technological breakthrough and complex economical networks combine to create an ever-expanding web of risks bearing down on the organizations. Each organization is part of a long chain comprising suppliers and subcontractors as well as customers. Furthermore, it is not enough to identify the risks of a given entity; the analysis must be expanded to include regional, state and even continental considerations. Zero inventories (procurement management) and zero defects (quality management) have increased both the frequency and severity of risks while widening the uncertainties involved.

Finally, what was perceived in the early 1980s as a new economical crisis, a new stage in the development process, is now clearly turning into a major shift in the worldwide markets. The phenomenon is so far-reaching that some call it a "rite of passage" from one era (the industrial) to the next (the post-industrial).

Indeed, some say we are leaving the era of the management of opportunities to enter the era of the management of risks. Opportunities refer to favourable uncertainties, the chances of gains, whereas risks should refer to both "unfavourable" uncertainties, the chances of losses only, i.e. threats, and opportunities. Therefore risk management is really the management of all uncertainties.

As far as local authorities (in France municipalities, departments and regions) and their associated bodies (in France SIVOM, SIVU, district and urban communities, etc.) are concerned, they are still far from having a clear vision of the exposures they are facing, although the movement is gaining momentum.

When contrasted with private entities, they have specific features that must be taken into account; laws define their missions. While they are shielded from some of the market risks, they must fulfil their purpose in the public interest under any circumstances. This is why they must follow a different logic while they enjoy some immunity. In many countries, they are controlled by specific jurisdictions, like the CPA in the UK, the Regional Chambers of Accounts in France.

Local authority could benefit considerably from a "strategic approach to risk management" when considering the impact it could have, not only on the entity itself, its employees and its constituents, but also all the small and medium-sized businesses located within its jurisdiction. Over and above the traditional role of the risk manager professional as "keeper of the organization's own survival and well-being", in a local authority the risk manager could:

- Preserve and enhance public safety: plan for land occupation, industrial zoning, and public security (police), etc.
- Participate in recovering from natural and industrial catastrophes: responsibility for restoring public services, essential action plans for protecting people and property.
- Enhance economical well-being of the area: following a major catastrophe, the local authority may play a key role in the mending of the "economic cloth" or help to prevent a catastrophic impact by assisting small and medium-sized firms to develop some sort of risk management capacity.

In other words, the local authority may play a key role in transforming "reactive" risk management into "proactive" risk management in all economic actors under its jurisdiction; i.e. to turn risks into opportunities. In such a changing world, any student of risk management must therefore build his approach on a model that must remain his guideline throughout his study to ensure a certain degree of coherence.

But to enter the world of the management of uncertainties, a number of concepts must be defined as there is no clearly accepted language, outside of the ISO 73 document, not yet universally used and currently under revisions.

Definitions

The expression "risk management" is an open concept, still subject to a number of different interpretations, especially in Europe. Each professional has his own definition, based on his personal background and experience and the specifics of the firm's "culture" whose risks he manages. This reality does not enhance fruitful discussions between specialists. To make things worse, the same words are sometimes used to express different concepts.

Organization is the dynamic interaction of resources combined to achieve some defined permanent objectives. Resources can be broadly classified into five categories:

- *H*uman
- *T*echnical
- *I*nformation
- *P*artners (upstream, suppliers and subcontractors, and downstream, customers)
- *F*inancial

Risk (pure, speculative, and mixed) has many meanings and so we will try to avoid using it in this. However, it is so commonly found in risk management and insurance presentations that one must be aware of its possible meanings. There are basically four concepts described by this term:

- The uncertain event provoking the loss (see below "Peril").
- The resource exposed (see below "Object of risk").

- The financial consequences (see below "Loss").
- A global and subjective appreciation of the preceding factors (like the final comment by a field inspector in an insurance company after visiting an insured site: "good risk in its category").

The most common use refers to the first definition: the original cause of the loss suffered by the organization. In this sense, it is the uncertain event generating the loss that is the risk (*pure risk*) as opposed to those events that may result in either a gain or a loss (*speculative risk*). Those risks that cannot be easily classified in either category are called *mixed risks*.

In the original limited definition of the function, risk managers were only dealing with pure risk. Some use an even more restrictive term, i.e. "insurable risks". However, in this case, the risk manager is merely an insurance purchaser. It is clear that both adjectives are not equivalent.

The new "holistic" or "strategic" approach to risk management tends to blur this classification that for a long time was the cornerstone of risk management. Therefore, it is essential to introduce a further distinction.

Systematic and unsystematic risk

The systematic risk (nondiversifiable risk) is generated by nonprobabilistic events, i.e. that may happen simultaneously rather than due to pure chance. This means that the systematic risk does not lend itself to diversification, which requires constituting a large portfolio of uncorrelated risks. Losses generated by general economic conditions represent a systematic risk and all the economic actors suffer at the same time. When money markets tighten, interest rates increase for all organizations.

Typically these risks are not insurable. Imagine an insurance company offering a cover to protect the insured against a rise in interest rates. The company would not be able to build a diversified and balanced portfolio to mutualize this risk, as all their clients would be suffering losses simultaneously.

The unsystematic risk (diversifiable risk) is generated by a series of events the occurrence of which is fortuitous; they happen according to different probability distribution.

These risks are specific to each economic entity. For example, fire in a building is fortuitous and in a sufficiently diversified portfolio of buildings geographically spread, fires represent an unsystematic risk.

An insurance company can build a diversified portfolio by insuring a large number of buildings against fire provided they are sufficiently dispersed in a large territory. In using the impact of the law of large numbers, the insurance company is able to forecast with a good degree of precision the number, frequency, cost, and severity of the claims it will have to indemnify in a given insurance period. Therefore, it can offer the cover and compute a premium for each insured that will allow it to pay the total annual claims arising from fire in the insured buildings.[1]

Insurable risks

They are risks for which there exists an insurance market. That is to say, that some insurers are ready to grant cover in exchange for a premium (offer) acceptable for some potential buyers (demand). It would be of little interest to develop here a treaty on the elements that make a risk not only insurable and but also attractive for an insurance company to underwrite. The nonspecialist reader could easily read one of the many insurance initiation books. It suffices

---

[1] Cf. below: Insurable risks.

Table 1.1   Classification of perils

	Economic	Human		Natural	Industrial
		Intentional	*Unintentional*		
		Wise guy *Criminal activity*			
Endogenous					
Exogenous					

here to state that the insurance process is based on the existence of a mutualization opportunity. The basic insurance principle is to share among many the financial burden of indemnifying the few that incur a given loss. In other words, from an individual's perspective, an exceptional uncertain threatening financial loss (claim) is transformed into a certain recurring limited annual cash outflow (premium).

It would be clearly unacceptable to use an outsource concept like "insurable risks", to define the domain of action of the risk management professional. Clearly, such an approach would call for a constantly modified boundary by the conditional existence of an insurance market rather than by an actual in-house process of exposure identification and evaluation.

Object of risk is any resource used by the organization and that is "at risk", i.e. that an adverse uncertain event (see below "Peril") can damage, destroy or make unavailable for the organization's use for a period of time, or indefinitely.

This term "object of risk" has been preferred to other terms like resources because it is a clearly defined concept already in use in the risk management information system GESTRISK based on the specifications drafted by the French risk managers association. It must be understood in a broad sense to include not only tangible assets, but also intangible assets and activities, with the cash flow thus generated. Objects of risk can be classified into five categories, based on the five categories of resources identified above.

Peril is the uncertain event (i.e. with probability strictly more than 0 and less than 1) that would generate a loss to the organization when it happens (any time in the future). The loss results from damage or destruction or unavailability of a resource essential for an organization's normal (or nominal) operations. In order to develop appropriate risk control and financing strategies, the perils can be best classified according to three criteria summarized in Table 1.1.

This table may require some explanation.

For the first column:

Endogenous:	versus	**Exogenous:**
An event that is generated by the organization itself or within the limit of the activities it controls (a fire starting on the premises, the release of a dangerous chemical into the atmosphere, the manufacturing of a substandard product, etc.).		An event that is generated from outside the area under the organization controls (a strike in a nearby factory creating unrest and blocking access to an industrial estate).

For the first line:

Economic:	Human:	Natural:	Industrial:
Resulting from an unexpected change in market conditions in the economic environment of the organization generating a sudden and tight constraint on it.	Resulting from human action (a fire breaks out in a warehouse from sparks during ill-protected welding operations, robbery in a jeweller's shop, etc.).	The probability of the event and its occurrence results from the action of nature – acts of God – (earthquake, hurricane, etc.).	Resulting from human activities but is not directly linked to a human act, voluntary or involuntary, like a fire while a factory is empty, water damages, etc.

In the case of "human perils", it can be:

Unintentional:	Intentional:
Resulting from error or negligence in the performance of a task:	The act of a person modifying a system intentionally to "improve" it but failing to properly document the changes for the other users.

OR

Unintentional:	Intentional:
At the time of the loss (cigarette butt close to a flammable material)	The act is performed or abstained from with the intention of generating a loss to a third party or gaining an illegal benefit for the person. In most cases, it is a criminal activity under the law in most countries. It should be further split between:
Before the loss occurred (absence of proper lining in a basement built in an area subject to flooding)	*"For profit"* where the person or organization involved in the attack is pursuing their personal financial interest (industrial spying, for example, blackmail, etc.).
	"Not for profit" where the person or organization is seeking to further a cause or remedy a wrongdoing (arson by an ex-employee, terrorist attack, etc.). *The terrorist attacks on New York and Washington on 11 September 2001 have illustrated how both essential and difficult it is to manage this peril.*

One final distinction must be made between perils and hazards (a common phrase in English insurance policies). It is of particular significance when applied to liability exposures where the hazard is generated by the action increasing potential liabilities (manufacture of a faulty product), whereas the peril itself is the claim put forward by a third party suffering the damage.

Loss (financial) is the negative financial consequences for an organization hit by a peril. Insurers usually estimate it either as:

- A *maximum loss* – possible or probable – (two concepts well known to the insurers either as PML or EML), whereas in the USA there is a third concept to take into account – the level of protection, or
- An *annual aggregate loss* (i.e. expected value annual loss due to several events).

Exposure

Based on the concept defined here above, an exposure is fully described by three elements, i.e. the financial consequences of a peril striking a given resource of the organization. But that definition should be revisited to include opportunities as well as threats. That is to say:

- Object of risk (resource at risk) – the resource that may be impacted by the outcome.
- Event (peril) – the random event that may impact positively or negatively the resource.
- Consequences on objectives (financial and other consequences) – as far as possible, they should be quantified in monetary terms, but some social and environmental impacts cannot always be translated into hard money.

Management

This is the term used to refer to the actions within an organization aimed at the following results:

- Plan (the team work)
- Organize (the team resources)
- Lead and motivate (team)
- Control and audit performance

This definition clearly positions the risk manager as a "manager" in charge of a budget and leader of a team. He must also report to an executive, justify the costs involved, and prove the efficiency of his operation, just like any other manager in the organization.

Risk management

Risk management is a continuous process to insure that proper consideration is given to uncertainty in all decisions made within the organization and that the proper documentation is kept for internal and external controls.

It comprises three steps: diagnosis of exposures, treatment of risk and audit of the risk management programmes.

> *Risk management is a continuous process for making and carrying out decisions that will reduce to an acceptable level the impact or uncertainties of the exposures bearing on an entity, i.e. within the risk appetite of the organization balancing opportunities and threats.*
> *The decision process is divided into three steps. Implementing these decisions requires each practitioner to ensure proper management.*

This definition clearly refers to an essential part of sound risk management, the continuous feedback loop. The "audit step" includes not only outside validation by a third party but also monitoring and reporting, i.e. understanding and tracking the risk decisions that have been made and how they relate to the objectives that have been set forth and also how they are implemented and reviewed periodically to ensure continuous pertinence with the evolution or the internal and external contexts as well as the organisation's own objectives.

Risk management objectives

An organization has been defined as a dynamic combination of resources organized to reach a set of goals and missions. Therefore, the definition of these objectives is a key element of any organization management.

In any event, economic efficiency will dictate the allocation of resources in the most economical way, i.e. to reach the most ambitious goal with the limited amount of resources available. This is the founding principle of the liberal economy system.

Under these conditions, it is clear that the unavailability of all or part of a given resource could prevent the organization from reaching its goals. The reasons for this "nonavailability" of resources include the occurrence of perils, or uncertain "accidental" events.

Within this framework, the objective of the risk management process can be defined as *the availability, under any set of circumstances, of the resources at a level compatible with the fundamental objectives of the organization*. This level can be refered to as "vital".

As a corollary, the risk manager must reach this goal while using as few resources as possible. Then again, a closer look at the organization's objectives is necessary to reach an operational definition of the goal of risk management.

Organizational objectives

The word organization is preferable to the more economic term of the firm so long as the risk management process can be applied not only to a profit seeking entity (firm) but also to a nonprofit organization and a public entity as well as a public or private hospital.

Individual organizations' goals may vary widely in content and wording; however, they can be usually classified into three broad categories.

Economic efficiency   This concept can be expressed in a number of ways but it is always a variation on the central theme of the liberal economy system; i.e. the maximization of profit. Clearly for publicly traded companies as well as companies where ownership is distinct from management, the current expression would be creating long-term stockholder value which will have direct consequences for the "post-event objectives" below.

For a nonprofit organization it amounts to reaching the goals with the minimum possible resources or the maximum output for a given level of resources.

In public entities, like local government, the goal is always to minimize budget requirements to meet the constituents' basic needs. At a governmental level, a goal could be to minimize the defence budget while still providing for an adequate level of protection in times of both peace and war.

Environmental issues   These focus on protecting the quality of the environment (air, water, and soil) and consist in essence of:

- Complying with legal and statutory obligations.
- Protecting the elements of the biosphere (environment in the traditional sense).
- Respecting the cultural traditions in all locations.

Ethics and good citizenship   This encompasses a number of nonfinancial issues that executives must take into consideration in making decisions also refered to a "enterprise social responsibility": social improvements, humanitarian conduct, and artistic support. Among others:

- Artistic donations.
- Humanitarian foundations.
- Actions to improve life conditions.

Functional objectives   The main departments of the organization are centred on the five classes of resource as listed above, i.e.:

- *H*uman (human resources VP)
- *T*echnical (operations VP)
- *I*nformation (information system VP or C.I.O.)
- *P*artners (marketing VP and purchasing or logistic VP)
- *F*inancial (CFO)

The main objectives of the organization (*permanent goals*) can be reached only if the main functions reached their subobjectives (*critical goals for the CEO*). More specifically the specific role of the finance director is to find the financial resources needed for the organization's smooth operation (*cash and fund management*) in the most favourable conditions (*cost of capital*).

Operational objectives (pre-event and post-event objectives)

In risk management manuals, objectives are often referred to as pre-loss and post-loss. This situation is due to the impact of the insurance terminology on risk management practices but the term event should always be preferred. On the other hand on a long-term vision the word "dysfunction" would encompass a broader spectrum of possibilities.

Risk management objectives have been derived traditionally from the objectives of the major departments that risk management is meant to assist in coping with their specific exposures.

This could be summarized in one sentence: *the risk manager's job is to ensure that, in any emergency situation, the organization has at its disposal adequate resources to allow it to attain its objectives under even the most strenuous circumstances.*

Among the resources that will be needed to get through the difficult phase is hard cash to face increased expenses and/or decreased revenues following the event. It is often the risk manager's direct responsibility to ensure that funds are available in the quantity and quality required.

More specifically, it is appropriate to distinguish pre-event and post-event objectives. If risk management is about planning ahead to reduce the uncertainties of the future, then it should be concerned in priority with post-event objectives.

Post-event objectives (rupture in the production process)   In any case, the minimum objective will be the organization's survival. However, for each of the four main classes of resources a continuum of objectives may be derived from the basic survival:

- *Technical, information and commercial*: continuity of operations is in fact a very demanding objective. However, it is inescapable sometimes in an industry where public health and safety is at stake, or permanence in a market is a prerequisite to stay in business. One may think of the registrar office in a municipality, the primary school system, or in healthcare of the electricity supply for an operating theatre. The continuum is based on the maximum downtime allowed. Clearly the shorter it is, the most expensive the investment in risk control. Therefore it is very important to measure with great care the "acceptable downtime".
- *Financial*: beyond survival, the financial objectives can be classified in increasing constraint order.
  - *No loss*: keep the organization in the "black" even in the year in which the loss occurs.
  - *Maintain profit level*: the "average" profit level achieved in the past is maintained even when the loss occurs.
  - *Sustain growth*: the growth is maintained throughout the period whatever happens.
  When a very large public holds the company stocks, the firm's financial results are essential for its enduring independence. Sudden variation in the earnings per share or dividend can be heavily penalized at the stock exchange with sharp declines in share prices. This may attract raiders and endanger also the executives' jobs! The finance theory would show that the long-term growth rate is a key to the profit learnings ratio.
- *Humanitarian*: these goals encompass all the negative impacts that the organization's activities may have on its socio-economic and cultural environment. This includes suppliers and subcontractors, customers, local communities and the labour force.

Pre-event objectives (economic efficiency)   Before the events' occurrence, it is clear that the risk management goal will be centred on economic efficiency, i.e. the risk management programme must be as lean as possible while providing for the completion of the post-event objectives assigned to it.

Other significant objectives

- *Reduce uncertainties*, i.e. the variability (standard deviation) of the financial results to a level compatible with top management "appetite for risk" (some say that the risk manager's job is to "buy his boss a good night's sleep").
- *Abide by the common laws and all the statutory laws* that apply to the organization's activities and locations.
- *Harmony with the "society" goals*: it can be useful to remember that the society or community goals can be reflected at two levels:
  - The *laws* that represent the wishes of the people through the electoral bodies representing them (legislative power).
  - *Ethic and "good citizenship"* for which the strict adherence to the law is not enough and the organization must strive at anticipating the cultural and humanitarian expectations of the society.

Conflict between objectives
It is easy to understand, with no need for lengthy explanations, that as one escalates along the continuum of post-event objectives, one will draw more on the financial resources of the organization and therefore will tend to increase, rather than decrease, the overall cost of risk.

Risk management decision process

The analytical approach to managing risks is defined through a matrix to reflect the dual activity of the risk manager practitioner:

- A manager, as such, must go through the managing process of planning, organizing, leading, and controlling (horizontal axis).
- A decider going through the three steps routine of the risk management decision process as described below (vertical axis).

Step 1–Diagnosis of exposures

The diagnosis of exposures cannot be conducted without a clear understanding of the organization's goals and strategy. A systems approach to risk analysis allows the risk manager to define a portfolio of exposures for the firm and to draft a risk map to illustrate the major risks that should draw top management's attention. The objectives and mission of the organization should also be subjected to a risk analysis, in light of the ethics and values publicly announced by the organization and in the light of public beliefs.

Exposure identification is the single most vital part of the risk management process; it consists of listing the exposure "portfolio" of the organization in terms of resources and the perils that may affect them. The analysis is aimed at measuring the probable or possible impacts on the organization of each exposure in terms of probability and severity. The financial consequences should have priority but others like social, human, and environmental should also be factored into the best of the ability. The assessment phase will take into account the existing treatment mechanisms to measure their efficiency and assess further improvements needed.

Actually, once an exposure is recognized, uncertainty is somewhat reduced as a volatility can be assessed and a problem once identified can lead to some kind of solution. The "hidden exposure" is always more threatening as, evidently, when it strikes, there is no plan to cope with it, no risk management technique to either reduce the consequences or finance them.

The risk management practitioner can use a number of tools during the investigation process, and these are listed below. However, tools without a method lead nowhere and we will describe one such method for using properly all the tools available. The one we have chosen is called "risk centres".

Identification tools   It is all too obvious that, for a given organization, exposure identification requires a thorough understanding of both the organization itself, for endogenous perils, and of its environments, for exogenous perils. The term environment refers here not only to the economic partners of the organization, the entities it is trading with. It encompasses the overall economy, the social, legal, and cultural components as well.

Therefore, the risk identification tools are instruments to describe and analyze the organization and its environments.

- Financial and accounting records:
  These are key to understanding what the main features of an organization are. They consist of the following documents.
  - The *balance sheet* gives a first approach to the physical assets held by the organization and on the liability side; it may be possible to spot any outstanding liability stemming from that exposure. It gives also a hint to the current situation of the organization, the main ratios, where it stands in working capital and debt to equity ratio.
  - The *income statement* gives an idea of the profitability of the organization, its main profit centre and their contribution to the profits (a key to evaluating losses of revenues).
  - The *sources and uses of funds statement* identifies the main flow of long-term funds and the congruence between sources and uses.
  - The *annual report* contains also other valuable information such as the auditors' report, lease equipment, some contracts, and human resources status.
- Marketing, purchasing and other documents:
  All documents given to customers, including packaging and user's notice may be instrumental in understanding potential product liabilities. Procedure manuals can illustrate potential defects in the administrative processes leading to quality problems, etc. Reading union panels may point to possible safety questions and other morale questions raised by the workers' representatives. Special attention must be given to all contractual agreements as they bring potential liabilities.
- Production and flow charts:
  These identify the flows of goods and services within the organization and with its main economic partners, both up-and downstream, suppliers and customers. They help in identifying bottlenecks and locating the weaknesses in the logistics or distribution network.
- Standards questionnaires:
  They are sometimes called also "checklists"; they were formerly regarded mainly as guidelines for the insurance underwriters. If limited to a short-list of questions, they can offer the newly appointed or assigned risk management professional a quick approach to all the sites from his office. Each operational manager answers the same set of questions, which allows for a quick consistent overview.
  Their limit is twofold. Being "standards", they are not always well adapted to the specifics of a given organization, or of each site. If they are designed to be broad in scope, both for resources and perils, they could be long and fastidious. But the operational managers might not take the time to answer.
  On the other hand, often they emanate from insurers. Therefore, their focus is mostly on "insurable risks" that may not be the most serious facing a given organization. In that case, they are based either on the covers generally granted or on the exclusion of the "all risks" policies.
- Historical data and scenario analysis:
  As illustrated in the recent book by Peter L. Bernstein,[2] the first breakthrough in modern management dates from the day when Pascal established the founding stone for what was to become modern statistics. Trying to establish a trend for the future from the experience

---

[2] Bernstein, Peter L. 1996. *Against the Gods. The Remarkable Story of Risk*, John Wiley & Sons, Inc., New York.

of the past was the first break from the "fear of the gods", the first step towards modern management.

The use of historical data, i.e. past losses experience, of a given organization remains the first source for establishing forecast as to the level of losses for the years to come. However, there are serious limits to the use of probability or trending, the first being to have a sufficient number of adequate data (law of the large numbers) and the second the underlying hypothesis calling for a stable environment (probability) or a stable evolution of the environment (trend analysis).

Therefore, it is clear that historical data are most useful for large organizations and high frequency losses, which lend themselves to probability laws. Such is not the case for high severity, low frequency losses. For this category, it is possible to tap from others' experience through statistics gathered by the insurers and consolidated by their professional associations.

It is also important to analyze the chain of events that led to losses or potential losses with techniques like fault tree analysis.

- Internal and external experts:
Risk managers are necessarily generalists with some knowledge of all the activities in which the organization engages. Conversely, they cannot be experts in all these varied areas and therefore must rely occasionally on experts' opinion.

They may be specialists in given scientific or technical fields but also in financial matters (bankers or financial institutions), insurance (brokers, underwriters, reinsurers) or legal (lawyers). In some cases, psychologists or sociologists may prove useful to understand specific populations or reaction under stress, for example.

- Site inspection (visit):
However, direct contact with operational mangers on their sites cannot be replaced by "homework". The risk management professional has a specific perception for risks and a fresh look at things that may allow for the unearthing of specific exposure going otherwise unnoticed.

Risk centres method   The various tools listed above provide the risk management professional with a general idea of the main exposures that the entity is confronted with. However, this paperwork is not enough and must be enhanced by visits to the various sites of the entity. This must be done in a systemic and logical manner.

Practically, each consultant has developed a method for identifying and analyzing clients' exposures. However, few have published it in an orderly fashion. The method developed here is one of the few "public" views. First published by Yves Maquet,[3] a consultant, it is reproduced here with substantial changes introduced by the authors.

This method is built upon a model that views the entity as a dynamic combination of five main categories of resources to reach a goal, or a set of goals, assigned to the board of directors by the stockholders' annual meeting. The five categories of resources are the following for this model:

- H = human: beware, not all human resources are "employees".
- T = technical: here limited to the plant and equipment under the control of the organization itself, whether owned, leased or under custody and care.

---

[3] Maquet, Yves 1991. *Des Priues d'assurance an financement des risques*, Bruglant, Brussds.

- I = information: all information flows within the organization as well as those exchanges with all its socio-economic partners, whether stored or processed, be they computerized or not.
- P = partners: all the goods and services exchanged with the partners both upstream (suppliers and subcontractors) and downstream (customers and clients) but also administrations and consumers' unions, etc.
- F = financial: all financial flows running through the organization. In a free market economic model it represents the reverse flow of goods and services with its natural and necessary "accumulation" to allow a correct operation of the "economic pump".

In this approach, we are still concerned with reaching goals and objectives. Losses are only seen in light of their impact on these goals and objectives. An exposure is worth consideration only insofar as it threatens those goals.

Thus the risk centre method stems from a strategic vision with success as the only acceptable outcome. But success for the whole organization relies on the individual success of each manager. Thus the entity, or system, is divided into subsystems, or risk centres, using its reporting hierarchy as a guideline.

One must only remember that a "permanent" objective of a manager is divided into as many critical objectives as he has people reporting to him. The idea being that if all of these critical objectives are not met, the manager will not be able to meet his own permanent objectives. The permanent objective of the manager is a critical objective for his boss, and conversely, all his critical objectives are permanent objectives of his subordinates.

Hence, following down the lines of authorities in a given organization, it can be split into as many small entities as necessary. These small or "individual" firms represent the "risk centres".

Where should the process stop? Each individual risk centre must still be a "living entity" with all five classes of resources and a clearly defined objective necessary to the overall firm objectives. It is a "monocellular" firm in which the "boss", the manager, can grasp the frontier of his domain and thus has a good vision of his exposures while still enjoying a degree of freedom to decide how best to manage his "micro business".

In fact, the risk centre method is one more application of a universal approach to "big problems", often used in physics and mathematics. A problem that is too big and unmanageable should be split into as many small problems as necessary to be manageable.

The various identification tools are then used to establish a diagnosis of the exposures facing each individual risk centre. However, at this stage, the interview with the risk centre manager will play an essential part in the success of the process. As it is a time-consuming process, the centres should be ranked on the basis of their contribution to the overall goals of the organization, or better even their capacity at ruining the chances of reaching those goals. Therefore, an overview of the main exposures should be developed as early as possible in the risk management process, if only to establish a list of priorities for the risk manager's efforts.

The way to conduct such an interview with the risk centre manager is summarized in Table 1.2.

Questions 1 and 2 aim at evaluating the manager's understanding of the expectation of his superiors, his position in the overall organization and the resources he uses to achieve his own missions. Questions 3 and 4 try to develop a contingency planning specific for the centre.

Question 3 puts the manager in an impossible situation where he would not have access to a vital resource, plant, and equipment or personnel. He is then threatened in his inner security

Table 1.2   Interview with a risk centre manager (Example)

Question 1–Goals and Objectives
What are the goals and objectives, the missions of your service or department?

Question 2–Resources
- What is your organization?
- What are your personnel, your office space, work area tools and equipment?
- Where do your products, your raw materials, your information come from?
- Where do you send your production, information?
- What means of communication do you use?

Question 3–Key Scenarios
Assume your entire location burns down tonight, without injuring any of your employees. *Tomorrow morning when your employees report to work, how do you manage to start production again?*

Assume now, on the contrary, that you have no workers reporting to work tomorrow morning (strike, no access open, etc.) while your plant is intact.
How do you manage to start production under these circumstances?

Clearly the purpose of these questions is to assess what resources are "vital", and which are "additional" when the question is survival of the organization under extreme duress . Therefore, the questions assume total lack of one of the resources.

Question 4–How Do You Propose To Fend Off These Exposures
- Now
- pre-event: prevention/reduction
- Later
- post-event: survival or contingency planning, crisis management

and forced to imagine a disaster from which to recover. This artificial stress may bring out some creative solutions to be used in the crisis management manual.

Question 4 aims at designing a new harmony between objective and resources that was temporarily destroyed by the unfortunate scenario. The question is a management one where the peril is secondary and the absence of the resource for whatever cause is the central idea. Insurance and classical risk controls are not essential here. The concept of "vital" resources refers to those resources just barely sufficient to live temporarily through a difficult time.

The next step consists of taking into account the difficulties in implementing different loss control measures than nobody knows better than the centre's manager himself. He, more than anybody else, can determine what level of tolerance for uncertainty and the level of mishap that is acceptable for his "constituencies". It is even possible that, with a good risk mapping, the manager will be able to reallocate his resources before the occurrence of any traumatic experience. He could thus avoid any catastrophic consequence (loss reduction) and provide for the contingency planning to be implemented in case of an emergency to preserve as far as possible the goals assigned to him by the organization (survival planning). Most of the time the investment cost involved will prove to be limited as the field manager will know where to go to get the most cost-efficient "alternative resource". He job is to know all the threads of his trade.

However, this microscopic approach at the "risk centre" level is not sufficient, and it is essential to have a broader view, a system's approach that will include the relationship between all the risk centres, their interaction with each other, and their environment(s). The overall planning, the consolidation process, requires an understanding of the organization and of its long-term strategy that is conceivable only at the executive level.

It is clear that this process will follow the hierarchical pyramid from bottom to top. When a risk centre manager reaches the limits of his autonomy the ball must be passed on to the next level of management up to the CEO or the executive board. The risk manager must be a facilitator along this process and he is in charge of the presentation of the final picture to the board, laying down the options open for decisions.

Of course, along that line, the risk mapping is reduced to the essential issues, those exposures that could send the organization to the rocks.

No process can be totally exhaustive, however qualified are the persons in charge. It is there-fore always necessary that a review be done regularly, whenever possible by outside expertise (consultant, internal audit, peer review). This is implied in step 3 of the risk management decision process. The "circle of risk management" may prove useful at this stage.

Step 2–Risk treatment

The loss control aspect of the risk mediation process is challenged to transcend traditional hazards to cover all types of potential losses: legal, procurement, production, markets, partners' and contractual. The risk financing portion of mitigation must be integrated in a global finance strategy – not only to benefit from the new alternative risk transfer offerings but also because it simply makes sense. With all risks in the same portfolio, the financing possibilities open up. Modern risk financing is no longer a simple dosage between retention and transfer, i.e. buying insurance with different levels of deductible, per occurrence or per accumulation over a period.

Some economists even theorize that insurance mechanisms may be rejected entirely by large concerns (where it is viewed as economically inefficient) since each individual stockholder can mitigate risks through a balanced portfolio diversification. This theoretical approach, however, does not take into account the fact that small investors cannot sufficiently diversify. And it negates the social efficiency of insurance mechanisms. While reducing profit fluctuations induced by large losses, insurance may protect employment as well as the assets of small investors. (The choice of systematic insurance transfer should be revisited, however, for large holding companies, especially in a time when the price of insurance is experiencing manifold increases.)

In order to effectively treat all the exposures identified and analyzed during the diagnosis process, the first step is to proceed with as wide a check as possible of all measures that could be applied to the situation. In other terms, what instruments of loss control or loss financing could be included in a risk management programme acceptable to top management, fulfilling the goals and objectives of the organization and reasonably easy to implement by all those involved.

Review of risk management alternatives (step 2.1)   For each exposure, there should be an exhaustive "brainstorming" session to insure that no stone remains unturned. For the risk management professional, hired as a consultant to audit a risk management department, the most striking defect is the failure to use one's imagination to find new solutions to new risks. It seems that most risk managers stick to old recipes. For each instrument that could be used, their impact on reducing long-term uncertainties should be measured against their cost.

The risk management professional must always keep in mind that he has two sets of tools, loss control and loss financing:

- Loss control techniques:
  These techniques are to be planned ahead, before any event causing loss has occurred. However, some are activated at all times (pre-loss measures) or only at the time of the event or after (post-loss measures). They are all aimed at reducing the economical impact of adverse events on the organization. Basically, they reduce one of the two major components of the economical consequences: Frequency (or probability) and Severity.

  The techniques aiming at reducing Frequency are broadly classified under the term *"loss prevention"*: they prevent accidents from occurring (*by acting on the chain of event, or causes, leading to them*).

  The techniques aiming at reducing Severity are broadly classified under the term *"loss reduction"*: they prevent accidents from spreading damaging effects (*by acting on the chain of event increasing the losses, or consequences, after they occur*).

- Risk financing techniques:
  Except under some rare and specific circumstances listed in Chapter 2, loss control techniques do not reduce the risk to Zero. Therefore, the occurrence a sizeable loss remains a possibility that cannot be ignored due to the potentially severe impact it might have on the organization's current flows of cash. It is therefore mandatory for the organization to establish some kind of "safe source of cash" to be tapped under specific duress.

  As is described further in step 4, funds may come from within the organization itself or from without. The first case is called Retention, the second Transfer. Actually, theses crude definitions will be reviewed to reflect more recent developments in risk management. More specifically, in risk financing, the actual source of funds at the time of the claim (or need) is less important than who bears the uncertainties (the risk) to decide whether the programme is retention or transfer.

Risk management programme development and approval (step 2.2)   Organizational goals are at the heart of modern risk management, therefore the definition based on "success" is the right one: an exposure, a risk, is a potential chain of event or scenario that could prevent the organization from reaching its goals. This stresses that designing an appropriate risk management programme will always mean designing a programme that best allows the permanent or long-term goals to be reached.

In other terms there can be no "best risk management programme" without a direct reference to long-term organizational goals, but also each departmental goal. At this stage, it is essential to have a comprehensive or global approach. There are different words used to describe it: holistic (France), integrated (UK) or enterprise (USA). Strategic risk management is of the essence of any strategy. Some authors have coined an expression to refer to a traditional "pure" risk or "insurable" risk approach naming it "suboptimal risk management".

Therefore, the risk management mission is to guarantee the long-term "safety" or achievement of the organization's goals. That is why some use the phrase "strategic risk planning" rather than "risk management programme" which may have too narrow a connotation (limited to pure risk).

At the end of the day, the final say in such an important matter has to rest with the board of directors whose job is to make sure that top management goals are aligned with the shareholders' objectives, with due consideration given to other stakeholders' interest in order not to jeopardize the company's social licence to operate. In simple terms, it is the board that must set the "risk appetite" of the company and communicate it in operational terms for all in charge of implementing the risk management strategy.

Risk management programme implementation (step 2.3)   The circle of risk management (see below) represented 25-year-old breakthrough that led the risk management professional out of "insurance manager duties". It is like an orientation table for any risk manager. Placed at the centre, he has a key to understand his organization's risk management issues and responsibility.

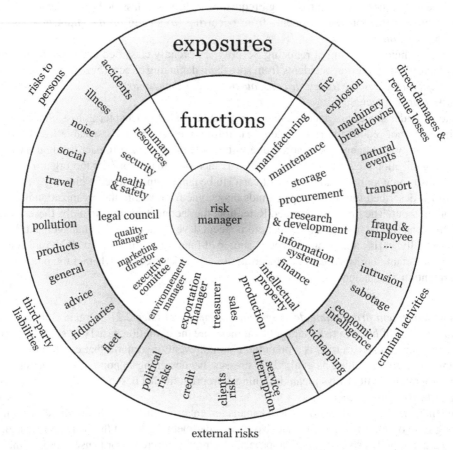

Circle of risk management

One of the primary concerns of risk management professionals is that they usually have a limited role in the actual implementation of the programme they have designed. In most cases, they only implement the global financing programmes. And even in that area, their direct implication is still too often limited to buying insurance covers.

However, this aspect should not be underestimated; the insurance budget in a large international conglomerate can be very substantial, even in excess of one billion euros. When they get involved in the management of captive insurance or reinsurance they are obviously more visible to top management due to the investment funds involved with the reserving practices.

For all the other elements of the risk management programme, dealing with organization, production facilities, products and distribution channels, suppliers, and subcontractors, the risk manager is only the coordination point. He is more in the position of an internal consultant and must be able to communicate and convince the managers. At the previous stage, the need to consolidate in one overall strategic risk management programme has also been stressed.

A comprehensive and rational risk management programme will aim at reaching the overall goals of the organization. Those who benefit from such an approach are not always those who have to pay the costs. Therefore, one of the keys to the successful implementation of all risk management programmes is the management costs allocation system. It must "naturally" drive the operational managers to implement at their level all the investments and the daily chores needed for a complete implementation. These points will be addressed again further.

Step 3–Audit and corrective actions

Top executives' interest in the audit process extends to the risk management sphere, and corporate governance issues have made this step a critical aspect of extended risk management. A case could be made for the internal auditor to be the natural owner of this step, but this remains an open debate.

However, the audit step of the risk management process cannot be performed only by a third party, be it internal or external; it is essential that all the operational managers in charge of managing the risks linked with their activity perform also the self-assessment audit with the assistance of the risk management professional. This monitoring and reporting exercise will allow for a proper documentation of the activities involved with managing risks and ensuring that the decisions have been made rationally taking into account the objectives and limitations of the organization, as well as the priorities set by top management and the board. Thus the continuous feedback loop will be effectively closed allowing for a proper evaluation of the changes in the organization's internal and external context as well as the evolution in the company's goals to adapt to stockholders' owners' social and economical circumstances. The risk register recommended by the Australian Standards is a good tool for assigning responsibility and following the risk management strategy implementation.

There is, however, a trend for internal auditors (encouraged by external audit firms ready to assist with their consulting branch) to go beyond the auditing phase and pose as the legitimate owner of the entire risk management strategy of the firm. Thus, the risk manager may be reduced to insurance buying and managing, or made redundant through a complete outsourcing of risk management competencies. Regardless of which department is in charge of the process, it should always be completed with the help and support of the risk management team. If the risk manager is an "internal consultant" with no hierarchical authority to implement most of the approved programmes, then he must directly, or through an internal audit department, make sure that the programme is not only fully implemented but also proves to be efficient in reaching the assigned goals.

The word "audit" is indeed appropriate at this stage. However, the word "diagnosis" is preferred for the first step where "audit" is still too often used. An "audit process" aims at comparing an ideal situation with the reality found. Reality is contrasted with a set of standards, both qualitative and quantitative and the sources for the differences are sought to explain and correct the situation when needed.

For those not familiar with audit processes, it is important to remember that there are essentially two classes of standards:

- *Result standards:* they help measure the progress made over a given period when comparing the standard at the end of the period with
  - Beginning levels,
  - Desired ending levels,
  - Results for the main competitors (benchmarking).
- *Activity standards:* they measure the efforts deployed during the period without references to the results achieved.

The main benefit of using such a classification to measure the efficiency of the risk management department is that it is parallel to those used when auditing any department in an organization.

However, one must always keep in mind that it is much more reliable to use such an approach constantly for "frequency exposures" where it is relatively easy and safe to measure the improvements, the reduced number of incidents and the reduced overall "costs of risk". Such is not the case with "severity exposures" where efficiency is hard to trace as costs may be relatively "hard numbers" whereas the results may require a long period to be evaluated.

Let us illustrate briefly. Even in the wake of such ecological catastrophes as the Exxon Valdez and more recently the Erika, some challenges still remain. Tankers pay dues in the harbours on the basis of their draft and double-hulled tankers are penalized as they can carry less crude oil due to the internal "skin"! Even though new tankers have to be double skinned, some of the old ones, which are not, are still allowed to sail until phased out.

STATE OF THE ART AND THE TRENDS IN RISK MANAGEMENT

Risk profile, risk map or risk matrix

Prior to examining more closely the different techniques to mediate risks, it is essential to stress again that risk management is an "economic function" and that the impact is usually measured on the basis of two parameters. In the long run, the cost is measured by the expected value:

$$\text{Frequency} \times \text{Severity}$$

However, using the multiplication sign is potentially misleading, as, in a human time scale, this may be totally irrelevant as a basis for decision making. It is more proper to use the vector (F, S) to draw a curve that will separate, for each organization, each board of directors, the acceptable and the unacceptable. In fact bearing in mind the definition of risk as the uncertainty of the outcome of a situation, or the spread of result, one could argue that the vector to consider has three dimensions (F, S, σ) where σ is the standard deviation of the annual cost.

On the other hand, the product $(F \times S)$ can be used as a reliable measure of the expected cost of risk for the "frequency" exposure class where the probability of occurrence is such that the law of large numbers applies: thus the organization can budget its expenses on the basis of the expected value of the cost of risk (see D below).

As a conclusion from an exposure diagnosis process, the exposures of a given organization could be summarized in a four quadrant matrix where both frequency and severity are qualified as "high" or "low". *Each organization has to decide for itself what it will call "high" and what it will accept as "low" based on a number of considerations among which are financial strength, stability of cash flows, profits levels and stability, and other subjective elements.*

The four quadrants can be read as follows:

Table 1.3   Simplified risk matrix

Severity	Frequency	
	Low	High
Low	(A)	(C)
High	(D)	(B)

- (A) – Low frequency and severity: these are exposures that have practically no significant impact on the profits. They can be dealt with if and when they occur, as the cash in hand is sufficient to take care of them. They can be practically ignored and do not require any monitoring.
- (B) – High frequency and Severity: these are exposures that no organization should allow to exist. They are typically treated by the risk "avoidance" or "suppression" techniques: do not engage in such a project or get out of it as fast as possible when identified. These extreme situations are rare and should not happen when the risk manager is taken on board any project team very early in the process.

For all practical reasons, the risk manager domain is restricted to the two last quadrants.

- (C) – High frequency, low severity: as mentioned above, this is an area where the laws of statistics can apply even within the limits of the organization. There is enough "risk mutualization" to forecast with a "reasonable" degree of precision the losses for next year based on the past experience and the likely evolution. Let us say that the forecast can be held true within a range that does not interfere seriously with the budgeting process.

However, this implies that the organization has collected and recorded reasonably dependable statistical data on past losses as a basis for forecasting future losses and measuring the probable impact of proposed loss control measures.

In effect, this quadrant contains not so much "risks" as costs to be contained and budgeted as accurately as possible. However, it must be kept in mind that:

- "Loss prevention" (reducing the frequency or probability of a loss) measures have both immediate and long-term costs for the organization,
- Claims management is crucial for cost monitoring and that, if no insurance cover is purchased where the insurer does it within the "insurance premium", the organization will incur costs if it is done internally or fees if it is outsourced from a third party,
- All scenarios should be analyzed including the chances for a very bad year with exceptional frequency and/or severity to place an unbearable burden on the organization.

On the whole, this class of exposure lends itself well to retention financing where a first line can even be budgeted and charged against current cash flows with no specific exceptional risk financing mechanisms.

- (D) – Low frequency, high severity: this is the quadrant where the risk management professional expertise is most essential. Expected losses in the long run may require a century or a millennium time span to have any meaning. Therefore, this is utterly incompatible with the framework of a human organization. Should the event take place, the consequences for the organization are such that it cannot start up again without a massive injection of external funds. This is one of the main functions of the insurance community, to bring in fresh capital at a time of extreme duress. Hence, the expression coined by some: "the insurer is the banker of the exceptional situations".

That is to say, the covers offered are adequate for a reasonable premium, reasonably stable through time and above all secured by adequate solvency. *The insurer must be able to pay the large claims when called upon to do so!*

This is also where "loss reduction", i.e. limiting the severity of any claim, is essential.

Furthermore, all perils, all dysfunction cannot be assured; some are not insurable by law or by statistical impossibility. In some cases not enough insurers are attracted for a functional market to exist. Then, if and when such an event will occur internal sources of funds will have to be tapped, including investment money set aside for some new development programme that may have to be shelved temporarily as priorities are changed by an unexpected chain of events.

The preceding matrix is but a simplified version of what is now commonly called a risk map or risk matrix.

Risk mapping is a tool that allows classifying, comparing, and prioritizing exposures so that efficient action plans can be developed to mediate or treat them, or benefit from them to draw a competitive edge, putting to best use all available resources. In other words, it is a dynamic graphic representation of the ever-evolving organizational risk profile. Hence, each organization must develop its own specific risk map.

Risk mapping is also an excellent audit and communication tool both internally and externally for the risk manager and the executives of the organization.

However, the model used above, a matrix with only four quadrants may prove far too limited to gain an understanding of one organisation's risks. In practice at the cross, point, representing the mean probability and the mean impact the bulk, more than 80%, of the cost of risk is concentrated. Therefore, risk evaluation will be greatly improved with matrices that will be 4×4, 4×6, 6×4 or 6×6 depending on how fine an assessment is needed. Note that it is highly recommended to select an even number of possibilities on both axes to prevent those involved in the assessment process to take "the middle road."

Furthermore, the categories must be meaningful in the eyes of the "assessor", i.e.

– On the probability axis: Once a day, once a month, for high frequency, once a year, once every two years, once every five years, for the medium frequency as it is likely to happen during the tenure of any executive, and once every fifty years, once a century, once a millennium, for rare event that no one should have to live through and yet be prepared for should it happen due to the dire consequences;
– On the impact axis: for low impact refer to annual profit give a good grasp to a board of director (less than one per mil, one percent, etc.) whereas for medium range impacts a reference to the annual cash flow or gross revenues may prove more meaningful and finally for the very severe impacts may be compared to total assets, or net worth, some times more than a 100%!

This approach will give an immediate insight into what is "essential" or "strategic" and what should be left to the field managers to cope with.

Finally, it should be noted that more than a "permanent risk map" the risk matrix is only a temporary tool to help decision maker that is immediately obsolete when the deciders have moved forward and changed the "risk landscape."

Risk financing and strategic financing

Strategic risk management is still a long way from being the norm. On the other hand, large conglomerates participating in the globalization process have already perceived the gains to be made at the efficient frontier in managing risks in a holistic fashion. Financial analysts and CFOs have been trained in the same universities where the gospel is diversification and uncorrelated risks, pure and speculative alike.

The two fundamental objectives of the finance department remain solvency and optimum return on assets. That means conducting a long-term sustained growth, protected from most uncertainties. At this stage, one must keep in mind that the current development in finance theory rests on the assumption that strategies are built on arbitrage between risk and return and that at the efficient frontier, the board's appetite for risk is key to the return achieved. If the stockholders want more return, they have to bear more risk, as measured as the volatility of future results.

When applied to the realm of risks, beyond the specific financial risks from which it was designed in the first place, the portfolio approach to risk financing leads to a first and fundamental choice between pre- and post-financing of risks. In order that the value to the stockholders be maximized, i.e. the long-term market price of the stock, post-financing will always provide a higher present value of future flows of cash as the funds can be invested in higher return assets. However, two considerations are essential:

- Risk management fundamental mission: it is not so much to eliminate exposures or even to curb the cost of risk than to make sure that only those risks that provide a good return are borne by the organization, i.e. it will cope with the volatility of the cash flows generated by the uncertainty of the outcomes.
- Retention/transfer optimal choice: as mentioned earlier, the origin of the funds, from inside or from outside the organization, is originally the key to distinguishing between retention and transfer. Within the framework of portfolio analysis, the main question is who bears the risk in any given situation, i.e. the uncertainty of the outcome. Therefore, when risk is measured by the standard deviation of the outcome, even the purchase of insurance cover transfers the volatility to the insurer, i.e. the risk, at least according to the terms and conditions of the insurance contract. The optimal equilibrium will have to trade off return for a chance of failure through the "cash flow at risk approach".

From risk management to strategic risk management

Beyond the traditional definition of risk management including only the management of accidental risks, the following lists illustrate some of the "risks" that could be associated with the concept of risk management in a much broader sense.

- Financial risks like:
  - *Banking risks (or lenders' risk)*: loan officers in the banking industry use the term to refer to the quality of a portfolio of loans, that is to say, the ability of the borrowers to repay the instalments in full and on time.
  - *Liquidity risk*: CFOs and treasurers are responsible for the congruence between in- and outflows of cash. They must make sure that the organization will meet is obligation at all times (including those times following a large accident when exceptional sources of funds must be secured).

- *Foreign exchange risk*: brokers at the exchanges are very attentive to fluctuations in interest rate and currency movements, as they have to hedge daily their positions to avoid risk or seek return.
- *Interest rate risks*: long-term financing bears an interest and the change in the time structure of interest may have an impact on the solvency or the return of the actors in the financial markets.
- *Investment risk*: Whether dealing with large individual projects or large stock funds, investment managers are aware of the fundamental finance principle: risk and return are linked, the higher the risk, the higher the return. In the case of portfolio, the fiduciary must understand the investor's risk appetite and whether they are in for a long haul of short-term gains. In the latter, the choice concerns when to buy and when to sell using short-term up or down trends in the market. In the former, the strategy must rely on the fundamentals of the corporation whose stocks or bonds they keep, sell or contemplate buying.
- Nonfinancial risks like:
  - *Health risk (or hazard)*: healthcare specialists are trained to stop epidemics and pandemics, restore or maintain public hygiene, and more generally promote a healthy environment for the general public.
  - *Project risk*: pilots of major projects like the construction of a dam, a power plant or skyscraper, or the launching of a satellite have two key indicators to follow: time and costs. Therefore they must swiftly manage any incident occurring during the construction or preparation. (Project risk management is key to project management and a specialty of risk management where cost and timing are the main factors.)
  - *Military risk (foreign war)*: the members of the strategic defence staff of any country must be very careful with the confidentiality of their decisions and proposals. They also have to prepare alternative strategies for any foreign operations.
  - *Weather conditions risk*: meteorologists work at developing models to predict tornadoes and other climactic situations impacting the life of the people as early as possible to enhance decision-making processes.

Clearly, all these examples illustrate situations where it is legitimate to use the concept of risk management. Indeed, in all these situations, the aim is to find appropriate means to manage uncertainty, to reduce the range of possible outcomes, and to develop a capacity to react when confronted with adverse conditions.

Some academic circles and even some professionals fear that the term "risk management" is tainted by its origin in the insurance world – even in workers' compensation covers for that matter. This is the reason why a new phrase has been coined: "strategic risk management". The underlying idea is that in all situations where there is uncertainty about the future, a probabilistic approach is difficult. The main differences between the traditional view of risk management and this new approach can be summarized in three points:

- Strategic risk management is concerned with all risks, pure as well as speculative.
- Strategic risk management's central goal is economic efficiency. It is not limited to restoring a situation following an accident. Therefore, it is geared towards growth; change management in an essentially positive approach rather than the negative approach of the traditional view of risk management. (*Economic efficiency or growth could be even replaced by optimum value to stakeholders in a more ethical centred approach.*)
- Strategic risk management is in essence systemic. It is not only analytical, it views the organization as an open living body, as a whole. If the identification of individual exposures

remains essential, combining them in a dynamic system is the key to this approach. All the objectives of the organization must be assessed, the strength and weaknesses evaluated as well as opportunities and threats stemming from its environment. A global optimum for the system is the only possible mission.

In this broader perspective, traditional risk management is not obsolete. It appears only as one of the many facets of strategic risk management. When the term managing risk is changed to managing uncertainty, it must be applied to all dimensions of the organization's strategy.

From managing physical assets to managing reputation

In the last two decades of the twentieth century the world economy experienced what must be seen now as a complete paradigm change. Globalization is only the most visible part of the iceberg; in fact the rise of a 'nonphysical' economy as the major proportion of the world's wealth is undoubtedly the most significant evolution. The value of intangible assets became the most important part of the market value of any firm traded on the stock exchange: when compared to the value of the physical assets, the total value of the firm (measured by the share price multiplied by the number of outstanding shares) reached peaks that ranged from 10 to 100 times.

The financial explanation is simple: the value of the firm is equal to the present value of the future stream of dividends expected from that firm, discounted at a rate which takes into account of the level of risk and the expected growth.

However, the model could not explain the level of shares in a company that had never turned any profit and might not in the near future; in fact what gave them value were *expectations*. This "added value" is now commonly called "reputation". Does it really exist? The stock market provides the answer: even after the collapse of the stock market in 2002/2004 only partially recouped since then with some significant recent rebounds, the value of "not-accounted-for" intangible assets – the difference between physical asset value and market price – is still significant. As a matter of fact, this is not only true for traded shares but even for private transactions when smaller firms are integrated into larger concerns. Reputation, whether it exists or not, has a significant impact on the economy, representing probably between 60 and 70 % of developed countries' wealth.

In short, up until recently risk management has been dealing with what has become less than a third of the wealth of the organizations it serves. It is high time reputation risks were assessed and mitigated.

All information – whether written, spoken, or via a computer programme – that flows in, through, and out of the organization is of vital importance. It is a source of exposure, through loss of data, degradation, or disclosure resulting from equipment failure, human error, or wilful intrusion. It contributes to the survival of any organization because of the importance of the "intangible assets" value stemming from the flow of information. It is so important that a specific diagnosis and risk management programme for information exposures is essential. (Among major information exposures, the "Y2K bug" was an illustration of a well-managed exposure resulting in only minor interruption.) Internet connections and firewalls remain a constant challenge. Nevertheless, all CEOs should remember that the human brain is the easiest way to carry information (and secrets) out of the organization: the best risk control technique is a proactive human resource policy. Furthermore, all human beings are not only rational but also emotional and social animals, and using a purely rational approach to information risk as a way to manage it when intangible assets are exposed would be very short-sighted. Indeed, most organizations, with sometimes a push from public opinion, consumers' associations or even trading partners, are being made more and more aware of a major exposure: *the risk to reputation (image, brand)*.

This is the risk that an organization's reputation can be tainted, either by real mismanagement or simply in the public's or its economic partners' perception. For the purpose of this chapter, "reputation" is defined broadly and includes both the stakeholders' subjective appreciation of the organization and the intangible assets like brands and image that can be separately valued. The degradation may have different origins: dramatic accidents, questioning of management's wisdom, product defect and ill-organized or untimely product recall, or defamation, to quote but a few.

Consider Exxon and the pollution of Alaska waters by the *Exxon Valdez*, or Shell and the consumers' boycott following the *Piper Alpha* affair more recently BP and the Alaskan pipeline; Perrier never fully recovered after toluene traces were found; whether Firestone has rebounded after the SUV tyre recall? (Thanks largely to out-of-court settlements in most of the cases, coupled with the effort made in Formula 1 car racing that resulted in tremendous success since the 2003 world championship – outstanding adherence under slippery conditions!) We can add more recent examples: British Airways flights grounded for several days in the summer of 2005 over social unrest at its outsourced catering supplier, KPMG admitting to illicit advice to clients, major brokers drawn into a controversy over commissions and tempered tender offer processes, major pharmaceutical firms delaying recall of major products, etc.

The media's increased scrutiny, relaying public interest in all aspects of each organization's management, imposes on all boards of directors a need always to act as if under a "glass roof", where every move and every thought can be made public. In all areas of management, therefore, decisions and their implementation must be at all times consistent with the set of values set forth by the organization.

This is of the utmost importance in the areas grouped under the heading "corporate social responsibility" – encompassing employment practices, impact on the environment and sustainable development, human rights, involvement in local communities (especially in emerging economies) and relationships with business partners.

To summarize, reputation is the result of a lengthy project to build trust, through consistent efforts, with all stakeholders, while the world is growing less and less trusting and the different stakeholders may have diverse, indeed contrary interests in the organization.

The main consequence for risk managers is that maximizing value to stockholders will require managing risks in such a way that reputation is enhanced and risks to reputation mitigated. Clearly, sound risk management is one of the pillar of good governance.

From risk manager to chief risk officer

As briefly explained above, in the recent past risk management went through a tremendous evolution and appears to have grown from a set of technical skills into both a discipline in itself and a part of the broader field of management sciences.

Since the mid-1990s, this reality has been illustrated in many organizations by the creation or expansion of the internal risk management professional's status. However, more recently, in the UK among others, a reverse trend has appeared with the separation of risk financing (assigned to the CFO) and loss control (to the operational), thus questioning the pertinence of a risk manager altogether. In the meantime, corporate governance tends to be embodied in a new function. Could it be then that one of the major risks to be managed by a risk manager would be his own career?

But in the same time, both Australian and British corporations are encouraged to create risk committees in their board staffed only with independent directors, i.e. nonexecutive, to ensure proper consideration is given to these important issues.

Whatever the framework, consultant, part-time executive or manager, depending on the size and scope of the risks to be managed, there is an ever-broadening field of competencies for the next generation risk management professional.

These apparently conflicting trends can be reconciled when one realizes that risk management is truly transversal as risks will stem from and touch all the activities conducted within and without the organization. Therefore, the risk management professional is only a facilitator of the risk management process that must be owned by the risk management practitioners, i.e. all in charge of an activity for the organization.

In the USA, some corporations, mostly in the financial sector, have recognized the necessity to include the risk management process at the highest level, i.e. in the executive suite. For those risk persons who sit in the executive meetings, they have forged a new title reflecting their executive status.

Traditionally, members of the executive committee have become "chief officer", like the chief executive officer, chief administrative officer, chief financial officer, etc. So the new person would be the CRO (chief risk officer), and should report to the risk committee at the board level.

French entrepreneurs could smile at this recent discovery made in the New World. As early as 1898, Henri Fayol, a French engineer and entrepreneur, considered as one of the founders of modern management, identified "safety", i.e. protecting persons and assets, as one of the six main functions of a firm.

He identified clearly the strategic security director, the ancestor of the CRO. It took nearly 60 years for Fayol to be translated in English and 40 more years for the American establishment to read him. But how much longer will be needed for the French establishment to rediscover him?

Will this new risk manager, this new CRO, whatever the title, be the person to find a new "meaning" for words such as risk, safety, security, threat and opportunity, sustainability?

Why is risk quantification needed?

In the context within which organizations must operate today, it is all too clear that the traditional and reactive approach of the insurance purchaser protecting the assets of the organization must be replaced by a dynamic and proactive vision aimed at achieving the organization's mission, goals and objectives under any stress or surprise. It requires a new expanded definition of "risks". The "new" risk manager must think and look beyond the organization's frontiers, more specifically to include all the economic partners, indeed all the stakeholders of the organization. Special attention will have to be devoted to the procurement chain and the interdependences of all parties.

This is a major reason why risk management professional conferences in Europe and Australia as well as in America have given some thought to developing a new title to evidence the evolution of the risk management scope and duties. How to name this new strategic manager of risks when clearly purchasing insurance is no longer the sole answer to managing risks?

With this rapid evolution of the "risk domain" comprising more and more noninsurable risks, new approaches to risk management have become necessary to be an effective risk manager.

Defining the competencies required is a very daunting task, let alone finding the individual to possess them!

The Australian standards were revised in 2004, and the British standards developed jointly by ALARM, AIRMIC, and the IRM are now accepted by FERMA and have been translated into more than 20 languages. If interpreted as a road map to effective ERM (enterprise-wide risk management) rather than a compliance reference, then these frameworks do provide a track to explore an ISO commission an RN chaired by K. Knight is currently developing an international "RN framework" inspired from the Australian Standards. But whatever the itinerary preferred, all managers will need to develop a risk register and quantify the possible or probable consequences of risks to make rational decisions that can be disclosed to the authorities and the public. In many circumstances the data available are not reliable and complete enough to open the gates for traditional probability and trend analysis, other toolboxes may be required to develop satisfactory quantification models to help decision makers include a proper evaluation of uncertainty in any strategic or operational decision.

RISK QUANTIFICATION – A KNOWLEDGE-BASED APPROACH

Introduction

In the first section of this chapter, we have presented what we believe are the foundations of risk management:

- The definition of an exposure: object or resources at risk, peril, and consequences. Thus defining an organisation as a portfolio of exposures.
- The three-step risk management process: diagnosis of exposures, risk treatment, and audit; the risk treatment step being further decomposed in design, development, and implementation phases of the risk management programme.

We have also demonstrated that quantification is the key element for strategic – or holistic – risk management, as only a proper evaluation of uncertainties allows for rational decision making.

In this section, we will show how a knowledge perspective on risk could support the design of a risk management programme, at both tactical and strategic levels. One of the key tasks of the risk manager, i.e. to design a risk management programme and have it approved, can be represented as an "influence diagram".

Causal structure of risk

Risks are situations where damaging events may occur but are not fully predictable. Recognizing some degree of unpredictability in these situations does not mean that they are totally random events.

Most of the risks that we will consider throughout this book are partially driven by a series of factors, or drivers. These drivers are conditions that would make the occurrence of the risk more probable, or more severe.

From a scientific viewpoint, causation is the foundation of determinism: identifying *all* the causes of a given phenomenon would allow predicting the occurrence and unfolding of this event. Similarly, the probability theory is the mathematical perspective on uncertainty. In situations where an event is totally unpredictable, the laws of probability can help to envision and quantify the possible futures.

Knowledge is the reduction of uncertainty – when we gain a better understanding of a phenomenon, the random part of the outcome decreases compared to the deterministic part.

Some authors introduce a subtle distinction between *uncertainty* and *variability*, the latter being an intrinsic randomness of a phenomenon that cannot be reduced. In the framework of deterministic physics, there is no such thing as variability, and apparent randomness is only the result of incomplete knowledge. Invoking Heisenberg's "uncertainty principle" in a discussion on risk quantification may seem disproportionate. However, in so doing, we understand the principle as stating that the ultimate knowledge is not reachable, rather than that events are random by nature: "In the sharp formulation of the law of causality (if we know the present exactly, we can calculate the future) it is not the conclusion that is wrong but the premise".[4]

Uncertainty and knowledge

For the purpose of this discussion, we can summarize our position as follows: uncertainty results from an incomplete knowledge, and complete knowledge is unreachable.

Our perspective on risk quantification will rely heavily on this dialectic between knowledge and uncertainty.

Specific knowledge of a phenomenon is represented by a causal structure. When working with a specific device or machine, the possibility of a misuse leading to an accident depends both on the experience of the user and on the complexity of the device. "Experience" and "complexity" are key drivers for this risk.

However, these drivers are not sufficient to create a deterministic model. If we know that the user is "experienced" and the machine "simple", this does not mean that there is no risk at all. Several other factors can interfere: the user may be tired or disturbed, the machine may not have been reset properly by the previous user, etc. The occurrence of the risk is still a random event, but the probability of this event depends on the drivers.

Thus we simply recognize that (1) some key drivers have some influence on the possible occurrence of the risk, and (2) even if these drivers are known, the occurrence of the risk remains unpredictable.

The formalization of causal probabilistic graphs (Bayesian networks) is particularly adapted to represent this mixture of knowledge and uncertainty. We will use this formalism as a tool throughout this book. Causal graphs and Bayesian networks will be described in detail in Chapter 2 Toolbox. We provide here only a brief introduction to this formalization.

Figure 1.1 represents the causal structure – the "knowledge", i.e. the causal relationships between the *nodes* (the variables).

Here, both the "User experience" and the "Machine complexity" influence the possible occurrence of an "Accident". Since the actual occurrence of an accident cannot be predicted from the knowledge of these two causes only, the "Accident" is a random variable. The probability distribution of this variable is conditioned by the two drivers. As "Accident" is a binary (yes/no) variable, its distribution is fully characterized by the probability of occurrence of an accident.

Of course, each node can be determined by one or more drivers, and can be the driver of other nodes in the more complex graph. For instance, in the elementary illustration here, we could introduce the idea that the experience of the user cannot be measured directly, but is

---

[4] Heisenberg, W. 1927. Über den ausch aulichen Inhalt der quantentheoretischen Kinematik und Mechanik, *Zeitschrift für Physik*, 43, 172–198.

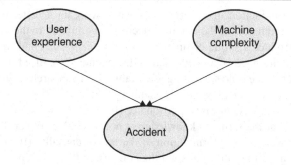

Figure 1.1   Illustration of causal structure of a risk

partially conditioned by her age. Older users are typically more experienced, although they can be new in the job.

A risk management programme itself can be described through an abstract causal graph. Before introducing this graph, which represents the cornerstone of our approach, we need to introduce two other types of nodes in causal graphs.

Decision nodes represent drivers that are chosen rather than observed. If we use the above model for a prospective risk analysis in a workshop, the choice of an equipment supplier can be a driver of the machine complexity. On the other hand, the management could increase the level of qualification of the users by implementing a training programme. Therefore, the final probability of accident would be – partially – influenced by some management decisions, Figure 1.2.

Utility nodes usually represent cost, or profit, variables driven by other variables. They can also represent other quantifiable measures, which cannot be reduced to costs, such as human casualties.

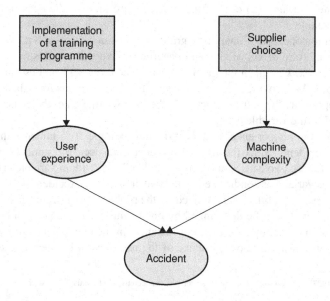

Figure 1.2   Management decisions in the casual structure of a risk

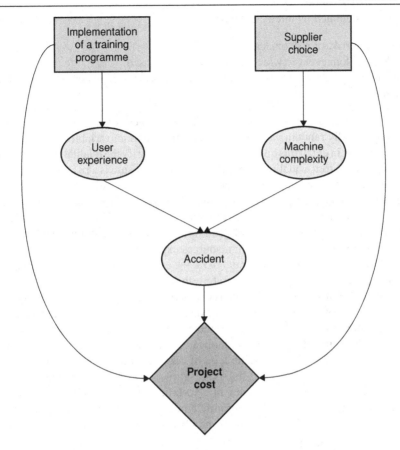

Figure 1.3 Probabilistic economic analysis of a project

Further to the factory point of view risk analysis initiated above, a probabilistic economic analysis can be carried out, through the introduction of cost elements: total accident costs, training costs, and machine costs, Figure 1.3.

Figures 1.1–1.3 are built according to the conventions used in "influence diagrams". An influence diagram is a visual representation of a decision problem. Influence diagrams offer an intuitive way to represent decisions, uncertainties, objectives, and their mutual interactions.

We will use the following conventions throughout this book:

- A rectangle represents a decision.
- An ellipse represents a random variable.
- A diamond represents an objective, cost or utility.
- An arrow represents an *influence*, or *causal dependency*.

We will now try to generalize this simple example to show how causal graphs can be used to formally represent the risk management process.

Building a quantitative causal model of risk

In the first section of this chapter, we have shown that risk assessment is supported by the notion of *exposure* as the basic concept of risk.

An exposure is defined by three elements:

- The resource at risk, or risk object.
- The peril or random event to which the resource is exposed.
- The consequence, i.e. the possible impact – financial or other – when the resource is "hit" by the peril.

For each of these notions, we propose a quantitative counterpart, which would be generally described as a partially random variable – a conditioned random variable.

Before describing in detail this quantification, we must clarify the qualitative and quantitative notions of exposure. From a qualitative point of view, an exposure is a risk. From a quantitative point of view, the exposure will measure the number of resources exposed to a risk.

The exposed resources are quantified by exposure. Exposure is measured by an appropriate quantitative measurement of the exposed resource, such as typically the number of units, the acreage, the volume, etc. In the context of quantifying operational risk for a bank (Basel 2), an apparently similar risk can have different resources exposed, and, hence, different exposures. When considering credit card *external* fraud risks, the exposed resource is the credit card itself. Credit cards can be lost or stolen, and therefore the number of cards is the measurement of exposure to this risk. On the other hand, when considering *internal* fraud risks, the risk can result from a group of employees able to duplicate existing cards and issue fraudulent transactions under some circumstances. In this situation, the exposed resources are the employees of the firm, not the cards. Rather, the number of duplicated cards would be a factor of severity.

In the case of natural events, the same type of distinction may apply. Resources exposed to a tropical storm would be houses, since the storm would hit each of them individually. As a consequence, the number of houses in a specific area would be the correct exposure measurement. On the other hand, the appropriate measurement for a tidal wave, or tsunami, exposure would be the coast length. Here, the number of houses built close to the shore would be an indicator of severity rather than of exposure.

The peril is quantified by a probability of occurrence. This probability is defined as the average expected number of disasters that may happen for one unit of exposure during one unit of time. If the probability of a factory fire in a particular area is estimated at 0.05 %, this means that on average, we expect that 1 of 2000 plants will experience a fire next year.

Exposure and probability of occurrence must be defined in a consistent way. Consider the risk of terrorist attacks on planes. Assume that the main risk is that a terrorist would succeed in boarding a plane with a bomb. Assume further that the probability that he would succeed is 10^{-6} (one in a million), given the quality of controls in place. The appropriate exposure is neither the number of passengers – depending on which plane is involved, an Embrayer, a Boeing 727 or 777 or an Airbus A380 – nor the number of planes in a given company fleet. The appropriate exposure is obviously the number of *flights*. In the same domain, assume that the probability of an individual suffering a heart attack within one year is 0.1 %.[5] We can then estimate the probability of both the pilot and the co-pilot being struck during the same flight. In this example, the appropriate exposure measurement is not the number of flights, but rather the cumulated hours of flight for this company.

Most perils can be described by a binary indicator: the peril will or will not happen. For some of them, such as earthquakes or other natural hazards, the peril occurrence must be further

---

[5] This evaluation would be focused on the typical airline pilot profile (male, 35–55, good physical condition).

qualified by intensity. For instance, earthquake intensity is usually measured on either Richter or Mercalli scales.

Occurrence and intensity

Intensity is a general notion that could be used for all perils, provided that, as a convention, only 0 and 100 % intensity are observable for "yes or no" perils.

   This would also make the three notions of exposure, occurrence and severity more consistent: they are random variables characterized by a probability distribution. The specific case of the yes/no peril can be described by only one figure: the probability of occurrence.

   The consequences of a peril are quantified by a severity or impact indicator: financial losses, human casualties, breach of ethics, long-term impact, etc.

   When quantifying the consequences of a peril, the disaster is assumed to have already happened. The occurrence is considered certain, but the consequences are still uncertain, and will be represented as a random variable.

   When a continuous intensity measurement is applicable, it should not be confused with severity or impact. An earthquake may be very intense, but still have no impact at all, if happening in the heart of a desert.

   Fire is a particular case, which in our opinion should be considered as a yes/no peril, even though it can be limited or catastrophic. Indeed, a fire ceases if it is not fed by oxygen and flammable goods. Therefore a fire's intensity is defined only by its consequences.

Quantification of a risk

Exposure, occurrence (or intensity), and impact are the three random variables that fully define a risk. Quantifying these variables is the first step of risk quantification, which corresponds to the "Risk assessment" step of the risk management three-step process described above.

This assessment is probabilistic, since each of these variables is potentially random.

Exposure, frequency, and probability

The risk management literature often qualifies risk using two main concepts: frequency and severity. Severity is the expected cost of an accident or a disaster, or, more precisely, the distribution of this cost when an accident occurs. We believe that frequency is not a well-defined concept since it measures the probability of an accident or a disaster *given the present resources exposed.* Change of frequency may have two causes: change in exposure, or change in probability.

   For instance, since 1970 the probability of an airline accident has constantly decreased to about 1.5 accidents for 1 million take-offs or landings in 2000. However, the exposure – i.e. the number of take-offs or landings – is constantly increasing, and hence the number of accidents does not show a clear downward trend, Figure 1.4.

   This gives the public the wrong perception of an increasing risk, whereas the individual traveller is now more than 10 times safer today than in 1970.

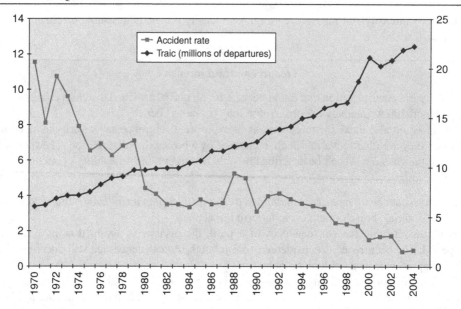

Figure 1.4   Parallel evolution of airline accident rate and traffic

This example also shows the importance of an appropriate definition of exposure, as the *number of resources "independently" exposed to a given peril.*

Some studies on transport safety use a "km.passenger" as a measurement of exposure, usually reporting the "casualties per 100 million km.passenger" as a measurement of frequency. This may be an appropriate indicator from an economic point of view, but "km.passenger" is not a correct measurement for exposure, at least for air transport. Indeed, a "km.passenger" is not a resource independently exposed to the risk of a take-off or landing crash – which are by far the most dangerous phases of a flight. When a crash occurs on a long-distance flight, several hundreds of thousands of "km.passengers" are hit simultaneously. It is not possible to define the individual probability of one "km.passenger" being hit.

A change of transport structure, for instance increasing the share of long-distance flights would artificially reduce the risk, although the overall safety would not be improved. This is shown in Figure 1.5, where the casualties per 100 million km.passenger have decreased three times faster (from 0.05 to 0.005 in 10 years) than the number of accidents per million departures (from 3.25 to 0.9), during the period from 1996 to 2004. This is probably due to an increase in long-distance and large carriers' share of the overall traffic.

Another problem with this measurement is that it also entangles exposure, probability, *and* severity.

This "casualties per 100 million of km.passenger" indicator may increase if either: (1) the short-carrier share increases, (2) the actual safety of aircrafts decreases, or (3) the size of air carriers increases. Again, this might be an interesting indicator for a global "cost-of-risk" analysis, but this will not help in understanding the drivers of this cost.

Exposure, occurrence, and impact drivers

Each of the three variables described above can be influenced, at least partially, by some drivers.

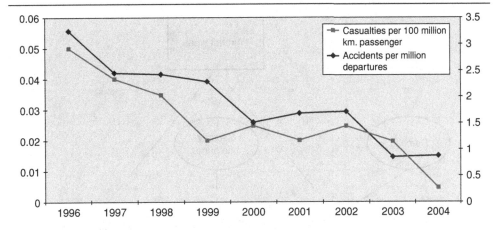

Figure 1.5 Parallel evolution of different frequency measurements for airline accidents

For instance, an airline company may analyse the risk exposure attached to a partial renewal of its fleet with large aircrafts. This would decrease the exposure to terrorist attacks since it would lower the number of flights. Similarly, a reduced number of flights would lower the workload of the security officers, and allow more thorough checks, finally reducing the probability of an attack. On the other hand, should a disaster occur, obviously it would have more severe consequences, since on average twice as many passengers would be on board.

But if the traffic increases due to economic conditions leading to a higher demand for air travel, the company would have to increase the number of flights anyway.

In that particular case, we see that:

- Drivers to exposure (number of flights) are: demand and company policy.
- Drivers to occurrence are: workload of, which is in turn driven by number of, flights and number of security officers.
- Drivers to severity are: demand and airline policy.

Controlling exposure, occurrence, and impact

Controlling exposure, occurrence and impact reflects the three main approaches to risk reduction.

Controlling exposure is related to *avoidance*: a resource exposed to risk is usually a resource exposed also to an opportunity. If an airline decides not to increase its traffic, its exposure to take-off or landing accidents will not be increased, but this means also that some opportunities would be lost.

Controlling occurrence is related to *prevention*: reducing the probability of a given risk is performed through an analysis and improvement of the situation before the accident happens.

Controlling impact is related to *protection*: reducing the severity of a given accident is performed through an analysis and improvement of the hypothetical situation if the accident would happen.

Controllable, predictable, observable, and hidden drivers

Four categories of drivers can be identified:

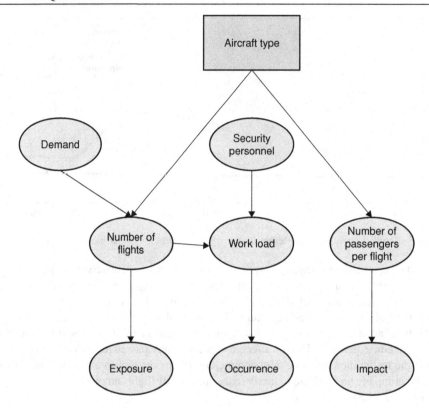

Figure 1.6   Drivers of risk exposure variables (exposure, occurrence, and impact)

- *Controllable drivers* can be influenced by some decision: in our example, the number of passengers per flight will be modified by the aircraft type selection.
- *Predictable drivers* cannot be really influenced by a decision, but their evolution can be predicted to some extent: in our example, the demand can be partially predicted – using external economic forecasts.[6]
- *Observable drivers* cannot be influenced, or predicted. They can be only observed after the facts, a posteriori. Observable drivers should not normally be included in a causal model of risk, since they cannot be used in a prospective evaluation.
- *Hidden drivers* cannot be measured directly, not even a posteriori, but may be controlled to some extent. For instance, the hostility of potential terrorists cannot be measured; however, it can be reduced through communication actions.

Cost of decisions

This first analysis shows that controllable drivers are obviously the most interesting: they are the levers of risk control or mitigation.

---

[6] In that particular example, the airline could partially drive its demand on this line through its pricing policy which could drive its market share. However, since the reaction of the competition cannot be predicted, it could be more rational to consider that demand is not controllable.

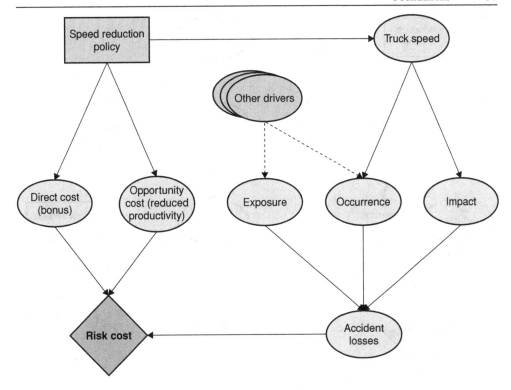

Figure 1.7   How risk mitigation actions impact risk cost

In most cases, implementing a risk control measure will:

- Change the distribution of some risk driver, at either the exposure, occurrence, or impact level.
- Have a direct cost, related to the implementation itself.
- Have an indirect or opportunity cost, related to the potential impact on business.

For instance, consider a cargo company deciding to take a harder line on truck speed limitation. The company may decide to award a bonus to the compliant drivers. This company will incur directly the cost of the bonus (direct costs), but may also initially face a drop in revenue, or need to hire more drivers to serve its customers. Of course, this policy will reduce the probability and impact of accidents.

Risk financing

The second element in the treatment step of the risk management process is usually to develop a risk financing strategy, including a more effective use of insurance and other sources of capital.

This strategy will have an impact on the cost of the retained risks and on the cost of financing, which could also be analyzed through an influence diagram.

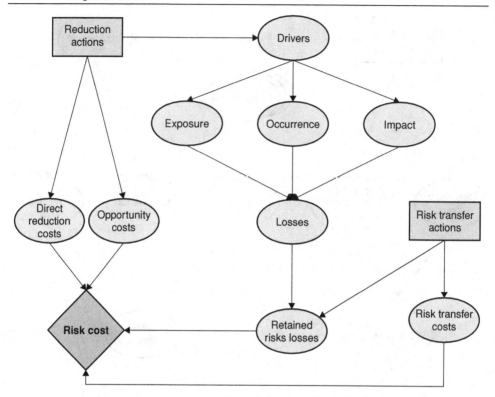

Figure 1.8   The risk management programme as an influence diagram

Risk management programme as an influence diagram

From this first general analysis of the risk management process, we can derive a general causal graph for risk management, Figure 1.8.

This graph can be analysed in detail as follows:

- "Exposure", "occurrence", and "impact" are random variables partially determined by risk "Drivers". These "Drivers" may of course be multiple and potentially dependent. This type of dependence is not represented in this abstract version of the graph, but would be in a specific model for a particular risk or risk portfolio.
- "Losses" is a random variable whose distribution depends on exposure, occurrence, and Impact. "Reduction actions" modify the "Drivers", and, consequently, the "Losses". "Reduction actions" are human decisions. The choice of actions will of course depend of the risk cost analysis, but it is considered to be free. This is why decisions have no direct causes in this graph, or more generally in influence diagrams.
- The cost of reduction actions, "Direct reduction costs", depends on the reduction actions implemented, as does "Opportunity costs".
- "Risk transfer actions" implement various methods for financing the possible losses. The "Retained risk losses" distribution depends on both the total losses distribution – before financing – and the risk transfer actions selected.

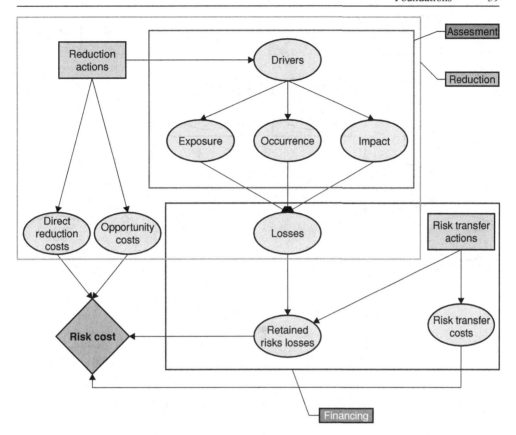

Figure 1.9   Risk assessment, control, and financing as parts of the risk management influence diagram

- The final objective node, "Risk cost", is computed as the sum of reduction costs, opportunity costs, retained risk losses, and risk transfer costs.

This diagram captures most of the risk management process. The three steps of this process (assessment, reduction, and financing) are represented by subparts of these graphs, as shown in Figure 1.9.

Modelling an individual risk or the risk management programme

Before going further in this discussion, there is one point we would like to make clear. The formalization of causal graphs allows describing a model for both a single risk and the global risk management programme.

   The airline terrorist risk model and cargo road accident model are examples of individual risk models. Such individual models may be simply juxtaposed when designing a risk management programme. They would certainly interact, at least through the limitation of financial resources. Figure 1.10 shows how the constraints on money allocation for risk mitigation could be represented in a causal graph.

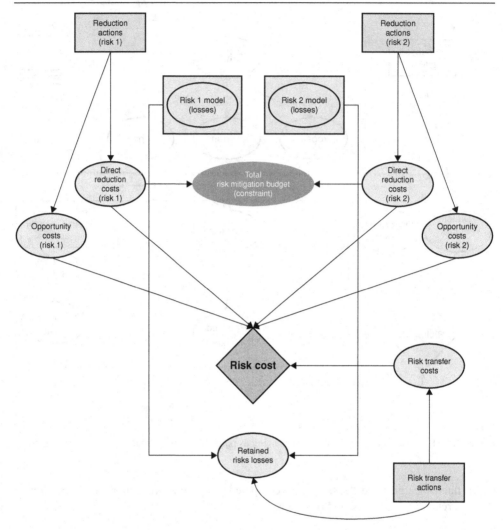

Figure 1.10   Interaction of multiple risks

In this example, we consider only two risks risk1 and risk2, although the discussion could be easily extended to any number of risk models. Causal models of loss distribution for each of these risks are represented in a compact way. Reduction actions are available for each of these risks. These actions cannot be selected independently, as the total budget allocated for risk mitigation expenses is limited: therefore the total costs undertaken for reduction of risk1 and risk2 cannot exceed the budget.

Although it is in theory possible to aggregate all individual risk models into a global model, in practice this would be far too complex. The global risk model of the organization should be considered at a synthetic level. Each risk model would be replaced by a simplified risk cost model, and risk costs models would be aggregated into a global risk model. In Chapter 3, we will discuss how a specific risk model can be transformed into a synthetic risk cost model, and also exhibit risk models considered at different levels.

SUMMARY

Risk management is currently maturing into a fully fledged branch of managerial sciences dealing with the handling of uncertainty to which any organization is confronted due to more or less predictable changes in the internal and external context in which it operates as well as evolutions in their ownership and stakeholders that may modify their objectives.

Global risk management is involved in the design and implementation of strategies that will incorporate provisions for adaptations to these changing conditions and provide sentinel events to warn of possible ruptures as early as possible. This will deliver value by facilitating prompt reaction and pre-emptive actions to allow managers to reach their objectives, goals, and missions under any circumstances and cope with surprises, even of cataclysmic proportions.

However, this organizational resilience can be achieved only through the implementation of a continuous process of risk management at all levels in the organization stemming from a clearly defined risk management strategy approved by the board in which risk appetite is defined and communicated. This three-step process, diagnosis of exposures, risk treatment or mitigation plan, loops through the review and audit process of the risk management programmes to ensure that the key objectives are at the centre of all decision making and achieved through a proper implementation of the plans.

Judgement can be applied to decision making in risk related issues, but rational and transparent processes called for by good governance practices require that risks be quantified as widely as possible. When data are insufficient, unavailable or irrelevant, expertise must be called upon to quantify impacts as well as likelihoods. This is precisely what this book is about. It will guide the reader through the quantification tools appropriate at all three steps of the risk management process: diagnosis to set priority, loss control and loss financing to select the most efficient methods with one major goal in mind – long-term value to stakeholders and audit to validate the results and improve the future.

2
Tool Box

PROBABILITY BASICS

Introduction to probability theory

Probability theory is the fundamental mathematical tool to quantify uncertainty. Mathematically, the nature of a probability is simply a measure over the subsets of a given set. Only measures that satisfy the axioms of this theory can be called "probabilities".

These axioms are due to Kolmogorov, and are extremely simple. They can be expressed in plain English. We will limit our presentation to probabilities over finite sets, although the theory can be extended to infinite sets.

If E is a finite set then P is a probability over E if it satisfies the following constraints:

1. The probability of any subset of E is a number between 0 and 1.
2. If A and B are two exclusive subsets of E, then the probability of the subset obtained by merging A and B is the sum of the probabilities of A and B. (if $A \cap B$ is empty, then $P(A \cup B) = (P(A) + P(B))$.
3. The probability of the total set E is equal to $1 - P(E) = 1$.

The role of these axioms is to represent our intuition of uncertainty. As for most axiomatics, we would normally expect that an inference drawn from these axioms would not violate our intuition, or commonsense. There is no theoretical guarantee, however, that this will be the case. In particular, once stated, these axioms will "live their own life", and, through mathematical inference, produce a lot of theorems, which won't always be as self-evident. Before unfolding a (small) part of this theory, let us spend some time checking that these axioms are actually in line with our intuition.

First, we must understand which sets we are talking about in probability theory. The total set E is *the set of all possible outcomes* of a future – or unknown – event. To illustrate this notion, we will consider the casino roulette game. Gambling in a casino is possibly the domain where our intuition of uncertainty is the clearest, maybe because the games are simple and the risks are quantitative by nature.

In the European wheel roulette game, the set of possible outcomes of a spin is $E = \{0, \ldots, 36\}$ (Figure 2.1). The probability of a subset A of E represents a measure of how certain we are that the outcome will be part of A.

If we believe that the ball cannot jump out of the wheel, or break, then *we are certain* that the outcome of the next spin will be in E. The probability of E is equal to 1 (third axiom). The first axiom, which requires that the probability of any subset should be between 0 and 1, is a pure convention, but is in line with everyday language: we are 100 % certain that the next outcome will be in E, or 50–50, about even (actually a little bit less).

The second axiom is also quite intuitive. If we believe that the wheel is fair, then each outcome should have the same probability, say p. We should *rationally* believe that the probability of

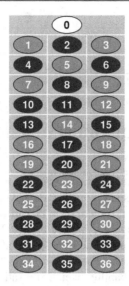

Figure 2.1 Outcomes of a roulette game

getting an odd is the sum of all single probabilities of 1, 3, ... , 35, i.e. $18p$. Similarly, the probability of getting an even would be $18p$, and finally the probability of getting 0 would be p. Getting either 0, or an even or an odd is *certain*, so finally $37p = 1$, or $p = 1/37$.

The important point here is to understand that a rational person *should* use the second axiom to combine its beliefs about uncertainties. If your belief about getting the "5" is 1/37, and similarly for all numbers, then you *should* believe that the probability of getting an odd is 18/37, and accept a payoff on 1:1 for this bet (assuming that you accept to give the usual long-run advantage to the casino). If you believe that this probability is higher, then you would be ready to accept less payoff on this bet, and you would be a very interesting gambler for the casino. If you believe that this probability is lower than 18/37, then you would ask for more payoff and never find a place to gamble.

The axioms do not say that you should believe the probability of getting a "5" is 1/37. Actually they do not say anything about this probability. They only say that if you believe that this probability is 1/37, and the probability of getting a "6" is also 1/37, then you should normally believe that the probability of getting either "5" or "6" is 2/37. If you have some reason to think so – in other words if you know that the wheel is not fair – you may very well believe that the probability of getting a "5" is 1/3, as is the case for getting a "6". But if you do believe so, probability theory recommends you also believe that the probability of getting either "5" or "6" is 2/3.

The second axiom works only for mutually exclusive events, i.e. subsets where mutual intersection is empty.

Consider for instance the four following subsets of the roulette total set:

- Odd = {1, 3, ..., 35}
- Even = {2, 4, ..., 36}
- Red = {1, 3, 5, 7, 9, 12, 14, 16, 18, 19, 21, 23, 25, 27, 30, 32, 34, 36}
- Black = {2, 4, 6, 8, 10, 11, 13, 15, 17, 20, 22, 24, 26, 28, 29, 31, 33, 35}

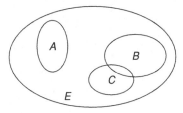

Figure 2.2   Venn diagram

If you bet at the same time on odd and even, you would lose your money only if the outcome is 0. The probability that the outcome would be either odd or even is 36/37, i.e. the sum of probability of each set.

If you bet at the same time on odd and red, you would lose your money if the result is 0 or any of {2, 4, 6, 8, 10, 20, 22, 24, 26, 28, 29}. The probability that the outcome would be either odd or red is *not* 36/37. Odd and red *are not mutually exclusive* events.

In this example, using the axioms of probability, we were able to build the probability measure for the European wheel roulette from only one single assumption: the wheel is fair.

This assumption led us to a very usual measure that can always be used to define a probability over a finite set. This measure is the *cardinal*, i.e. the number of elements of the subset. With this measure, $P(A)$ is Card(A)/Card(E), i.e. the number of elements in A divided by the number of elements in E. The underlying assumption is that each individual element has the same probability.

This measure is also the foundation of "Venn diagrams" generally used to provide a graphic interpretation of probabilities, Figure 2.2.

Using Venn diagrams, you can simply reinterpret the axioms of probability using surfaces, the probability of any subset of E being its surface compared to the total surface of E:

- The probability of any subset of E is a number between 0 and 1: the surface of any subset of E is between 0 and the surface of E.
- If A and B are two exclusive subsets of E, then the probability of the subset obtained by merging A and B is the sum of the probabilities of A and B: the total surface of two separate subsets is the sum of their surfaces, which is not true if the two subsets share an intersection (B and C in Figure 2.2).
- The probability of the total set E is equal to 1: the surface of E is 100 % of the surface.

Conditional probabilities

Conditional probability is possibly the most important notion when trying to use probabilities to support decision, because it introduces the use of prior information.

The theoretical definition of conditional probability is very simple. If P is a probability defined over E, then for any subset B of E, and provided that the probability of B, $P(B)$, is not 0, you can define a valid probability measure P_B. This new probability is simply defined by the ratio of two probabilities, $P(A \cap B)$, and $P(B)$:

$$P_B(A) = P(A \cap B)/P(B)$$

$P_B(A)$ reads as "the conditional probability of A given B", and can also be written as $P(A|B)$.

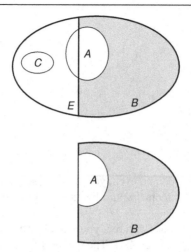

Figure 2.3 Conditional probabilities using Venn diagrams

This definition can be visualized using Venn diagrams as shown in Figure 2.3.

In the first diagram, three subsets, A, B and C, are represented in relation to E. The probability of A as a subset of E is the surface of A relative to the surface of E.

In the second one, which represents the conditional probability with respect to B, B is now the total set. Anything outside B is ignored, and the surfaces are now measured relative to the surface of B. The C subset has vanished from the second diagram because it does not have any intersection with B. In other words, the probability of C given B is now 0.

Let us return to the roulette example to discuss this notion.

When you arrive at a casino, a reasonable belief is to assume that the wheel is fair. This implies in particular that any number can come out of a spin. The total set of possible outcomes is $E = \{0, 1, 2, 3, \ldots, 36\}$.

Now imagine that you catch a "secret" conversation between two croupiers, and that it turns out that the wheel is loaded, and that the "5" cannot come out, due to some magnetic system in place. If you do believe this conversation, the interesting set to consider is $B = \{0, 1, 2, 3, 4, 6, 7, \ldots, 36\}$, and you may now use the conditional probability P_B to gamble. You will probably consider playing "even".

The formalization of this reasoning, according to the conditional probability, is as shown in Table 2.1.

There are a couple of important remarks we would like to emphasize when talking about conditional probabilities.

Conditional probabilities are about revising the beliefs on some uncertain events as getting some information about these events. When you deal with a *future* event, you may revise your probability if you get information on this future event, and not on a past or present event.

The "probability of A given B" reads "my belief that A will happen given that I know that B will happen", and not "my belief that A will happen given that I know that B has happened".

It may make sense, however, to use conditional probability to deal with present information relative to future outcomes, provided that you define properly the working sets.

Suppose that you are interested in whether the stock market will increase of decrease tomorrow. Assume further that you have noticed in the past that the stock markets have a slight

Table 2.1   Revising probabilities as new information is gained

---

Just arriving in casino (a priori)

P(The "1" will come out) = 1/37
P(The "2" will come out) = 1/37

...

P(The "5" will come out) = 1/37

...

P(The "5" will not come out) = 36/37

After getting the confidential information (a posteriori)

Relatively to the initial set, all probabilities remain unchanged.

P(The "1" will come out) = 1/37
P(The "2" will come out) = 1/37

...

P(The "5" will come out) = 1/37

...

P(The "5" will not come out) = 36/37
P(Even will come out) = 18/37

The set of interest is now $B = \{$The "5" will not come out$\} = \{1, 2, 3, 4, 6, \ldots, 36\}$
Conditionally to this set, the probabilities have changed, and beliefs on the future should be expressed conditionally to this new set.

P_B(The "1" will come out) = (1/37)/(36/37)
P_B(The "2" will come out) = (1/37)/(36/37)

...

P_B(The "5" will come out) = (0)/(36/37) ...
P_B (The "5" will not come out) = (36/37)/(36/37) = 1
P(Even will come out) = (18/37)/(36/37) = 1/2

---

tendency to "mean-reversal". You have done so by collecting a long history of stock movements, and sorting them into four categories:

- UP–UP = The market went up two consecutive days
- UP–DN = The market went up then down
- DN–UP = The market went down then up
- DN–DN = The market went down two consecutive days

The statistics you have collected are summarized as shown in Table 2.2.

If you believe that these statistics are still representative of markets' behaviour, you may infer some probabilities:

- P(Reversal) = P($\{$UP–DN, DN–UP$\}$) = 52 %
- P(UP–*) = P($\{$UP–UP, UP–DN$\}$) = 51 %
- P(*–UP) = P($\{$DN–UP, UP–UP$\}$) = 51 %
- P(DN–*) = P($\{$DN–UP, DN–DN$\}$) = 49 %
- P(*–DN) = P($\{$UP–DN, DN–DN$\}$) = 49 %

Table 2.2 Two days stock market behaviour statistics

UP–UP	25 %
UP–DN	26 %
DN–UP	26 %
DN–DN	23 %

Now you can ask yourself the question "What is the probability that the market will go up tomorrow given that it went down today?"

You can do so because the *uncertain event* is not "the market direction tomorrow", but the couple (market direction today, market direction tomorrow), which is still *uncertain* today.

However, you have a valid piece of information for this question: you know that the outcome of this uncertain event will be (DN–*), i.e. part of {DN–UP, DN–DN}. Now you can calculate $P(*-UP|DN-*) = 26\%/51\% = 51\%$.

Using conditional probabilities is in practice a powerful tool for reasoning about uncertainty.

Imagine that all your 1000 employees have passed a colour vision test. The final results are as shown in Table 2.3.

Now imagine that you find a test report with no name, for which the result is positive (the person is colour blind). What is the probability that this person is a man?

To answer this question, we can visualize the situation using a Venn diagram. The surface of a represented subset is equal to the number of persons in this subset, Figure 2.4.

According to this diagram the surface of the "Women" set is equal to the surface of the "Men" set, both equal to 500. Using the basic probability measure (the cardinal), the probability that a test report belongs to a man is 50 %.

Considering only the color blind persons reduces the discussion to the small "Colour blind" subset, Figure 2.5.

In this subset, the surface of the "Women" part is equal to 5, while the surface of the "Men" part is equal to 40. In this subset, the probability that a test report belongs to a man is 40/45, i.e. around 89 %.

From a mathematical point of view, we have simply used the definition:

The initial probability measure P gives the following values:

- $P(\text{Men}) = 0.5$
- $P(\text{Women}) = 0.5$
- $P(\text{Colour blind}) = 0.045$
- $P(\text{Men} \cap \text{Colour blind}) = 0.04$

    •

Table 2.3 Results of a colour vision test

	Men	Women	Total
OK	460	495	955
Colour blind	40	5	45
Total	500	500	1000

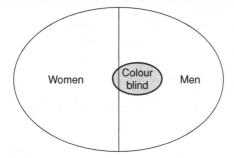

Figure 2.4 Using conditional probabilities for inference (a)

- $P(\text{Women} \cap \text{Colour blind}) = 0.005$
- etc.

The conditional probability P_{CB} is defined as:

$$P_{CB}(A) = P(A \cap \text{Colour blind})/P(\text{Colour blind})$$

So:

$$P_{CB}(\text{Men}) = 0.04/0.045 = 0.89$$

Independence

If A and B are two subsets of E, they are independent if and only if:

$$P(A \cap B) = P(A).P(B)$$

Considering your 1000 employees again, you may also test them for myopy, and get the result shown in Table 2.4.
We can check that:

- $P(\text{Men}) = 0.5$
- $P(\text{Myopic}) = 0.4$
- $P(\text{Men} \cap \text{Myopic}) = 0.2 = P(\text{Men}).P(\text{Myopic})$

The two subsets "Men" and "Myopic" are independent. You can check with the color blindness data that "Men" and "Colour blind" are not independent, as:

- $P(\text{Men}) = 0.5$
- $P(\text{Colour blind}) = 0.045$
- $P(\text{Men}).P(\text{Colour blind}) = 0.0225$
- $P(\text{Men} \cap \text{Colour blind}) = 0.04$

Figure 2.5 Using conditional probabilities for inference (b)

Table 2.4   Results of a myopy test

	Men	Women	Total
OK	300	300	600
Myopic	200	200	400
Total	500	500	1000

Independence can also be expressed using the conditional probability notation (if $P(B) \neq 0$):

$$P(A|B) = P(A)$$

This form is possibly easier to interpret. If getting some information does not change your belief about a possible uncertain outcome, then this outcome can be considered as independent from this information.

Bayes' theorem

Using the formal definition of the conditional probability:

$$P(A|B) = P(A \cap B)/P(B)$$

We can also write:

$$P(B|A) = P(A \cap B)/P(A)$$

And notice that:

$$\boxed{P(A|B) = P(A).P(B|A)/P(B)}$$

This result is known as the Bayes' theorem, which is quite simple from a formal point of view, but needs some comment to be interpreted.

In this equation, we can identify each element as parts of a "belief revision" process. A typical context to illustrate the belief revision process is a criminal investigation, Table 2.5. Initially, you may have some beliefs about the potential murderer, beliefs which are revised as you collect new pieces of evidence.

Table 2.5   Example of belief revision process (a)

A	Uncertain event of interest	The murderer is Miss Scarlett
$P(A)$	Initial belief about A	I have a certain belief that the murderer is Miss Scarlett
B	New information gained	The crime has taken place in the kitchen
$P(B)$	Initial belief about B	I have a certain belief that the murder has taken place in the kitchen
$P(B|A)$	Likelihood of B if A is true	It is unlikely that Miss Scarlett would have killed anyone *in the kitchen*
$P(A|B)$	Revised belief about A	Since I know that the crime took place in the kitchen I should revise (decrease) my belief about Miss Scarlett being the murderer

Table 2.6 A simplified Cluedo game

People	Weapons	Places
Colonel Mustard	Spanner	Lounge
Miss Scarlett	Dagger	Hall
Mrs White	Rope	Dining room
Professor Plum	Candlestick	Kitchen

Bayes' theorem can be considered as the "engine" of any belief update. A possibly more intuitive expression of Bayes' theorem is:

Posterior belief ∝ Prior belief · Evidence likelihood

If you have a strong belief for a particular outcome of an uncertain event, and if you collect pieces of evidence that are not consistent with this outcome, or at least would be very unlikely, then you should revise your belief.

This is a continuous process: you permanently revise your beliefs when you get new pieces of information.

Let us now examine in detail this type of belief revision in the context of a Cluedo game. We consider in Table 2.6 a very simplified version of this game, with only four cards of each type.

You have been given three cards: Colonel Mustard, Spanner, and Lounge. You have two fellow players, each one having also three cards. And finally there are three cards in the murder envelope, which you are trying to guess.

When Player 1 calls for "Professor Plum, in the Kitchen, with the Candlestick", it turns out that Player 2 has some cards (1, 2 or 3) matching the suggestion. Of course, you do not know which cards matched. How can you use this piece of information to revise your beliefs?

Before getting this information, you know that the murder envelope contains one people card among {Scarlett, White, Plum}, one weapon card among {Dagger, Rope, Candlestick}, and one place card among {Hall, Dining Room, Kitchen}. Altogether, you have 27 possible combinations. *Before Player 1's suggestion*, you should rationally believe that each combination has a probability of 1/27.

Now it is your turn to make a suggestion and you consider calling for "Miss Scarlett, in the Kitchen, with the Rope". What is the probability of this suggestion given the piece of information you have collected?

The calculation of these probabilities is tedious but simple.

If we make *no assumption about the cards in the murder envelope*, there are also 27 possible combinations for the game of Player 2. Among those, 19 of them would match some cards in

Table 2.7 Example of belief revision process (b)

A	Miss Scarlett, in the Kitchen, with the Rope
$P(A)$	$1/27 = 0.037$
B	Player 2 had some cards matching "Professor Plum, in the Kitchen, with the Candlestick"
$P(B)$	$19/27$–see calculation below
$P(B|A)$	$6/8$–see calculation below
$P(A|B)$	$1/27.6/8/(19/27) = 0.039$

Table 2.8   Situations matching the suggestion with no prior

Scarlett	Dagger	Hall
White	Dagger	Hall
Plum	*Dagger*	*Hall*
Scarlett	Rope	Hall
White	Rope	Hall
Plum	*Rope*	*Hall*
Scarlett	*Candlestick*	*Hall*
White	*Candlestick*	*Hall*
Plum	*Candlestick*	*Hall*
Scarlett	Dagger	Dining room
White	Dagger	Dining room
Plum	*Dagger*	*Dining room*
Scarlett	Rope	Dining room
White	Rope	Dining room
Plum	*Rope*	*Dining room*
Scarlett	*Candlestick*	*Dining room*
White	*Candlestick*	*Dining room*
Plum	*Candlestick*	*Dining room*
Scarlett	*Dagger*	*Kitchen*
White	*Dagger*	*Kitchen*
Plum	*Dagger*	*Kitchen*
Scarlett	*Rope*	*Kitchen*
White	*Rope*	*Kitchen*
Plum	*Rope*	*Kitchen*
Scarlett	*Candlestick*	*Kitchen*
White	*Candlestick*	*Kitchen*
Plum	*Candlestick*	*Kitchen*

the suggestion "Professor Plum, in the Kitchen, with the Candlestick" (in italic character in Table 2.8).

In other words, $P(B) = 19/27$.

If we now *assume that the murder envelope contains the three cards "Miss Scarlett", "Kitchen", "Rope"*, there are only eight combinations left for the game of Player 2 (Table 2.9), and among those, six would have matched the suggestion "Professor Plum, in the Kitchen, with the Candlestick".

In other words $P(B|A) = 6/8$ (Table 2.7).

Table 2.9   Situations matching the suggestion with a prior

White	Dagger	Hall
Plum	*Dagger*	*Hall*
White	*Candlestick*	*Hall*
Plum	*Candlestick*	*Hall*
White	Dagger	*Dining room*
Plum	*Dagger*	*Dining room*
White	*Candlestick*	*Dining room*
Plum	*Candlestick*	*Dining room*

Table 2.10 Situations matching the suggestion with a different prior

White	Dagger	Dining room
Plum	*Dagger*	*Dining room*
White	*Candlestick*	*Dining room*
Plum	*Candlestick*	*Dining room*
White	*Dagger*	*Kitchen*
Plum	*Dagger*	*Kitchen*
White	*Candlestick*	*Kitchen*
Plum	*Candlestick*	*Kitchen*

From this information, we can calculate using Bayes' theorem that $P(A|B) = 3/76 = 0.039$.

This may seem counterintuitive as a typical player would normally reduce his belief about "Miss Scarlett, in the Kitchen, with the Rope", if he or she knows that at least one of the three cards "Professor Plum", "Kitchen", "Candlestick" is *not* in the murder envelope.

To get the full picture you must recalculate also the revised probability of other combinations. For instance, consider the combination "Miss Scarlett, in the Hall, with the Rope", and call this combination C.

If we now *assume that the murder envelope contains this C combination*, i.e. the three cards "Miss Scarlett", "Hall", "Rope", there are only eight combinations left for the game of Player 2 (Table 2.10). Among these, seven would have matched the suggestion "Professor Plum, in the Kitchen, with the Candlestick".

In other words $P(B|C) = 7/8$, and $P(C|B) = 0.046$.

This means that the combination "Miss Scarlett, in the Kitchen, with the Rope" has now a relatively *lower* probability compared to other combinations, and in particular those with no cards matching the suggestion of Player 1.

We chose on purpose to describe such a detailed example, to show that the actual application of Bayes' theorem is not always simple, and that results should be interpreted with care.

This example also illustrates an important point: although most Cluedo players would have had the correct intuition about the belief revision, no player would have actually calculated the probabilities involved. *Bayes' theorem is a quantitative tool for belief revision, where intuition, is,* when correct, *only a qualitative guide.*

Another important and useful form of Bayes' theorem is known as the *total probability theorem* and states that:

If $A_1, A_2, \ldots, A_n$ are mutually exclusive and collectively exhaustive subsets of E, i.e. $A_i \cap A_j = \emptyset$, and $\cup (A_i) = E$, then for any subset B of E:

$$P(B) = \sum P(B|A_i).P(A_i)$$

This is quite easy to establish from the axioms of probability, if you notice that $\sum P(A_i) = 1$ (second axiom).

The interpretation of this expression is quite simple. Returning to the simple "colour blindness" example, we can calculate the total probability of one of your employees being colour blind as:

$$P(\text{Colour blind}) = P(\text{Colour blind} \mid \text{Man}).P(\text{Man}) + P(\text{Colour blind} \mid \text{Woman}).P(\text{Woman})$$

Random variables

Consider a future or unknown event for which the set E of all possible outcomes has been defined. If we are able to measure a quantity for each possible outcome, then the set of all possible values of this quantity defines a random variable.

Mathematically, if E is a finite set and P is a probability defined over E, a random variable is any mapping from E to R.

In the roulette game, a simple example of a random variable is the possible net gain.

If I decide to bet $1 on "5", then my possible net gains are:

Outcome(s)	Gain
0	−1
1–4	−1
5	35
6–36	−1

If I decide to bet $1 on "even", then my possible gains are:

Outcome(s)	Gain
0	−1
1–3–5–7–9–11–13–15–17–19–21–23–25–27–29–31–33–35	−1
2–4–6–8–10–12–14–16–18–20–22–24–26–28–30–32–34–36	1

If I decide to bet at the same time $1 on "5" and $1 on "odd", my possible gains are:

Outcome(s)	Gain
0	−2
1–3–7–9–11–13–15–17–19–21–23–25–27–29–31–33–35	0
5	36
2–4–6–8–10–12–14–16–18–20–22–24–26–28–30–32–34–36	−2

Obviously, once a random variable has been defined, the set of all possible values of this variable can be considered, and a probability defined over this set. This is done simply by giving to each possible value of the random variable the probability of the subset of E mapped to that value.

For instance, considering X the possible gains when betting \$1 on "5" and \$1 on "odd" at roulette, the possible values for this random variable are 0, 1, and 37, with the following probabilities:

Subset of E mapped to X	X	Probability
0–2–4–6–8–10–12–14–16–18–20–22–24–26 –28–30–32–34–36	−2	19/37
1–3–7–9–11–13–15–17–19–21–23–25–27–29 –31–33–35	0	17/37
5	36	1/37

The table mapping the different possible values of X to a probability is called the *distribution of X*:

X	Probability
−2	19/37
0	17/37
36	1/37

Several random variables can be defined over the same set. For instance, if you consider rolling two dice, the set of possible outcomes is the set of 36 couples (1,1), (1,2), up to (6,6). You may define over this set the following random variables:

- $D1$ = The value of Dice 1
- $D2$ = The value of Dice 2
- Min = The minimum of the two values
- Max = The maximum of the two values
- etc.

Since each random variable can be identified to a partition of E (i.e. a set of subsets of E), it is possible to extend the definitions of conditional probability and of independence to random variables.

If X is a random variable defined over a finite set E, we note $(X = x)$ the subset of E that maps to $\{x\}$. For instance, in the rolling two dice example, (min = 5) is the subset $\{(5, 5), (5, 6), 6, 5)\}$.

The distribution of X conditionnally to Y is then the set of conditional probabilities $P(X = x | Y = y)$ for all possible combinations of x and y, typically arranged into a table:

	$Y = y1$	...	$Y = yj$	...	$Y = Yp$
$X = x1$					
...					
$X = xi$			$P(X = xi\|Y = Yj)$		
...					
$X = xn$					

In the rolling two dice example, the distribution of min conditionnally to max is (assuming that the two dice are fair):

Max / Min	1	2	3	4	5	6
1	1.000	0.667	0.400	0.286	0.222	0.182
2	0.000	0.333	0.400	0.286	0.222	0.182
3	0.000	0.000	0.200	0.286	0.222	0.182
4	0.000	0.000	0.000	0.143	0.222	0.182
5	0.000	0.000	0.000	0.000	0.111	0.182
6	0.000	0.000	0.000	0.000	0.000	0.091

Two random variables X, Y are said to be independent if for any couple $(X = x)$ and $(Y = y)$ are independent for any couple (x, y).

This can also be written $P(X = x|Y = y) = P(X = x)$.

This is clearly not the case for the two variables min and max, as shown in the table above, where we have merged the unconditional probability of min and the conditional probability of min given max.

You could have guessed this because since max $\geq$ min, having some information about max changes the belief of min. At one extreme, if you know that max $= 1$ then necessarily both values of the dice are 1, and min $= 1$ also. This type of reasoning is useful when thinking about independence: when you can find at least one situation $(Y = y)$ where some knowledge about Y changes your belief about X, then X and Y are not independent:

Min	Unconditional probability	|Max = 1	|Max = 2	|Max = 3	|Max = 4	|Max = 5	|Max = 6
1	0.306	1.000	0.667	0.400	0.286	0.222	0.182
2	0.250	0.000	0.333	0.400	0.286	0.222	0.182
3	0.194	0.000	0.000	0.200	0.286	0.222	0.182
4	0.139	0.000	0.000	0.000	0.143	0.222	0.182
5	0.083	0.000	0.000	0.000	0.000	0.111	0.182
6	0.028	0.000	0.000	0.000	0.000	0.000	0.091

On the other hand, the two random variables $D1$ and $D2$ are independent: is there a case of knowing when the value of $D2$ changes your belief about $D1$?

Bayes' theorem can also be extended to random variables. This is particularly interesting in the "total probability theorem" form, since this allows us to compute probability distributions of random variables as a "table product" operation.

We can apply the total probability theorem to any subset $X = x_i$:

$$P(X = x_i) = \sum P(X = x_i | Y = y_j).P(Y = y_j)$$

X	P(X)			Y / X	y_1	$\ldots$	y_p	↓	Y	P(Y)
X_1	$P(X = x_1)$			x_1	$P(X = x_1 | Y = y_1)$		$P(X = x_1 | Y = y_p)$		Y_1	$P(Y = y_1)$
$\ldots$	$\ldots$	=		$\ldots$				**X**	$\ldots$	$\ldots$
X_n	$P(X = x_n)$			x_n			$P(X = x_n | Y = y_p)$			
				→				↓	y_p	$P(Y = y_p)$

This operation of conditioning is very important in combining probabilities, and in particular for Bayesian networks, discussed below.

Moments of a random variable

Some important quantities can be defined for random variables.

The *expected value* of a random variable is the probability weighted sum of its possible value:

$$E(X) = x_1.P(X = x_1) + x_2.P(X = x_2) + \ldots + x_n.P(X = x_n)$$

For instance, considering X the possible gains when betting $1 on "5" and $1 on "odd" at roulette, the distribution of X has been calculated above and is:

X	Probability
−2	19/37
0	17/37
36	1/37

The expected value of X is approximately -0.05 (any random variable that you can build to represent your gains at the casino will have a negative expected value).

If the random variable is measured on a repeatable uncertain event, then the expected value represents the long-run average of the measures of this random variable.

For instance, the expected value of the roulette gain above is slightly negative: this means that in the long-run, you will always lose money at the casino–but you knew that already.

For any random variable X of expected value $E(X)$, you can define another random variable $X_c = (X - E(X))^2$. The expected value of X_c is called the *variance* of X. The square root of $E(X_c)$ is called the *standard deviation* of X:

$$V(X) = (x_1 - E(X))^2 \cdot P(X = x_1) + (x_2 - E(X))^2 \cdot P(X = x_2) + \ldots$$
$$+ (x_n - E(X))^2 \cdot P(X = x_n)$$
$$\sigma(X) = \sqrt{V(X)}$$

$X - E(X)$ measures how far X lies from $E(X)$. We square the difference so that they do not compensate when computing their probability weighted sum. The variance is then the expected value of the squared difference. The standard deviation can be thought of as how far the outcome will lie from the expected value on average.

If we consider two random variables X and Y, the *covariance* of X and Y is calculated as the weighted sum of the differences $X - E(X)$ and $Y - E(Y)$:

$$\mathrm{Cov}(X, Y) = (x_1 - E(X)) \cdot (y_1 - E(Y)) \cdot P(X = x_1 \text{ and } Y = y_1)$$
$$+ \cdots + (x_n - E(X)) \cdot (y_p - E(Y)) \cdot P(X = x_n \text{ and } Y = y_p)$$

The *correlation* between X and Y is defined as the ratio:

$$\rho(X, Y) = \mathrm{Cov}(X, Y)/(\sigma(X) \cdot \sigma(X))$$

The correlation (and covariance) has one very interesting property: if X and Y are independent, then $\rho(X, Y) = 0$. This can be easily checked by expanding the expression of covariance when X and Y are independent. The reciprocal is not true.

Consider a very simple case where X can take the values $\{-1, 0, 1\}$ with the following distribution, and $Y = X^2$.

X	Y	Probability
−1	1	1/3
0	0	1/3
1	1	1/3

Clearly X and Y are not independent: $P(Y = 1) = 2/3$, and $P(Y = 1|X = 0) = 0$. However, the X, Y correlation is 0.

Continuous random variables

The above discussion was focused on random variables with a finite number of possible values. Since we consider mapping from E to R, where E is a finite set, this will always be the case. However, the probability theory can be extended to infinite sets. Even if this discussion is beyond our scope, we can consider uncertain events for which the set of values of random variables cannot be easily defined a priori. Consider, for instance, the time you will spend driving today, the inflation rate in France for next year, the return of your stock portfolio at the end of this year: all these quantities are measures of a future state of the world, i.e. random variables.

Figure 2.6 US stock market (SP500)–Prices from 1870 to 2000

If you limit your evaluation to a given precision, you could very well define a list of possible values for these random variables, and try to estimate the probabilities for each value.

However, it seems more convenient to establish these probabilities for given intervals of the possible values.

This is the purpose of the *cumulative distribution function* (CDF), which is defined as $P(X \leq x)$. This function evaluates the probability that the outcome of a random variable is below x (actually between negative infinity and x).

Now consider a simple example: evaluating the return of your portfolio. To simplify the discussion, we will assume that you are not a stock market expert and thus (1) you simply purchased a SP500 tracker, and (2) you have no personal belief on how the market will evolve this year. So you decide to base your expectations on the historical behaviour of the US stock market. For this, you collect a series of US stock market total returns, from 1870, shown in Figure 2.6 in logarithmic scale.

From this series, you calculate a series of yearly returns, which you graph as shown in Figure 2.7.

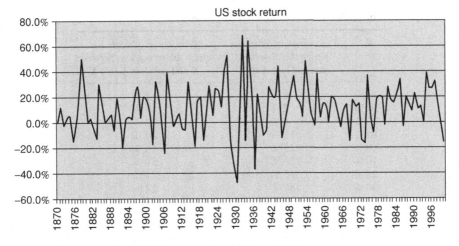

Figure 2.7 US stock market (SP500)–returns from 1870 to 2000

Table 2.11   US stock returns cumulative distribution

X	Number of years for which the observed return is less than X
−40 %	1
−30 %	2
−20 %	4
−10 %	17
0 %	38
10 %	65
20 %	93
30 %	115
40 %	125
50 %	128
60 %	129
70 %	131

After examining this series you decide to classify the years of observation by actual return offered, Table 2.11

From this table, you can read that, over 131 years of observation:

- 38 years had a negative return
- 66 years had a return above 10 % (=131−65)

You then decide to (1) express each figure as a percentage of the total number of years, and (2) add a column to this table, showing the difference between one line and the previous line, Table 2.12.

Now you can read clearly the percentage of years having a return between two particular values of return, and you decide to plot this table, Figure 2.8.

Table 2.12   US stock returns distribution

X	Percentage of years for which the observed return is less than X	Percentage of years for which the return was between X and previous line's X
−40 %	1 %	1 %
−30 %	2 %	1 %
−20 %	3 %	2 %
−10 %	13 %	10 %
0 %	29 %	16 %
10 %	50 %	21 %
20 %	71 %	21 %
30 %	88 %	17 %
40 %	95 %	8 %
50 %	98 %	2 %
60 %	98 %	0 %
70 %	100 %	2 %

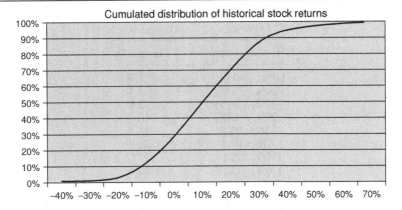

Figure 2.8 Cumulated distribution of historical stock returns

Now satisfied with your analysis, you decide to *set your beliefs of next year's return* at the observed distribution of historical stock returns, Figure 2.9.

This means that you will use the probability distribution for the "next year's return" as shown in Table 2.13.

With this example, we have introduced the cumulated density function (CDF) of a random variable. The CDF of a random variable is the F mapping such that $F(X) = P(X \leq x)$.

We have also introduced the histogram density which is a useful tool for reasoning about a cumulated density function.

Another important notion when dealing with continuous random variables is the "probability density function". The probability density function can be understood as the limit of the histogram distribution when the interval size becomes smaller and smaller.

Mathematically, the probability density function of a random variable is defined as the f mapping, when it exists, such that:

$$F(x) = P(X \leq x) = \int_{-\infty}^{x} f(t) \cdot dt$$

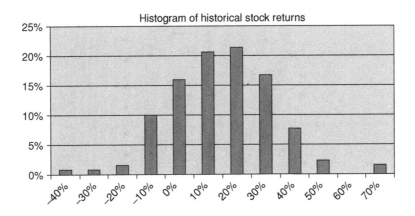

Figure 2.9 Histogram of historical stock returns

Table 2.13   Beliefs for US stock next year's return

Next year's return	Probability
[−∞, −40%]	1 %
[−40%, −30%]	1 %
[−30%, −20%]	2 %
[−20%, −10%]	10 %
[−10%, 0%]	16 %
[−0%, 10%]	21 %
[10%, 20%]	21 %
[20%, 30%]	17 %
[30%, 40%]	8 %
[40%, 50%]	2 %
[50%, 60%]	0 %
[60%, 70%]	2 %

Main probability distributions

Mathematicians have imagined a large number of distributions. Most of these distributions have been created to answer a specific need.

Introduction–the binomial distribution

This usually starts from considering a *stochastic process*, i.e. the repetition of a sequence of uncertain events. Let us illustrate this process with a simple example.

Before going to the casino, you may decide to spend at most $10, and, for instance, repeat the same bet exactly 10 times.

What would be the probability that you win 0, 1, ..., 10 times?

A simple way to address this question is to consider an event tree, describing all the possible sequences, Figure 2.10.

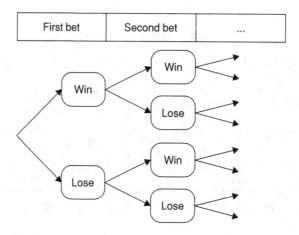

Figure 2.10   Event tree of binomial distribution

The "uncertain event" being examined is your situation 2 hours later when you go back to your hotel: how many times would you have won?

Reasoning with two bets, and assuming that they are independent, it is easy to verify that:

- $P(\{Win,Win\}) = p^2$
- $P(\{Win,Lose\} = p.(1-p)$
- $P(\{Lose,Win\} = (1-p).p$
- $P(\{Lose,Lose\} = (1-p)^2$

And finally that:

- $P(0 \text{ win}) = (1-p)^2$
- $P(1 \text{ win}) = 2.p.(1-p)$
- $P(2 \text{ win}) = p^2$

Now we can extend this result to n bets. If we denote by $P(n, k)$ the probability of having k successful bets among n bets, then:

$$P(n, k) = p.P(n-1, k-1) + (1-p).P(n-1, k)$$

In other words, to win exactly k times among n bets, there are two options: either win k times during the first $(n-1)$ bets, and lose the last, or win $(k-1)$ times during the first $(n-1)$ bets, and win the last bet.

Mathematically, this expression yields the following formula:

$$P(n, k) = \binom{n}{k} \cdot p^k (1-p)^{(n-k)}$$

where $\binom{n}{k} = n!/(k!(n-k)!)$ is the number of possible choices of k elements in a set of n elements.

From this result we can now establish the desired probability for 10 successive bets at the casino. The numerical results in Table 2.14 are shown for $p = 18/37$, considering that all bets would be placed on "even", for instance.

This distribution is known as the *binomial distribution* (Figure 2.11).

Table 2.14   Binomial probability distribution

k	$\binom{10}{k}$	Probability of k wins
0	1	0.001275
1	10	0.012079
2	45	0.051495
3	120	0.130094
4	210	0.215682
5	252	0.245196
6	210	0.193576
7	120	0.104793
8	45	0.037229
9	10	0.007838
10	1	0.000743

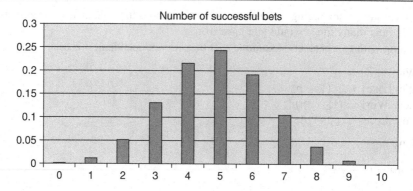

Figure 2.11   Histogram of binomial distribution

Overview of usual distributions

As we said before, there are many distributions described in the literature, and a whole range of discussions can be found regarding the appropriate distributions to use in order to represent a given phenomenon (see, for example, Vose).[1]

These distributions are created either from real-life models – such as Weibull distribution, used to represent lifetime of objects in reliability theory or from mathematical inference. For instance, the square value of a normally distributed variable follows a so-called chi-squared distribution.

All these distributions can be useful in some risk analysis applications. However, we have selected what we believe are the most usual distributions for a risk manager:

- The normal of Gaussian distribution, used to represent the impact of common events.
- The Poisson distribution, used generally to represent the frequency of events.
- The extreme value distribution, used to represent the impact of uncommon events.
- The general histogram distribution.
- The triangular distribution.

The normal or Gaussian distribution   The normal distribution, Figure 2.12, is typically used to model a variety of natural or behavioural phenomena. The wide use of this distribution is a consequence of the central limit theorem (below). In all situations, where many small effects are added together into an observable variable, the use of the normal distribution can be theoretically justified.

The Gaussian distribution parameters are:

- μ: the mean of the observed phenomenon.
- σ: the standard deviation of the observed phenomenon.

The PDF expression of this distribution is:

$$f(x) = \frac{1}{\sqrt{2\pi}\,\sigma} e^{-\frac{1}{2}\left(\frac{x-\mu}{\sigma}\right)^2}$$

---

[1] Vose, David 2000. *Risk Analysis, a Quantitative Guide*, 2nd edn, John Wiley & Sons Ltd, Chichester.

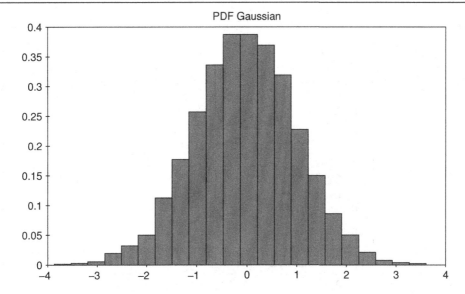

Figure 2.12 Normal distribution

The Poisson distribution   The Poisson distribution, Figure 2.13, is a discrete probability distribution. It expresses the probability of a number of events occurring in a fixed time if these events occur with a known average rate, and are independent of the time since the last event. In the field of risk management, it is often used to model the frequency of a given event.

This distribution has only one parameter:

- λ is the expected number of events during the considered period.

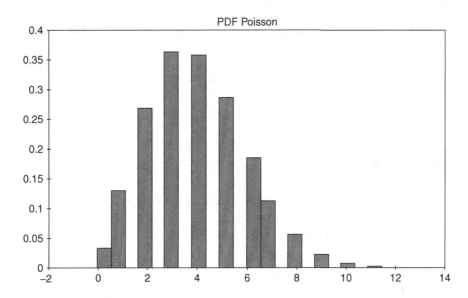

Figure 2.13 Poisson distribution

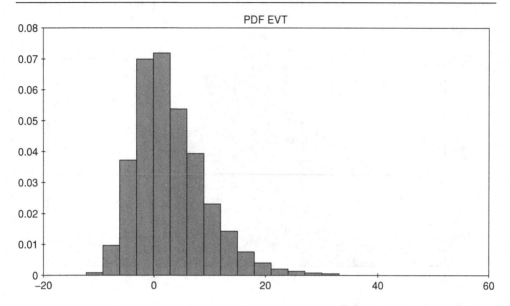

Figure 2.14 EVT distribution

The PDF expression of this distribution is:

$$f(x) = \frac{\lambda^x e_{-\lambda}}{x!}$$

The Gumbel distribution In the 1950s, the German mathematician Gumbel proposed a statistical theory of extreme events (EVT or extreme value theory), Figure 2.14. This theory has now abundant, applications, for instance when modelling large insurance losses, financial intraday risk, but also extreme floods or waves.

The Gumbel distribution is a special case of the Fisher – Tippett distribution, the PDF expression for which is:

$$f(x) = \frac{z.e^{-z}}{\beta}$$

$$\text{where } z = e^{\left(-\frac{x-\mu}{\beta}\right)}$$

The Gumbel distribution is obtained when $\mu = 0$ and $\beta = 1$.

The general histogram distribution Histograms are used to represent the distribution of empirical data, Figure 2.15.

The parameters of this distribution are:

- The minimal and maximal value of the available data.
- $\{x\} = \{x_1, x_2, \ldots, x_N\}$ is an array of intermediate values, assumed to stay between the minimal and maximal limits.
- $\{p\} = \{p_1, p_2, \ldots, p_N\}$ is an array of each interval cumulated probability.

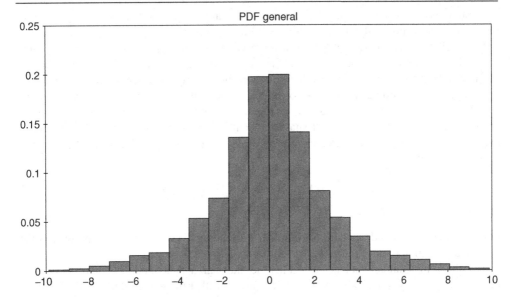

Figure 2.15 General histogram distribution

The PDF expression of this distribution is:

$$f(x) = p_i + \left[\frac{x - x_i}{x_{i+1} - x_i} \right] (p_{i+1} - p_i)$$

The triangular distribution   This distribution is generally used to represent an expert's view of a random variable. We will discuss the triangular distribution below, in "Estimating a distribution from expert knowledge".

Before closing this short catalogue of usual distributions, we would simply like to mention one important point. Most of the usual mathematical distributions are unbounded, which means that they can take infinite values, because they were usually designed as limits or generalizations of discrete distributions. Using unbounded distributions, and hence potentially infinite outcomes, may be nonsensical in risk management applications. We will go back to this discussion in the following sections of this book.

Fundamental theorems of probability theory

One of the most powerful tools of probability theory is the law of large numbers, which expresses the fact that a repeated series of random events converges to some sort of deterministic equilibrium.

The *weak law of large numbers* states that if $X_1, X_2, X_3, \ldots$ is an infinite sequence of uncorrelated random variables, where all the random variables have the same expected value μ and variance σ^2, then the sample average:

$$\overline{X} = \frac{(X_1 + X_2 + \cdots + X_n)}{n}$$

converges in probability to μ.

In other words, it is less likely, as the number of samples grows, that the sample average would be significantly different from the expected value.

When all the random variables have a finite variance, the *central limit theorem* extends our understanding of the convergence of the sample average by calculating the distribution of the standardized sample average. Regardless of the underlying distribution of the random variables, this standardized difference converges in distribution to a normal random variable.

If $X_1 X_2, X_3, \ldots X_n$ is a finite sequence of n independent random variables which are defined on the same probability space, and share the same probability distribution D, if both the expected value μ and the standard deviation σ of D exist then the distribution of standardized sample average:

$$S_n = \frac{((X_1 + X_2 + \cdots + X_n)n) - \mu}{\sigma \sqrt{n}}$$

has expected value 0 and standard deviation 1. Furthermore, this distribution approaches the normal distribution (convergence in distribution).

This theorem is fundamental because it justifies that a great deal of real-life distributions can be approximated by a normal law–be careful, however, that the prerequisites of the theorem are matched, and in particular the independence of individual variables.

Empirical estimation

Now we come to an important question. Where do the probabilities come from?

In our discussion above, we always assumed some initial probabilities, and derived other probabilities using the axioms and theorems of probability theory.

As we mentioned already, probability theory only gives you tools to combine "rationally" your initial beliefs, but does not give you any initial belief. We saw a very simple instance of that in the roulette example. If you believe that the wheel is fair, then you can rationally build probabilities for each possible outcome.

Our position in this book is that a probability is always the expression of a belief. You may collect evidence to support your beliefs – collect data, interview experts – but these beliefs will remain yours. And in practice, as a risk manager, you will have to have enough supporting evidence, or expert support, to convince others with your beliefs.

There have been many discussions about the "nature" of probability. We will spend some time to discuss this point below, but for now let us focus on the two main ways to collect evidence to support your beliefs: data and experts.

Estimating probabilities from data

The first way to estimate a probability is to use a set of data supposed to be occurrences of the process you are trying to evaluate.

For instance, using the simplest possible example, if you want to estimate the probability of getting heads or tails with a coin, you may flip the coin a certain number of times, and use the proportion of heads as the probability. For instance, if you have flipped the coin 10 times and observed 4 heads, you would use 0.4 as heads probability. How valid is this inference, and actually how could you evaluate its validity?

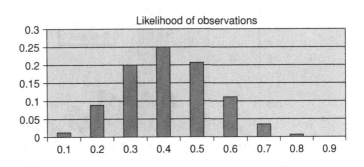

P	P(10, 4)
0.1	0.01116
0.2	0.08808
0.3	0.200121
0.4	0.250823
0.5	0.205078
0.6	0.111477
0.7	0.036757
0.8	0.005505
0.9	0.000138

Figure 2.16   Likelihood of observations

One possibility is to remember the binomial distribution and calculate the probability that you would have got 4 heads among 10 flips of the coin, making different hypotheses about the "real" probability of getting a heads for a flip.

If p is the current assumption of this probability, we know that:

$$P(10, 4) = \binom{10}{4} \cdot p^4 (1 - p)^6$$

We can calculate the value of $P(10, 4)$ for values of p ranging from 0.1 to 0.9, and get the results shown in Figure 2.16.

This simple calculation shows that "*the value of p for which the probability of observed results is maximal*" is actually 0.4. This result can be found rigorously. If we look for the maximal value of $P(10, 4)$ considered as a function of p, then we simply need to calculate the derivative of this function. This derivative will be 0 for the value of p maximizing the function:

$$\frac{d}{dp} \binom{10}{4} \cdot p^4 (1 - p)^6 = \binom{10}{4}(4 - 10p)$$

Assuming the derivative is 0 yields $p = 0.4$.

With this very simple example, we have introduced the important approach of *maximum likelihood* estimation of probabilities.

Does the fact that $p = 0.4$ is the maximum likelihood estimation of p mean that this estimation is good enough? Actually we cannot tell, but what we can tell for sure is that the estimation would have been better if we had based it on 100 samples rather than on 10. Indeed, if we plot on the same graph the likelihood of getting 40 heads out of 100 for different values of p and the likelihood of getting 4 heads out of 10 for those values of p, we get the picture (shown in Figure 2.17 the bars have been renormalized):

It is clear from the graph that the maximum likelihood estimator is better (has a much higher probability) with 100 samples than with 10.

Fitting a distribution from data

The same principles apply when trying to fit a distribution to data.

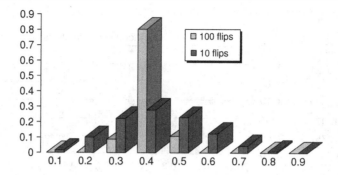

Figure 2.17   Maximum likelihood estimator

Returning to the stock return example, when we classified the observed historical returns in 12 categories, we actually fitted a histogram distribution on this data, Table 2.15 and Figure 2.18.

In most cases, this will be good enough in risk management applications, especially if you tend to approach your global risk management problem with Bayesian networks.

However, it is sometimes necessary to fit theorerical distributions on data, as we will for instance when we discuss the Basel II operational risk application – see Chapter 3.

This is usually done using the maximum likelihood approach, i.e. using the same principle as for probability estimation.

This works very simply:

1. Select a candidate theoretical distribution, which should be consistent with the phenomenon we try to represent. Here we need to be careful in particular when using unbounded distributions.
2. Calculate the likelihood of the observed data, assuming the underlying distribution is actually the one chosen in step 1. This likelihood is expressed as a function of the distribution's parameters, for instance the theoretical expected value and standard deviation.

Table 2.15   Empirical distribution of returns

Next year's return	Probability
$[-\infty, -40\%]$	1%
$[-40\%, -30\%]$	1%
$[-30\%, -20\%]$	2%
$[-20\%, -10\%]$	10%
$[-10\%, 0\%]$	16%
$[-0\%, 10\%]$	21%
$[10\%, 20\%]$	21%
$[20\%, 30\%]$	17%
$[30\%, 40\%]$	8%
$[40\%, 50\%]$	2%
$[50\%, 60\%]$	0%
$[60\%, 70\%]$	2%

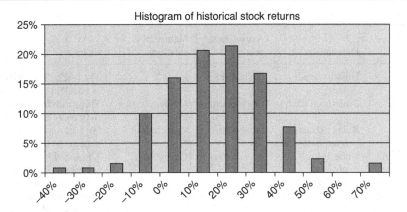

Figure 2.18 Fitting histogram distribution from data.

3. Calculate the partial derivatives of the likelihood with respect to the distribution parameters. The maximum value of the likelihood occurs when the partial derivatives with respect to the parameters equal 0.
4. Estimate the "goodness of fit", i.e. decide whether the maximum likelihood distribution actually fits the data. If not, consider revising the selection of candidate theoretical distribution in step 1.

Expert estimation

According to the online encyclopedia Wikipedia, "an expert is someone widely recognized as a reliable source of knowledge, technique, or skill whose judgment is accorded authority and status by the public or their peers".

Most definitions of "expert" include the reference to knowledge. An expert will help you in estimating some probabilities if the uncertain future that you are trying to quantify is more familiar to her. For instance, if you are project manager for the first time, and you try to analyze possible risks for your project, an experienced project manager would probably help you. In this case, the expert "simply" has a longer recorded experience than you do. In other words, in this situation, the expert estimation is still empirical, i.e. based on data. She has lived through the situation you are unfamiliar with a number of times, and her probabilities are, as usual, calculated as a frequency. Her database has, however, some specific feature. It is a set of *memorized* events. We will return to this point later.

Now imagine that you have to assess the risk of a terrorist threat, or of a new virus? You would probably try to rely on experts, such as intelligence agents, or biologists. How can they help you to assess probabilities on an uncertain event they have never experienced themselves? The underlying assumption is that they can connect this unknown event to past events and then estimate frequencies from a larger class of situation.

From data to knowledge

Without entering a philosophical discussion, we believe it is possible to clarify the concepts of data, information and knowledge.

Table 2.16   From data to knowledge

Object	Description	Acquisition process	Nature of relation	Example
Data	Unstructured facts	Collection	—	The truck driver #18 had an accident
Information	Structured data	Organization	Co-occurrence	The accident occurred on a freeway at 120 km/h
Knowledge	Rules extracted from data	Extraction	Correlation	60 % of severe accidents occur at high speed
Understanding	Underlying physical mechanism	Abstraction	Causation	The speed increases the probability of an accident because a driver has a minimum reaction delay. The speed increases the severity of an accident because of the kinetic energy involved

It is generally admitted that the difference between data and information is *structure*. The statement "The truck driver no. 18 had an accident" is a piece of data, among thousands of others.

Trying to organize this data into a structured way, such as collecting the data into a database, transforms data into *information*. Obviously, the structuring of data is the expression of some prior knowledge.

However, it is generally admitted that the actual and domain-specific *knowledge* process starts when looking for correlations in information. This process is at work in any experimental science, i.e. for any knowledge that describes some part of the real world.

Understanding is a further stage of knowledge. This stage is reached when an underlying mechanism can be exhibited that can account for the correlation observed. Finding such a mechanism will typically connect the limited data observed to a much wider domain of knowledge.

This discussion is important because it helps us to understand where the *confidence* in data and knowledge comes from. The underlying rule for any modelling is that "the same causes produce the same effects". When a rule has been verified in a number of situations, we believe we have captured the main drivers of these situations, i.e. the main causes.

Confidence comes from stability. In an unknown domain, when a rule is supported by many experiments, we have obviously more confidence in that rule than when it is based only on two or three experiments.

Why experts tend to have strong beliefs for some rules even though only sparse data are supporting this rule is the *nature* of expertise, i.e. understanding. Experts are capable of connecting observed data to the domain and, hence, to see apparently isolated data as observations of a more general, more abstract phenomenon.

In other words, confidence is always based on data support, either through collection of more samples, or through understanding, i.e. connecting the few samples that we have to a much larger sample set.

Confidence drives the way we consider data. When a model is considered as very robust, i.e. supported by a large amount of data, we tend to reject a single observation that would contradict the model. When a model is not robust, i.e. supported by few data points, we tend to question the model when a single observation contradicts it. In intermediate situations, we try to resolve the contradiction. This is usually done by introducing a new cause. We will probably decide that our model is still valid in a restricted context, but that a specific driver, a specific cause may also change the results in some particular situations.

From this introduction, we can suggest resorting to expert knowledge in three situations:

- To estimate probabilities of rare events.
- To estimate distributions of random variables, when only scarce data are available.
- To identify the causal structure of a domain.

Estimating probabilities from expert knowledge

As we defined it above, the task assigned to an expert when asked to estimate a probability can be decomposed into two parts. First, she has to connect the uncertain event for which the probability has to be assessed to a set of related events. Her expertise is assumed to be a guarantee that the set of selected events will be appropriate. Second, she has to recall her memories to evaluate a frequency.

Imagine that you are an operational risk manager in an international bank. Your mission requires that you evaluate the probability of some unexpected loss event, such as the scenario which caused the collapse of Britain's Barings Bank in 1995. You may require help from an experienced internal auditor in your organization, to evaluate the likelihood of such a scenario in your organization.

An export could implement the following type of analysis. First, she would consider the Barings scenario as a particular case of a more general situation (here the lack of control on a highly volatile activity). Second, review her knowledge of the organization to identify your organization's exposure to this particular scenario: are all highly volatile activities controlled by an independent and competent team. Finally, she would recall from past experience the probability that an individual or a group of individuals unsufficiently controlled would exceed their mission. Altogether, this analysis would allow the expert to evaluate a probability for this type of scenario.

This process may take place either implicitly or explicitly. Although this is not always possible, we recommend as much as possible to make it explicit. Indeed, in this case, only one probability is significant, and can be estimated with some confidence "the probability that an individual or a group of individuals unsufficiently controlled would exceed their mission". The likelihood of the scenario itself can be evaluated from this initial estimation, given the characteristics of your organization's activities and teams at risk.

Trying to elicit the expert's reasoning process increases confidence, in particular if you have to convince external people, for instance external auditors. Most people would tend to reject a simple probability estimate with no justification. In the Barings scenario above, since this scenario never happened in your organization, you cannot expect that your expert auditor would build her estimate on her memories. However, if urged to answer, she would probably be able to provide a qualitative estimate such as "less than once every 100 years". This type of estimate would certainly be questioned, if not rejected, by external supervision. On the other hand, you would probably be in a better position if you are able to explicitly ground this estimate on a causal structure as shown above.

The literature on probability elicitation is very abundant, and mainly addresses two topics:

- Identification and analysis of possible bias in expert judgement.
- Definition of protocols or methods for elicitation.

The first category mainly deals with the psychology of judgement under uncertainty, and shows that, depending on the protocol, experts may tend to under- or overestimate. In particular, there is a strong bias due to salience of events considered (*theory of perceptual salience*). People will tend to overestimate the frequency of recent, dramatic, or personal events while they would typically underestimate the likelihood of situations they can hardly imagine. Another source of error is the motivation of the expert, such as "the expert may want to influence a decision, she may believe that she is under evaluation, etc".

The second category tries to define elicitation tools or protocols to overcome these possible biases. For instance, the Stanford/SRI protocol involves motivating the expert with the aims of the elicitation process, structuring the uncertain quantities in an unambiguous way, conditioning the expert's judgement to avoid cognitive biases, encoding the probability distributions and verifying the consistency of the elicited distributions.

In the framework of risk management, however, we believe that the main issue is really the assessment of the probability of rare events. In this context, we would highly recommend implementing the simple principles discussed above, i.e. (1) try to analyze the rare event being addressed as a particular case of a more general class, for which some occurrence exists, and (2) derive the probability of the considered event.

Estimating a distribution from expert knowledge

In most cases, experts are *not* the appropriate knowledge source to estimate a distribution. One exception is when the event being modelled is quite frequent, but related data have simply not been collected. In that situation, experts can be of some help since they will generally have some internal representation of the distribution of the considered variable.

For instance, when considering internal fraud, the time extent of the fraudulent activity is a quantity of interest: how long can the fraudster operate before being detected? Usually, this information will not be available in recorded cases. Still, a fraud expert will have some sort of estimate of this duration.

The triangular distribution is a good way to represent expert belief. To be defined, this distribution requires only three parameters: the minimum, maximum, and most likely values. Once defined, these three values can be used to build a triangle whose surface is equal to 1. This triangle would then define the probability distribution function.

For instance, if the fraud expert considers that the minimum duration of a fraudulent activity would be one month, the maximum 24 months, and the typical one six months, the distribution would be as shown in Figure 2.19.

Identifying the causal structure of a domain

In general, the identification of a domain structure may be a complex task, in particular when it involves several experts.

The first task is to properly identify variables – and this is not the least in practice. Then, identifying the causal links is usually easier. It would be beyond the scope of this book to describe in full detail a methodology to catch the causal structure of a knowledge domain. In Chapter 3, we provide the general guidelines of such a method, focused on vulnerability models, with the exposure, occurrence, impact framework.

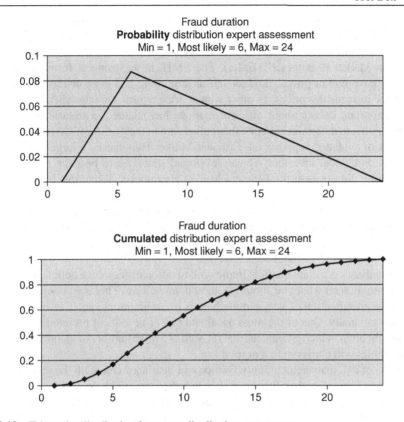

Figure 2.19   Triangular distribution for expert distribution assessment

Conclusion

As already stated above, our position in this book is that a probability is always the expression of a belief. As a risk manager, the evaluation of probabilities and distributions is your responsibility, and you have to decide in full knowledge.

Most of the literature on quantitative risk management is about mathematics. For a non-mathematician, this literature is often hermetic. There is one point that must be always kept in mind. Mathematical tools are used only to combine or derive beliefs in a rational way. In other words, all mathematical developments on probabilities build on top of a simple initial belief – or theory, if you prefer. This initial belief is then unfolded as much as possible using mathematical inference *within the framework of probability theory*, and yields quantitative results that may seem difficult to assimilate.

Let us describe a very representative example.

In 1900, Louis Bachelier[2] based his PhD dissertation titled "Theory of speculation" on the central assumption that the stock price returns are unpredictable, due to the uncountable factors that influence the investors' opinions. From this very simple belief (which anyone can understand and discuss), Louis Bachelier *derives mathematically one of the most important*

---

[2] Bachelier, L. 1900. Théorie de La speculation, *Annales Scientifiques de l'École Normale Supérieune Séries 3*, 17, 21–86.

ideas in the world of finance, i.e. that price returns are normally distributed (which most nonmathematicians would find mysterious). This work was indeed rediscovered in the 1950s and Eugene Fama published in 1965 "The behaviour of stock market prices,"[3] which introduced the "Efficient Market Hypothesis" (EMH). The EMH, in its strongest form, asserts that all information (past market prices, fundamental information, and even insider information) is fully reflected in securities prices. In other words, price returns are unpredictable.

A very important debate about efficient markets has resulted in thousands of empirical studies attempting to determine whether the markets are in fact "efficient". Although a tremendous amount of evidence supports the Efficient Market Hypothesis, a large number of people – traders, individual investors – have developed strategies to beat the market, showing that they simply did not trust the Efficient Market Hypothesis. Today this hypothesis is still controversial.

The mathematical derivation of Bachelier is not questioned (and not questionable): if the markets are efficient, *then* the price returns are normally distributed, according to the probability theory. What is questionable is whether the markets are indeed efficient. And this is an assumption that the maths cannot decide for you.

Probability theory is a mathematical framework to rationally combine beliefs. It will not give you any information on what you should or should not believe. This is an incredibly powerful tool: from the specification of very simple beliefs or assumptions, you can infer probability distributions rationally. One of the most usual and powerful tools of probability theory is the central limit theorem, which guarantees that the sum of a large number of identically distributed random variables will converge to a normal law.

In the field of risk management, only finance and insurance can really benefit from mathematical developments of probability theory, because these two fields deal with *frequent random events*. Indeed, at a cumulated level, *most random phenomena exhibit organized features*. When dealing with discrete and specific uncertain events, you have to build your own beliefs. To do so, you may rely on experts, specifically on causal models designed by experts, or you may simulate rave events.

C'est sur la régularité des résultats moyens des événemens considérés en grand nombre, que reposent divers établissemens, tels que les rentes viagères, les tontines, les assurances, etc.[4]

BAYESIAN NETWORKS AND INFLUENCE DIAGRAMS

Bayesian networks are a powerful tool to combine elementary beliefs in a rational way. A Bayesian network is comprised of:

- A causal graph which represents the knowledge structure of a domain.
- A set of "local beliefs", i.e. a set of local probability distribution, combined through the causal graph.

In this section, we will introduce the Bayesian network framework and its extension to influence diagrams. Probability basics have been presented above and will serve as a foundation for this discussion.

---

[3] Fama, E. 1965. The behaviour of stock market prices, *Journal of Business*, 38, 34–105.

[4] de Laplace, Pierre-Simon 1995. (*Théorie analytique des probabilités 1812–1820*), Jone VII des oeuvres complètes (Paris – 3e edition – 1820). Réédition Jacques Gabay.

As this book is mainly targeted at nonspecialists, we chose to introduce Bayesian networks on a simple example, inspired by road transport fleet risk management.

Introduction to the case

We consider a risk manager addressing the road accident risk for the company truck fleet. He wants to represent the three parameters (exposure, occurrence, and impact) of the vulnerability distribution using a Bayesian network.

For this particular risk, the appropriate *exposure* measure is the distance covered by the fleet during one period of time. Each kilometre covered by a truck is exposed to the occurrence of a road accident. The number of trucks would not be an appropriate measurement for exposure, since buying a new truck does not increase the risk of accident until the truck is on the road. Similarly, a driver participates in the risk exposure only when he is at the wheel.

This measure of exposure is generally used by national authorities, such as the *Observatoire national interministériel de sécurité routière*[5] in France.

The number of kilometres covered per year for the considered company is the selected measurement for exposure. From a prospective risk management point of view, this is clearly a random variable since we cannot know a priori the number of kilometres that would be covered next year.

Using the distance covered as a measure of exposure is only acceptable because we will analyze further the risk for each individual kilometre. We will examine whether this kilometre is covered by an experienced driver on a freeway or on a minor road, etc. This means that the probability of accident occurrence will be calculated "individually" for each kilometre, or at least for typical clusters of kilometres.

The drivers of the total distance covered during one year are mainly of a commercial nature: if we consider that the company will not change the structure of its activity next year, the exposure will be increased by a factor of growth – say 3 to 10 %, depending on the market growth, the policy of the company, the policy of competitors, and so on. On the other hand, a change of structure of activity – for instance, focusing on long distance transport – may have a more radical impact.

The probability of *occurrence* of an accident can be considered as dependent on various factors, among which the most significant would probably be:

- Truck driver qualification
- Truck driver condition
- Road used (freeway, urban motorway, minor road)
- Speed

Similarly, the severity of the accident, when it happens, will increase with speed, and possibly with the nature of the freight.

Since we try to build a simple introductory example, let us assume the simplified model:

- Exposure depends only of activity growth – no change in activity structure or competition.
- Probability of occurrence depends only of truck driver qualification, road used, and speed. Obviously speed depends also of the type of road used.
- Severity depends only on speed.

---

[5] National Observatory of Road Transportation Safety.

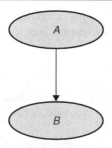

Figure 2.20   Representation of a causal dependency

Introduction to Bayesian networks

A Bayesian network is a probabilistic causal graph. The graph represents the structure of knowledge about a given domain: concepts or variables are connected by oriented links. A link is the expression of a causal dependency.

Figure 2.20 means that B is dependent on A. Since A and B are random variables, this means that the expected outcome for B depends of the previously observed outcome for B.

Mathematically, this means that the conditional distribution $P(B|A)$ is different to $P(B)$.

In the road transport fleet risk management example above, we could use a Bayesian network to represent the risk of accident for one unit of exposure, i.e. for one kilometre covered by a truck. Given the actual probability of accident (the order of magnitude being around 10 accidents for 100 million kilometres), we will rather consider a unit of 1 million kilometres.

Figure 2.21 can be read as follows.

Each kilometre covered by a given truck is exposed to the risk of an accident. *The probability of occurrence of an accident* depends on:

- The qualification of the truck driver at the wheel during this particular kilometre.
- The type of road on which this kilometre is covered.
- The speed at which this kilometre is covered.

If an accident does occur, *the cost (or impact) of the accident* will depend on the speed at that time. It is clear that these dependencies are not deterministic: for instance, an accident

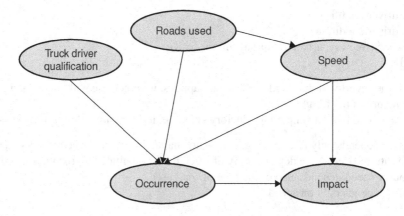

Figure 2.21   A causal graph for occurrence and impact of truck accident

Table 2.17   Variables and outcomes for the truck accident model

Variable	Possible outcomes	Comments
Truck driver qualification	Low Medium High	This variable represents the level of qualification of the driver at the wheel for the exposure unit considered (i.e. 1 kilometre)
Road used	Freeway Urban motorway Minor road	This variable represents the type of road on which the kilometre is covered
Speed	Low Moderate High	This variable represents the speed at which this kilometre is covered
Occurrence	0 1	This variable represents the occurrence of an accident under specific conditions
Impact	0–10 10–100 100–1000	This variable represents the cost of an accident, measured in some specific unit

can sometimes be serious at low or moderate speed, while in "lucky" situations a high speed accident may be benign[6]. The speed $\rightarrow$ impact dependency expresses that *on average* an accident would be more severe if it occurs at a high speed.

Nodes and variables

In a Bayesian network, each node represents a discrete random variable, i.e. a variable with at least two possible outcomes.

Bayesian networks can in principle deal with continuous variables, but discrete nodes are more usual. Furthermore, using continuous variables in Bayesian networks imposes restrictions for architecture and usable algorithms. In practice, as far as prospective risk analysis is concerned, the use of discrete or discretized variables would be generally appropriate and even recommended for a better communication of the models.

The road transport fleet risk management variables can be described as shown in Table 2.17.

Probabilities

Since each variable is considered random, its distribution must be defined. This means that the probabilities of the different outcomes must be defined.

In our example, it is easy to specify the probability of the two "root" variables: truck driver qualification and road used.

Provided the company has detailed information on its drivers it can rapidly establish that:

- 10 % of the truck drivers have not yet taken the training programme and can be considered as poorly qualified.
- 60 % of the truck drivers have taken the training programme and have 3–5 years' experience.
- 30 % of the truck drivers have taken the training programme and have 6–15 years' experience.

---

[6] The fact that dependencies are not deterministic has been discussed in Chapter 1. This simply means that other drivers exist, but cannot be captured, such as traffic density.

If we assume that drivers cover approximately the same mileage regardless of their qualification, this repartition can be extended to kilometres covered.

If we assume further that the company has detailed reports on its activity, the repartition of kilometres covered can be computed as follows:

- 70 % of the kilometres are covered on freeways.
- 10 % of the kilometres are covered on urban motorways.
- 20 % of the kilometres are covered on minor roads.

Therefore, if we consider a "random kilometre" for this company, we can reasonably assume that the expected outcomes for qualification and road type would be:

Truck driver qualification	Low	10 %
	Medium	60 %
	High	30 %
Road used	Freeway	70 %
	Urban motorway	10 %
	Minor road	20 %

This would not hold if the company had a specific driver assignation policy. For instance, if the company assigns only experienced drivers to distance where a significant distance is covered on minor roads, this would introduce a dependency between the "Road used" and the "truck driver qualification", as shown in Figure 2.22.

In this case, the repartition of kilometres covered per type of road would still be of interest, but would not be enough to quantify the network: the probabilities of "Road used" conditional to "Truck driver qualification" would be required.

Note that this could be again easily computed from activity reports and would look Table 2.18.

Now we need to analyse the speed on each type of road, Table 2.19.

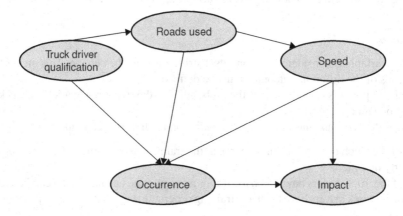

Figure 2.22   A management decision introducing a causal dependency: assigning experienced drivers to difficult missions

Table 2.18 Probabilities of "Road used" conditional to "Truck driver qualification"

Road used \ Driver qualification	Low	Medium	High
Freeway	90 %	77 %	50 %
Urban motorway	2 %	6 %	20 %
Minor road	8 %	17 %	30 %

In this simple example, we have used three qualitative modalities of speed: low, moderate, high. In practice, these indicators may be some ratio between the actual speed and the speed limit per type of road.

The last required information is relative to accident occurrence and accident cost. First, you need to express how the three drivers (truck driver qualification, road used, and speed) influence the probability of an accident, and then how the speed will increase the severity of an accident.

Hopefully you will not have enough statistics in your activity reports to have a reliable belief on this question. You may collect national statistics, or discuss with experts.

The result is come out with these tables, which express your present "belief" about the question, based either on national statistics, or on expert interviews.

For the probability of accident given the different conditioning variables (truck driver qualification, speed, and type of road), we will use Table 2.20, showing a differentiated accident probability for 1 million kilometres.

The two extremes are "Experienced truck driver at a relatively low speed on a freeway": around one accident for 100 million kilometres, and "Inexperienced truck driver at a relatively high speed on a minor roard": around seven accidents for 100 million kilometres.

And for the distribution of accident severity, depending on speed, see Table 2.21.

Table 2.21 expresses that, when an accident occurs at low speed, the cost of this accident is less than 10 in 70 % of situations, between 10 and 100 in 20 % of situations, and above 100 in 10 % of situations. This distribution is changed as the speed increases, for instance 60 % of the accidents that occur at high speed cost between 100 and 1000.

Dependencies

A link in a Bayesian network is intepreted as a causal relationship, i.e. $A \rightarrow B$ means that A is one of the causes of B. In other words, if A and B are uncertain variables, and the causal relation $A \rightarrow B$ holds, then the distribution on B will be different for different outcomes of A.

Table 2.19 Probabilities of "Speed" conditional to "Type of road"

Speed \ Type of road	Freeway	Urban motorway	Minor road
Low	20.0	33.3	50.0
Moderate	30.0	33.3	30.0
High	50.0	33.3	20.0

Table 2.20   Conditional probabilities of "Accident" occurrence

Speed	Truck driver	Road used	No accident	Accident
Low	Low	Freeway	97	3
Low	Low	Urban motorway	96	4
Low	Low	Minor road	95	5
Low	Medium	Freeway	98	2
Low	Medium	Urban motorway	97	3
Low	Medium	Minor road	96	4
Low	*High*	*Freeway*	*99*	*1*
Low	High	Urban motorway	98	2
Low	High	Minor road	97	3
Moderate	Low	Freeway	96	4
Moderate	Low	Urban motorway	95	5
Moderate	Low	Minor road	94	6
Moderate	Medium	Freeway	97	3
Moderate	Medium	Urban motorway	96	4
Moderate	Medium	Minor road	95	5
Moderate	High	Freeway	98	2
Moderate	High	Urban motorway	97	3
Moderate	High	Minor road	96	4
High	Low	Freeway	95	5
High	Low	Urban motorway	94	6
High	*Low*	*Minor road*	*93*	*7*
High	Medium	Freeway	96	4
High	Medium	Urban motorway	95	5
High	Medium	Minor road	94	6
High	High	Freeway	97	3
High	High	Urban motorway	96	4
High	High	Minor road	95	5

This is exactly what we showed just above by introducing the dependency between the "Truck driver qualification" and the "Road used" nodes.

Introducing a dependency in a Bayesian network should be considered only if you can quantify it. Introducing a dependency requires more explicit knowledge and has a certain cost. In some situations, you may be positive about a qualitative dependency, but unable to quantify it. In other situations, you may have evidence supporting a dependency, but no way to use it in your application. For instance, even if it is established that driving on drugs increases the probability of an accident, it would be extremely difficult to get statistics on how many kilometres are covered by drivers on drugs for your fleet.

Table 2.21   Conditional probabilities of "Accident" severity

Severity \ Speed	Low	Medium	High
0–10	70 %	20 %	20 %
10–100	20 %	60 %	20 %
100–1000	10 %	40%	60 %

Adding a cause to a node is also expensive in terms of statistical analysis, or expert inter-view: for instance, the distribution of "Occurrence" has 27 lines, each of them representing the probability of an accident for 1 million kilometres, given the values of the three causes identified. Adding another cause to "Occurrence" would have multiplied by three the volume of this table, if this new cause had three possible outcomes.

Inference

The main use of Bayesian networks is inference.

A Bayesian network represents the dependency structure of a knowledge domain. Once the graph has been created and the probability tables defined, a Bayesian network software will calculate the overall distribution of the set of variables.

Throughout the book we will illustrate the different examples with the Bayesian network tool Hugin. A very brief list of Bayesian network tools for risk analysis is proposed below.

Figure 2.23 shows the Bayesian network for the truck fleet risk, shown with "monitor windows", i.e. distribution windows. This means that each variable is shown with its actual distribution:

- The distribution of "Truck driver qualification" corresponds to what we have initially defined (this is the actual repartition of our drivers).
- The distribution of "Road used" corresponds also to what we have initially defined (this is the actual statistics of the distances travelled by the company).
- The distribution of the "Speed" does not look familiar: actually it has been computed by the Hugin tool from the distribution of "Road used", and the conditional distribution of "Speed" given "Road used". We will return to this calculation below.

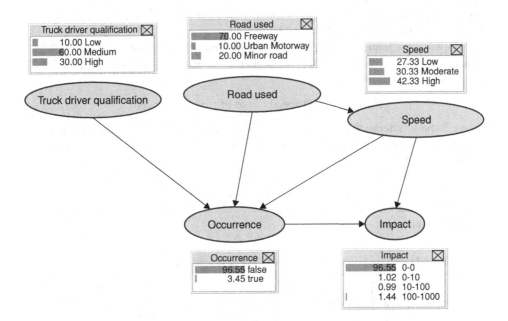

Figure 2.23   The truck accident Bayesian network: graph and probability tables

Table 2.22 Product of distribution tables: calculation of "Speed" distribution (a)

Road used		
Freeway		70 %
Urban motorway		10 %
Minor road		20%

Speed \ Type of road	Freeway	Urban motorway	Minor road
Low	20.0	33.3	50.0
Moderate	30.0	33.3	30.0
High	50.0	33.3	20.0

- The distribution of "Occurrence" shows that altogether the probability of an accident for 1 million kilometres is 3.45 %.
- The distribution of "Impact" shows again that in 96.55 % of cases, the cost incurred for 1 million kilometres will be 0 (no accident). This is consistent with the previous node. This node shows also that for around 1 % of cases, a cost of 0 to 10 will be incurred. For another 1 % of cases, a cost of 10 to100 is incurred. Finally, for around 1.5 % of situations, a cost of 100 to 1000 is incurred.

The first result that we get from defining our model and entering the data in the tool is the actual distribution of the costs incurred for one unit exposed (here 1 million kilometres).

How is this calculation performed?

We will illustrate this with a simple example: the calculation of "Speed" distribution.

We start with the two tables (Table 2.22).

The "Speed" distribution is computed as a simple product of the two tables (Table 2.23).

What is exactly this table's product? It is simply the application of the "total probability theorem" version of Bayes' theorem.

$$P(\text{Speed}) = P(\text{Speed} \mid \text{Type of road}) \cdot P(\text{Speed})$$

Now we come to inference per se. Inference in a Bayesian network is simply using Bayes' theorem. Consider the "accident" situation. This means that we would like to calculate the distribution of the other variables *given that we know that an accident has occurred*.

In a Bayesian network tool, this is simply done by entering a piece of evidence. Here we have selected "True" in the "Occurrence" node, Figure 2.24.

Now we see that the distributions of most variables have changed compared to the initial, unconditional situation:

Table 2.23 Product of distribution tables: calculation of "Speed" distribution (b)

70 % ×	20.0	+ 10 % ×	33.0	+ 20 % ×	50.0	=	27.33
	30.0		33.0		30.0		30.33
	50.0		33.0		20.0		42.33

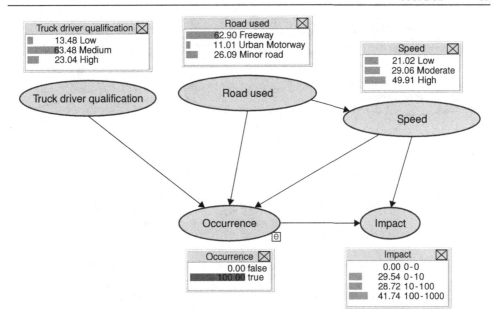

Figure 2.24   Inference in Bayesian networks–entering a piece of evidence: an accident has occurred

- First, the distribution of "Impact" has changed: obviously, since we assume now that an accident has occurred, the cost cannot be 0. We can see that 29.5 % of the accidents cost between 0 and 10, and so on. Note that these figures could have been simply deduced from the initial distribution.
- More interesting by, we see that the profiles of other variables have changed. The qualification of drivers has changed from Low: 10–Medium: 60–High: 30 to Low: 13.5 – Medium: 63.5 – High: 23. This seems intuitive since highly qualified drivers have less chance of having an accident.
- Similarly, assuming that an accident increases the probability of "Minor road" and "High speed".

Now we can try to understand the "typical" severe accident. For this, we will now select "100–1000" in the "Impact" node.

The results are quite intuitive: the typical severe accident would take place at a high speed, and on a freeway. The driver profile has not changed, Figure 2.25.

Learning

A Bayesian network contains knowledge in two different "forms":

- The causal structure of the graph.
- The probability tables.

We already discussed the fact that knowledge can be generally obtained from two sources: either empirically, i.e. from data, or from domain experts. This holds also for a Bayesian network, at least in theory. In practice, experts will help to build the causal structure of the

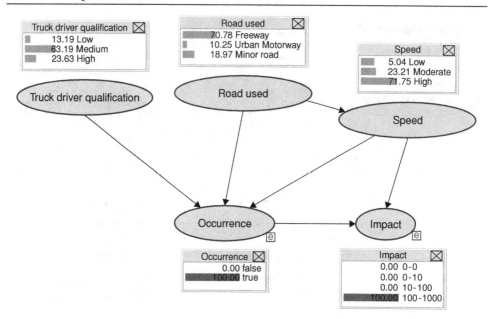

Figure 2.25   Inference in Bayesian networks–profile of a severe accident

model, and the quantitative part of the model (probability tables) will be inferred from statistical data. This is exactly what we did in the simple example above: the fact that speed increases both the probability and the severity of an accident can be assessed by an expert, but statistical data are required to assess precisely to what extent.

In theory, it could have been possible to derive the causal structure directly from data. Specific learning algorithms can be used for that purpose. However, building the model structure directly from data is usually not feasible because no statistical database would be available where all useful variables are simultaneously present.

Let us return to the truck fleet example:

• Assessing the conditional probability of impact given speed requires a national accident database.
• Assessing the probability of accident given road used and driver qualification requires company records.

Building the whole model directly from data would require a global database where all fields would be simultaneously present. But most probably, no national database will have any information regarding the driver qualification, and no company records will be large enough to be representative of accident rate.

Table 2.24 summarizes the best practices for knowledge acquisition in Bayesian networks. Although learning structure from data may be appropriate for some specific applications, such as data mining, we believe that these recommendations are valid for most risk management applications.

Table 2.24 Knowledge acquisition in Bayesian networks

	Expert assessment	Learning from data
Causal structure	Usual	Difficult, requires large amount of data
Probability tables	Difficult, reserve to undocumented events	Usual

Extension to influence diagrams

Bayesian networks represent specific domain knowledge in a probabilistic graph. In all their applications, and especially for risk management, this knowledge will be used to support some sort of decision.

Influence diagrams are extended Bayesian networks that can be helpful for decision under uncertainty. In influence diagrams, special nodes called "decision nodes" are used to represent various alternatives.

Let us consider a simple application. A local government has to decide about a vaccination policy for next's year seasonal flu.

The population is split into three groups:

- 0 to 19 years old
- 20 to 64 years old
- Above 65 years old

The probability of being ill depends on age, and is of course reduced by vaccination, according to Tables 2.25 and 2.26.

This knowledge can be represented using a simple Bayesian network, Figure 2.26.

Now the "decision" is about vaccination policy. Should the government encourage general vaccination, vaccination limited to the "high risk" groups (i.e. people above 65 years old) or recommend no vaccination at all?

A criterion has to be defined in order to compare the different strategies. Assuming we are dealing only with usual seasonal flu (we will introduce a complete example on pandemic flu in Chapter 4), the economic criterion may be appropriate. A vaccination dose is assumed to cost €10, while the cost of a contaminated person is estimated to be €200 on average.

Now we have all the information required to create an influence diagram, Figure 2.27.

Table 2.25 Probability of being contaminated (nonvaccinated people)

Illness \\ Age	0–19 years old	20–64 years old	Above 65 years old
Yes	8.0	6.0	20.0
No	92.0	94.0	80.0

Table 2.26 Probability of being contaminated(vaccinated people)

Illness \ Age	0–19 years old	20–64 years old	Above 65 years old
Yes	5.0	4.0	10.0
No	95.0	96.0	90.0

Compared to the present network, we have added:

- A decision node "Vaccination policy", with three states: "None" (no vaccination at all), "VHiRisk" (vaccinate only high risk people), and "VAll" (vaccinate everybody).
- A utility node "Cost".
- A link from "Age" to "Vaccination": this expresses the fact that vaccination is now dependent on age, according to the different policies.

The "Vaccination" node is now shown in Table 2.27.

In this augmented model, the probability of being vaccinated now depends on strategy and age: for instance, a person between 20 and 64 years of age will be vaccinated (100 %) if the policy selected is "VAll" (but only in this case).

Now, the "Cost" node is special: it has no probability table, but rather a table displaying the cost of each possible situation Table 2.28:

- If a person is vaccinated and contaminated, she will cost € 210(10 + 200).
- If a person is vaccinated and not contaminated, she will cost €10.
- If a person is not vaccinated and is contaminated, she will cost €200.
- If a person is not vaccinated and not contaminated, she will cost €0.

Now how will the influence diagram help us decide? Simply by displaying the expected cost of each strategy, Figure 2.28.

Now, in general, influence diagrams are simply extended Bayesian networks, including three types of node:

- Chance nodes (or random variables) are represented using ellipses (as usual).
- Decision nodes are represented using rectangles.
- Utility nodes are represented using diamonds.

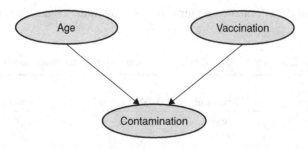

Figure 2.26 Simple "flu contamination" model

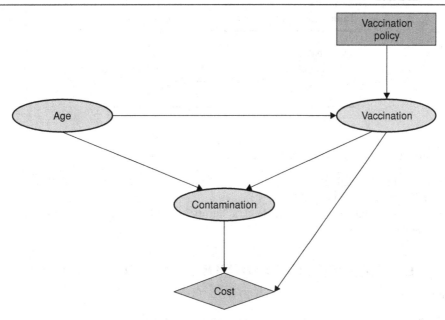

Figure 2.27 Vaccination policy influence diagram

Table 2.27 Probability of being vaccinated (decision model)

Vaccination strategy	None			VHiRisk			VAll		
Age	0–19	20–64	65+	0–19	20–64	65+	0–19	20–64	65+
Yes	0.0	0.0	0.0	0.0	0.0	1.0	1.0	1.0	1.0
No	1.0	1.0	1.0	1.0	1.0	0.0	0.0	0.0	0.0

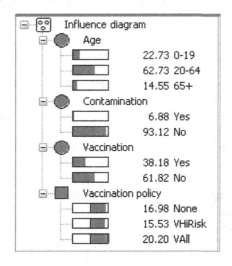

Figure 2.28 Compared "utility" of the different alternatives

Table 2.28   Cost of each possible outcome

Vaccination	Yes		No	
Contamination	Yes	No	Yes	No
Cost	210	10	200	0

The structure of an influence diagram must verify some constraints:

- There is a directed path connecting all decision nodes.
- The utility nodes have no children.
- The utility node has no "states". Instead, a "utility" must be defined for all configurations of the node's parents.

INTRODUCTION TO MONTE CARLO SIMULATION

Introduction

Sometimes you may be unable to effectively combine your beliefs (or local probability distributions). This may be impossible analytically, or you may have no mathematician at hand, or simply you may be too lazy. In any of these situations, you can use Monte Carlo simulation.

Monte Carlo simulation is a very powerful mathematical tool when dealing with uncertainty. It is widely applied in many application domains, such meteorology, finance, epidemiology, drug design, quantum physics, etc. The complete mathematical developments of Monte Carlo simulation are far beyond the scope of this book. Our purpose here is to introduce the basics of this technique for application in risk management.

A simple way to appreciate why you need to understand Monte Carlo simulation is that if ignore it, you may lose your money when dealing with people who do use it. It is clear for most people knowing the basics of probabilities that a casino owner is almost certainly rich. Thanks to Monte Carlo simulation, you will understand why some fund managers may become rich at your expense.

Introductory example: structured funds

A great deal of individual investors turned away from stock markets after the poor performances of the early 2000s, fearing to lose their capital, and indeed realized just in time that stock markets are risky. Some fund managers created special structured funds to overcome this fear and continued collecting money from the individual investors.

These funds are generally based on two promises: (1) whatever the market behaviour in the future, your initial investment is protected, and (2) if the market significantly increases, you will be awarded a significant part of this performance.

In this introductory example we will focus on a simple example, based on an existing fund actually marketed in France. The contract, which we will call the "Truffle Fund", is as follows. You have to keep your shares for at least 8 years. You can in theory sell at any time, but you would lose most of the performance. The initial fee is 6 %, and the yearly fee is 0.5 %. The fund is invested in the stock market. When selling back your shares after 8 years you will be

Table 2.29   Yearly returns of European stock markets

Period	European stock market total return
1998–1999	16 %
1999–2000	19 %
2000–2001	4 %
2001–2002	−21 %
2002–2003	−34 %
2003–2004	27 %
2004–2005	9 %
2005–2006	24 %

paid your initial capital (net of initial fee) plus 70 % of the total stock market performance during the period.

Let us consider a simple example – exactly as the salesman of the fund management firm would. If you invest 100, and the stock market went down 40 % (this happened for instance in Europe between 1997 and 2003), you would end up with 94, while someone who directly invested on the market would be left with only 60. On the other hand, if the market went up 100 %, (this happened in Europe between 1995 and 2000) your final capital would be around 160 (taking fees into account). In this case, the investor who directly invested in the stock market would beat you, since his capital would reach 200. Altogether, this seems a reasonable deal: you accept to give up part of your potential benefits, but your losses are really limited.

Being a risk manager, you decide to analyze in more detail the proposed offer. A first investigation would be to evaluate how this fund would have behaved on the last 8 years.

The actual yearly returns of the European stock market are as shown in Table 2.29.

Assuming a 100 index value on 1 January 1998, the stock market index would be 128.2 on 31 December 2005, 8 years later i.e. an overall performance of 28.2 %, or an annualized performance of 3.1 %. In these conditions, if you invested 100 in the Truffle Fund on 1 January 1998, you would have ended up with about 109 at the end of the 8 year period, Table 2.30.

In other words, the Truffle Fund annualized return would have been around 1.1 % over this 8-year period, i.e. about half the performance of the riskless asset (at least 2 %).

Now you feel disappointed. Before investing in the Truffle Fund, you need to analyze in more detail what could happen to your money in the next 8 years. For this you need to set your beliefs on the stock market for the next 8 years. This is not an easy task, so you decide to rely on specialists' beliefs.

Table 2.30   Simulation of fund performance

Initial investment, 1 January 1998	100
Entry fee, 1 January 1998	6
Management fees (0.5 %/year, 7 years)	3.3
Guaranteed capital	94
Performance (70 % of 28.2 %)	19.74 %
Total payback	109.3

First, from the efficient market hypothesis, already discussed above, you decide to assume that the stock market returns follow a normal law. Each year's return is assumed to follow independently the same law.

Second, you decide to evaluate the parameters of this distribution (mean and standard deviation) from history. This belief is consistent with the previous one, as you finally assume that the distribution of returns is stable over time.

Using these assumptions, you would like to evaluate the distribution of your future gains if investing in the Truffle Fund. This could be done mathematically for this simple case, but some structured funds have much more complex rules, for which Monte Carlo sampling would be necessary. We will first discuss how to sample random numbers according to a distribution, and then show how to combine these samples to draw some conclusions.

Sampling random numbers   Sampling random numbers is about creating a well-balanced set of possible results of random experiments. When you cannot repeat an experiment, for which some conditions are considered random, you may want to *simulate* it, i.e. run the experiment on "paper", or, more realistically, on a computer. If you would like the simulated experiment to be representative of the actual one, you need at least the random part of the real and simulated experiments to be similar, i.e. have the same distribution. If, for instance, the experiment

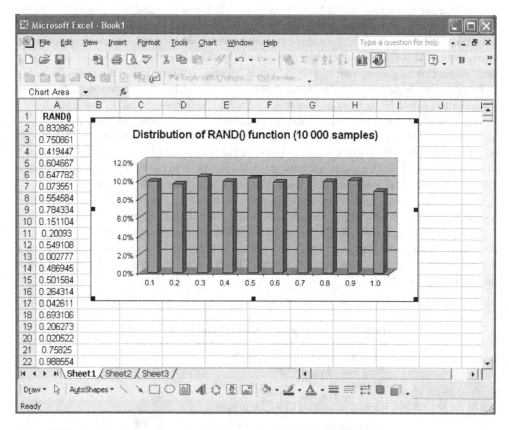

Figure 2.29   Sampling random number using Excel's RAND() function

Table 2.31 A histogram
distribution to sample from

Interval	Probabililty
[1,2]	0.2
[2,3]	0.4
[3,4]	0.3
[4,5]	0.1

involves some binary random event of probability 50 %, then you may flip a coin to simulate this. If the distributions involved are more complex, then you will need some computerized tools – there are no coins that you can flip to simulate a normal distribution.

The basic tool needed is a uniform sampler, i.e. a computerized function capable of drawing a number uniformly distributed between 0 and 1. Although, this is not a simple function to create, we will not enter this discussion here, and we will assume, for instance, that the RAND() function available within Excel is actually such a function, Figure 2.29.

With this function at hand, you can draw a number according to any distribution. Assume the distribution function is f, and the cumulated distribution function (CDF) is F. A theorem shows that if u is a random number uniformly distributed between 0 and 1, then $x = F^{-1}(u)$ is distributed according to f.

To get an intuition of this result, consider a random variable between 1 and 5, with a piecewise uniform distribution, as shown in Table 2.31.

The graph of the corresponding cumulated distribution function is Show in Figure 2.30.

If we draw u uniformly between 0 and 1, we know that u will fall between 0.2 and 0.6 with a 0.4 probability (this is an immediate consequence of the assumption of uniform distribution). Then $x = F^{-1}(u)$ will fall between 2 and 3, as shown above. Therefore, the probability of drawing x between 2 and 3 is 0.4, exactly as in the target distribution.

This holds for all intervals, as shown in Table 2.32.

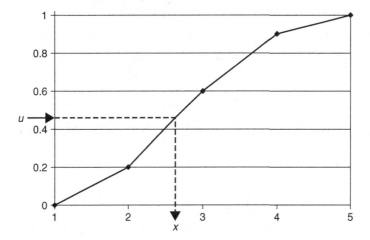

Figure 2.30 Sampling according to a histogram distribution

Table 2.32 Sampling according to a histogram distribution

u interval	Probabililty	$x = F^{-1}(u)$ interval
[0,0.2]	0.2	[1,2]
[0.2,0.6]	0.4	[2,3]
[0.6,0.9]	0.3	[3,4]
[0.9,0.1]	0.1	[4,5]

Sampling according to a normal distribution is then easy in Excel, using the NORMINV() function, which is the inverse function of the cumulated normal distribution function, Figure 2.31.

Building the structured fund simulation   In order to evaluate the structured fund future performance, we need to specify in detail the simulation process Table 2.33.

You can implement exactly the process described here within Excel. For this you simply need to sample the stock market returns during the 8 years of the simulation, using the RAND() and NORMINV() functions, Figure 2.32.

In order to evaluate easily hundreds of possible situations simultaneously, it could be more convenient to implement a single simulation in a single row.

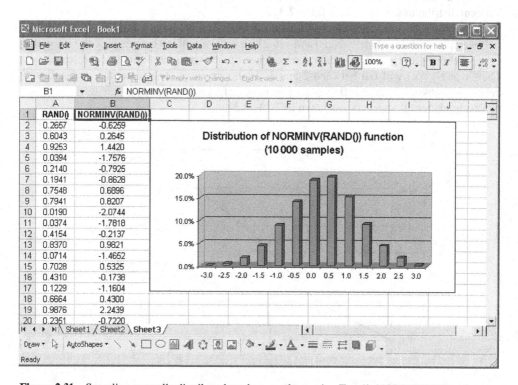

Figure 2.31 Sampling normally distributed random numbers using Excel's NORMINV() function

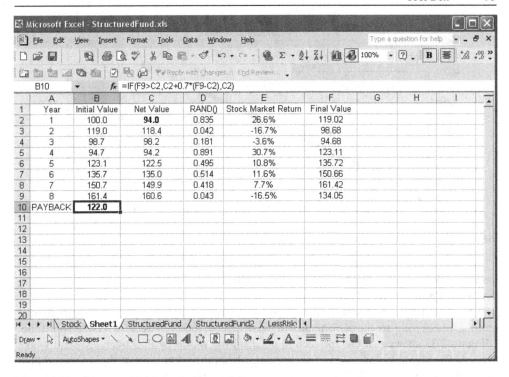

Figure 2.32   Structured fund simulation worksheet

One interesting analysis would be to compare the structured fund performance with a diversified portfolio holding 30 % of riskless asset and 70 % of stocks. By definition, this portfolio would offer 70 % of the stock market performance.[7] However, it would be more risky in

Table 2.33   Structured fund simulation process

Year	Initial value	Net value	Stock market return	Final value
1	V1 = 100	NV1 = 94	R1	FV1 = NV1*(1 + R1)
2	V2 = FV1	NV2 = 0.995*V2	R2	FV2 = NV2*(1 + R2)
3	V3 = FV2	NV3 = 0.995*V3	R3	FV3 = NV3*(1 + R3)
4	V4 = FV3	NV4 = 0.995*V4	R4	FV4 = NV3*(1 + R4)
5	V5 = FV4	NV5 = 0.995*V5	R5	FV5 = NV3*(1 + R5)
6	V6 = FV5	NV6 = 0.995*V6	R6	FV6 = NV3*(1 + R6)
7	V7 = FV6	NV7 = 0.995*V7	R7	FV7 = NV3*(1 + R7)
8	V8 = FV7	NV8 = 0.995*V8	R8	FV8 = NV3*(1 + R8)
	IF FV8>NV1			
		PAYBACK = NV1 + 0.7(FV8 − NV1)		
PAYBACK	ELSE			
		PAYBACK = NV1		

---

[7] Plus 30 % of the riskless asset performance.

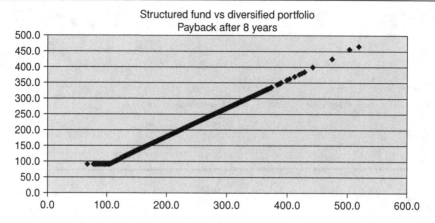

Figure 2.33   Structured vs diversified portfolio

unfavourable situations. But how often? We can have a partial answer to this question using the Monte Carlo simulation just designed.

If we draw 1000 samples of the next 8 years, according to the distribution of stock market returns, we can compare the performance of the structured fund versus the diversified portfolio.

Figure 2.33 shows that the "protection mechanism" set up by the structured fund works quite rarely (indeed in about 2 % of situations), while the performance of the structured fund is on average 76 % over the 8 year period versus a 95 % performance of the diversified fund.

Moreover, investing directly in the stock market – using for instance a tracker – would result in a final payback below 94 in only 3.3 % of situations, for an expected performance of 129 %! This means that, investing on the structured fund, you would give up almost 50 % of your expected performance to protect a quite unlikely risk.

Now we can understand the trick in the Truffle Fund offer. Losing part of one's capital *after one year* on the stock market is quite likely. Investors are willing to hedge this risk and feel reasonable giving up some performance for this. However, after 8 years, it becomes very unlikely to have a negative total return on the stock market – this happened only twice during the last 60 years on the European markets, and once on the US markets (between 1930 and 1938). So there is – almost – no risk to hedge, and certainly not at this price.

Conclusion   We have introduced the principle of Monte Carlo simulation, to show how to evaluate the distribution of some random variable, assuming it depends of other random variables, through a calculation or decision process. In the particular example studied, it would have been possible to calculate analytically the distribution of the return of the structured fund. This would not always be the case. As an exercise, you may consider the structured fund in Figure 2.34, for which the analytical calculation would be more complex.

Risk management example 1 – hedging weather risk

Description

Redwood Valley is a famous ski resort. During recent years, the resort has faced significant variations of snow levels. The weather during the winter at Redwood Valley makes the difference

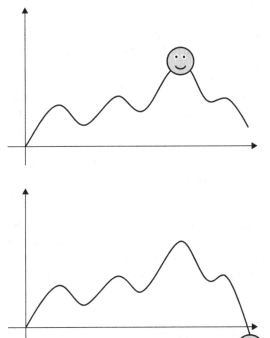

If the stock market return considered after 10 years is positive, the fund performance will be equal to the maximum performance recorded during this ten year period

Otherwise, the fund performance will be equal to the stock index performance (i.e., negative)

Figure 2.34   A more complex structured fund

between a worthwile profit and a significant loss. Only snowy winters attract enough tourists to cover the recurring maintenance expenses of the resort equipments.

Ed Grizzly is the Redwood Valley Lift Operators (RVLO) risk manager. The CFO of RVLO asked him to evaluate the risk of a financial loss this year. The main expenses to take into account are ski lift equipment operation expenses, which include maintenance, energy and salaries, and annual investments. Indeed, RVLO has launched this year a progressive renewal programme of all ski lifts with modern equipment. The policy of the RVLO is to try as much as possible to fund these expenses using current year lift pass income, minimizing the use of past years' cumulated profits.

Operation costs are evaluated at €7m for this year, while investments charge for ski lift renewal will be about €3m. These costs are considered certain – although they could also be subject to a certain volatility, for instance through energy costs. On the other hand, lift pass revenues are uncertain, since they depend on the resort activity, which in turn depends on snow level during the season. And obviously this parameter cannot be forecasted.

Given these parameters, RVLO would incurr a loss if lift pass revenue would be lower than €10m. A theoretical worse case scenario – although extremely unlikely – would consist of no revenue at all, i.e. a €10m loss.

This year, Ed Grizzly has to evaluate the likelihood of not being able to fund all expenses through lift pass revenue, and to propose a solution for this situation. In other words, the question he has to answer is: "How likely is it that the lift pass revenue would be lower than total ski lift expenses?" An additional concern to Ed is "How likely is a severe loss (more than €5m)?"

Collecting information

Since turnover depends on the number of skiers and snow level, Ed has to gather some statistical data guest occupancy about weather. Ed Grizzly obtains the following statistical data from the tourist office and local weather station.

The maximal housing capacity of the resort is 10 000 people. The ski season has three significant four week periods: December (Christmas holiday), February (winter school holiday) and April (spring school holiday). A weekly lift pass costs €300. From these simple figures, Ed evaluates that the maximal turnover would not exceed €36m (assuming full occupancy during the three periods), Table 2.34.

This maximum has never been reached in the past 10 years. Obviously some of the vacationers don't ski. Some of them only ski when the conditions are excellent, i.e. when the snow level is high. Statistical data show that 70 % of tourists ski when snow level is high. This rate decreases to 50 % for medium snow level, and to 30 % for low snow level, Table 2.35.

The occupancy per week depends on the period, the snow level and the snow level of the previous period. Snow level of the previous period has a significant impact on last minute vacationers, or people living close to the resort who may simply cancel their holidays. For instance, if the previous period snow level was high, the occupancy rate is as shown in Table 2.36 (shown as a percentage of the capacity).

Table 2.34 Maximal capacity and turnover

Maximal housing capacity	10 000
Number of periods	3
Number of weeks per period	4
Ski pass cost	€300
Maximal turnover	€36m

Table 2.35 Rates of skiers conditioned to snow level

Snow level	Skiers' rate
Low	30 %
Medium	50 %
High	70 %

Table 2.36 Occupancy rate conditioned to period and snow level

Period	Low	Medium	High
December	50 %	70 %	80 %
February	60 %	80 %	90 %
April	60 %	70 %	75 %

Table 2.37 December snow level statistics

Snow level	Frequency
Low	30 %
Medium	50 %
High	20 %

Table 2.38 Historical snow level correlations – February vs December

February \ December	Low	Medium	High
Low	30 %	15 %	5 %
Medium	40 %	50 %	10 %
High	30 %	35 %	85 %

Table 2.39 Historical snow level correlations – April vs February

April \ February	Low	Medium	High
Low	60 %	20 %	15 %
Medium	30 %	60 %	15 %
High	10 %	20 %	70 %

For example, if snow level is "medium" in February, the occupancy will be 80 % of the capacity (40 000). When the previous period snow level was only "medium", all figures in the Table 2.36 should be decreased of 20 %. Similarly, they should be decreased by 30 % for a "low" previous period snow level.

Now Ed decides to analyze the weather data. The local weather station provides the statistics in Table 2.37 for the December period snow level.

The weather station gives also the correlation tables, Tables 2.38 and 2.39. These tables read as follows: the greyed cell contains the probability that the February snow level would be Medium, given that it was "Low" in December. Analysed more carefully, these tables show that January and February snow falls can improve snow level, even if December was dry. On the other hand, March snow falls rarely compensate scarce snow falls in February.

Model

Now Ed will try to create a computational model for yearly lift pass turnover. It seems rather intuitive to present the model as a backward chaining process starting from the target variable back to the variables it depends on.

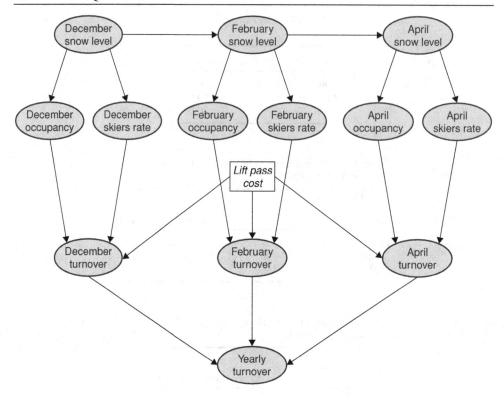

Figure 2.35   Causal graph of Redwood Valley yearly turnover

The target variable is thus the *yearly lift-pass turnover*, which is the sum of the *monthly turnovers* for December, February, and April. For each period, the turnover can be calculated as the product of the *number of skiers* and the *lift pass cost* (€300). The number of skiers is the product of the *occupancy rate* by the *rate of skiers* among the tourists.

The occupancy rate is a random variable. It depends on the *period*, the *snow level of the current period* and the *snow level of the previous period*. The dependency relationship is specified in Table 2.36.

The rate of skiers is a random variable. It depends on the snow level in the way specified in Table 2.35.

Snow level is a random variable. It depends on the period and on snow level of the previous period as specified in Tables 2.37, 2.38 and 2.39.

This model can be easily represented by a causal graph showing all dependencies between all variables. This causal graph contains both nonrandom (lift pass cost) and random variables (snow level), formula-type dependencies (yearly turnover is the sum of monthly turnovers) and random dependencies (occupancy rates depends on snow level), Figure 2.35.

This causal representation outlines the root variables for the computation process: snow level in December and periods. Once root variables are set, other variables can be either sampled from random dependencies or calculated through formulas.

Table 2.40   A possible
snow level sccenario

Month	Snow level
December	Low
February	Medium
April	Medium

Manual scenario

At first, Ed uses this model to manually play a scenario. He is pessimistic and he assumes that
the December snow level will be low (Table 2.37 gives a 30 % probability for this hypothesis).
Given this assumption, Table 2.38 shows that snow level in February should be distributed
as follows: low with 30 % probability, medium with 40 % probability and high with 30 %
probability. At this point, Ed assumes the most likely hypothesis, that is "medium". Now, if the
February level is medium the most probable snow level for April is also medium (Table 2.39).
As far as snow level is concerned, this scenario can be summarized in Table 2.40.

Building from these assumptions, Ed can now estimate resort occupancy.

In December, since snow level would be low, the occupancy rate should not exceed 50 %
of the total capacity and thus equals 20 000 (Table 2.36). In the same conditions, the skiers'
rates would be 30 % (Table 2.35), and finally the expected number of skiers in December
would be 6000.

In February, since snow level would be medium with a low snow level for the previous
period, Table 2.36 gives an occupancy estimate of 56 % (70 % of 80 %). The total number
of tourists for the period would then be 22 400 (56 % ∗ 4 ∗ 10 000). Finally, since the skiers'
rate would be 50 % (Table 2.35), the total number of skiers expected for the February period
would be 11 200.

Using the same method, we would find that the total number of skiers expected for the April
period would also be 11 200.

Lift pass turnover can easily be calculated for the three periods using the lift pass cost. These
turnovers are summarized in Table 2.41.

As a conclusion, this scenario yields a total turnover of around €8.5m, i.e. a loss of about
€1.5m!

Monte Carlo simulation

Ed realizes that he did not rely on the most pessimistic assumptions to build his scenario.
For example, he chose the most likely snow level for February and April. Should he select

Table 2.41   Expected turnover for this scenario

Month	Snow level	Turnover (€m)
December	Low	1.8
February	Medium	3.36
April	Medium	3.36
Total	—	8.52

the worse case assumption, expected loss would be much higher. Playing one scenario is not enough to embrace all possible situations and losses. To do so, Ed has now two options:

- Implement an analytical calculation, based on probability calculus. Ed does not feel very comfortable with this option.
- Implement a Monte Carlo simulation to simulate possible scenarios. This method seems easier to Ed since he already has a computational model at hand.

In this example, the Monte Carlo simulation would consist of playing many scenarios and computing the possible loss using the computational model. The computational model will be processed starting from the root variable – December snow level. All random variables involved in this process are discrete variables. Sampling such a variable simply requires a uniform sampler as shown in the introductory example.

In order to actually sample a discrete variable such as "December snow level", you just have to sample a random number X with a uniform sampler, and decide the target variable as shown in Table 2.42.

The computation process for yearly turnover calculation can be implemented as a simple spreadsheet, Figure 2.36.

As in the previous example, in order to run the simulation process 1 000 or 10 000 times, it could be more convenient to implement a single simulation in a single row, Figure 2.37.

Having run 1000 simulations of this process, Ed can now calculate the general statistics shown in Table 2.43.

This first analysis shows that the total yearly revenue will be less than €10m for 32 % of situations. This means that the resort has more than a two-thirds chance of having a balanced budget this year. Ed now wants to have more detailed statistics on the potential losses. He finds out that the repartition of potential losses is as shown in Table 2.44.

Before terminating his analysis, Ed realizes that when recalculating his Excel worksheet, the above figures change. He is worried about the robustness of his estimation, and tries to get a feeling for this as well.

To do so, he plays five simulations with 1000 runs, and five simulations with 10 000 runs, and writes down the probability of incurring a severe loss (more than €5M).

Although not a mathematician, Ed feels now that using a larger number of simulations should produce more robust estimates. He promises himself to read more detailed documentation about stability of Monte Carlo simulation.

Now, Ed has all elements at hand to evaluate possible hedging strategies. He could, for instance, decide to hedge this risk through the purchase of an appropriate weather derivative. Using Monte Carlo simulation, he will be in a clear position to evaluate if these options are fairly priced.

Table 2.42   Sampling a discrete variable

X	Probability	Snow level
[0, 0.3]	30%	Low
[0.3, 0.8]	50%	Medium
[0.8,1]	20%	High

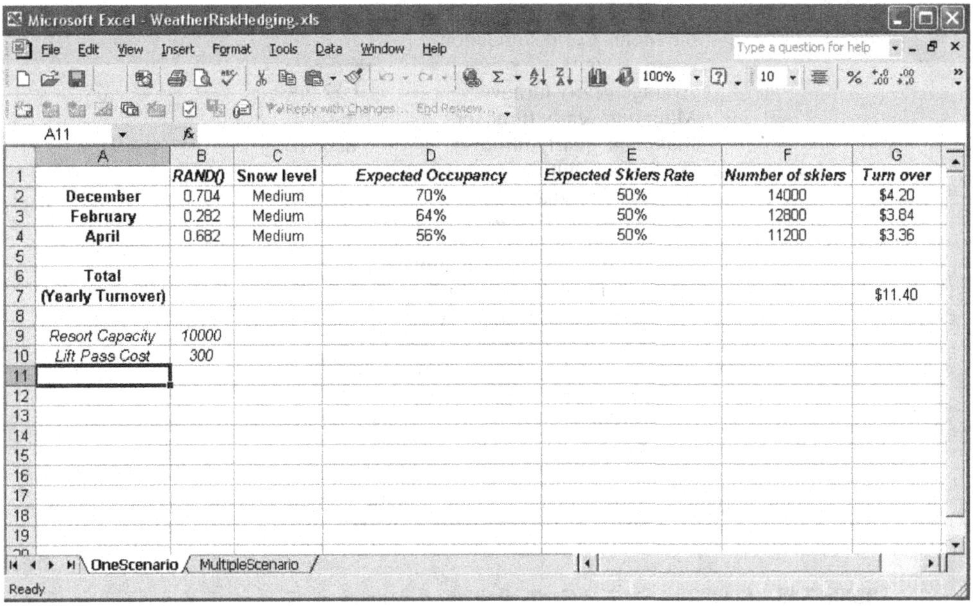

	A	B	C	D	E	F	G
1		RAND()	Snow level	Expected Occupancy	Expected Skiers Rate	Number of skiers	Turn over
2	December	0.704	Medium	70%	50%	14000	$4.20
3	February	0.282	Medium	64%	50%	12800	$3.84
4	April	0.682	Medium	56%	50%	11200	$3.36
5							
6	Total						
7	(Yearly Turnover)						$11.40
8							
9	Resort Capacity	10000					
10	Lift Pass Cost	300					

Figure 2.36 Single run simulation using Excel

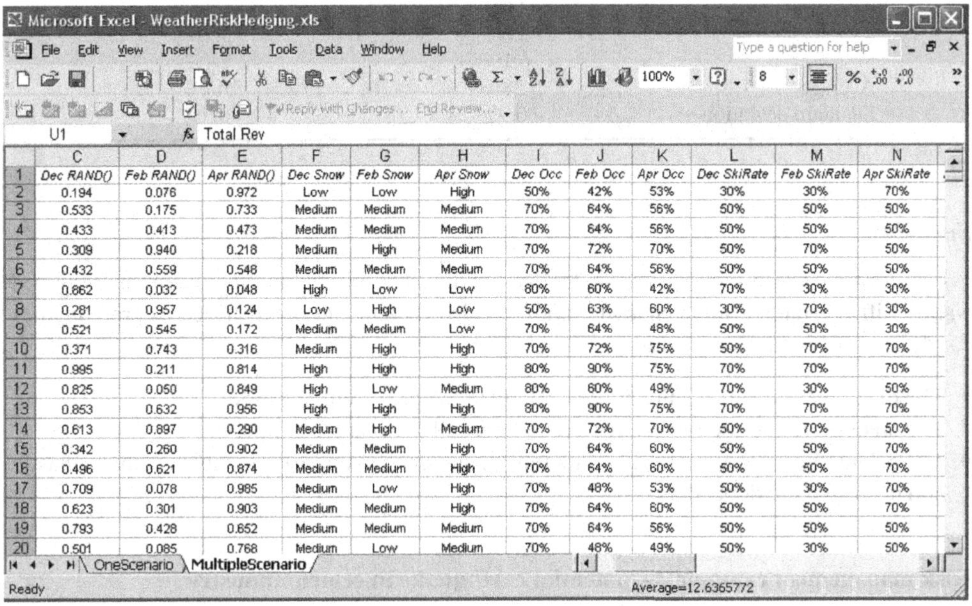

	C	D	E	F	G	H	I	J	K	L	M	N
1	Dec RAND()	Feb RAND()	Apr RAND()	Dec Snow	Feb Snow	Apr Snow	Dec Occ	Feb Occ	Apr Occ	Dec SkiRate	Feb SkiRate	Apr SkiRate
2	0.194	0.076	0.972	Low	Low	High	50%	42%	53%	30%	30%	70%
3	0.533	0.175	0.733	Medium	Medium	Medium	70%	64%	56%	50%	50%	50%
4	0.433	0.413	0.473	Medium	Medium	Medium	70%	64%	56%	50%	50%	50%
5	0.309	0.940	0.218	Medium	High	Medium	70%	72%	70%	50%	70%	50%
6	0.432	0.559	0.548	Medium	Medium	Medium	70%	64%	56%	50%	50%	50%
7	0.862	0.032	0.048	High	Low	Low	80%	60%	42%	70%	30%	30%
8	0.281	0.957	0.124	Low	High	Low	50%	63%	60%	30%	70%	30%
9	0.521	0.545	0.172	Medium	Medium	Low	70%	64%	48%	50%	50%	30%
10	0.371	0.743	0.316	Medium	High	High	70%	72%	75%	50%	70%	70%
11	0.995	0.211	0.814	High	High	High	80%	90%	75%	70%	70%	70%
12	0.825	0.050	0.849	High	Low	Medium	80%	60%	49%	70%	30%	50%
13	0.853	0.632	0.956	High	High	High	80%	90%	75%	70%	70%	70%
14	0.613	0.897	0.290	Medium	High	Medium	70%	72%	70%	50%	70%	50%
15	0.342	0.260	0.902	Medium	Medium	High	70%	64%	60%	50%	50%	70%
16	0.496	0.621	0.874	Medium	Medium	High	70%	64%	60%	50%	50%	70%
17	0.709	0.078	0.985	Medium	Low	High	70%	48%	53%	50%	30%	70%
18	0.623	0.301	0.903	Medium	Medium	High	70%	64%	60%	50%	50%	70%
19	0.793	0.428	0.652	Medium	Medium	Medium	70%	64%	56%	50%	50%	50%
20	0.501	0.085	0.768	Medium	Low	Medium	70%	48%	49%	50%	30%	50%

Average=12.6365772

Figure 2.37 Multiple run simulation Excel

Table 2.43   Some statistics derived from the Monte Carlo simulation

Average yearly turnover	€12.6m
Minimum yearly turnover	€4.8m
Maximum yearly turnover	€20.6m
% of runs resulting in a loss (turnover less than €10m)	29.2%

Table 2.44   Distribution of potential losses according to Monte Carlo simulation

Potential loss	Probability
>€5m	5.3%
€3–5m	5.1%
€1–3m	12.8%
<€1m	6.0%

Table 2.45   Stability of Monte Carlo simulation estimates

Run Number	1,000 steps simulation estimate	10,000 steps simulation estimate
1	5.3%	5.1%
2	6.0%	5.5%
3	3.9%	5.4%
4	5.6%	5.5%
5	6.1%	5.7%
Average	5.38%	5.44%
Standard deviation	0.9%	0.2%

Summary

Ed used Monte Carlo simulation to calculate the distribution of potential losses for Redwood Valley Lift Operators. Some characteristics of this problem can be identified as prerequisites for the use of Monte Carlo simulation:

- The objective is clearly defined: here calculate the probability of loss.
- The analytic resolution of the problem is impossible, or at least difficult.
- The calculation process can be completely described. This process involves both stochastic and deterministic dependencies.

Risk management example 2 – potential earthquake in cement industry

Analysis

Cementware is a global company which plans to open a new cement plant in the South Indian Ocean area. The Cementware board expects high returns. They are not worried about market risk as their activity is very profitable thanks to a technical competitive advantage, but they have serious concerns about a possible earthquake. The geological data available show that the selected area for the plant is a seismic high risk zone. The probability for a high magnitude earthquake happening during one year is estimated at around 0.4 %. This means that on average, a high magnitude earthquake would occur every 250 years. This may be considered as a rare event. Low magnitude earthquakes may happen but Cementware plants are always designed in compliance with the highest anti-seismic standards and should resist low magnitude earthquakes.

Considering this risk, the Cementware board of directors has decided to install a plant in the targeted zone only if the investment is expected to be profitable on the 10 future years with a minimal return of 10 %. In this example, we will study the interest in Monte Carlo simulation when performing cash flow analysis.

The objective set can be translated using the cash flow analysis keywords: "the net present value of cash flows over 10 years must be greater than the initial investment". Let us remind ourselves of some simple definitions used in cash flow analysis.

The *present value* of a cash flow C to be received in n years is the future cash flow value discounted by the return rate r for n years:

$$PV = \frac{C}{(1+r)^n}$$

The *present value* of an investment which generates cash flows during n years is the summation of cash flows' present values:

$$PV = \frac{C_1}{(1+r)} + \frac{C_2}{(1+r)^2} + \cdots + \frac{C_n}{(1+r)^n}$$

Each cash flow is calculated by substracting the cash outflow from the cash inflow.

This present value can be compared to the initial investment since they both represent amounts evaluated today.

The *net present value* (NPV) of the investment is computed by substracting the initial investment (10), an outflow today, to the present value.

$$PV = \frac{C_1}{(1+r)} + \frac{C_2}{(1+r)^2} + \cdots + \frac{C_n}{(1+r)^n} - I$$

To answer Cementware board of directors' question, we will introduce risk adjusted cash flows. In our example, a risk adjusted cash flow will be calculated by substracting potential losses from cash flows. A risk adjusted cash flow is therefore a random variable.

Oliver Acott, the Cementware risk manager, is in charge of evaluating the average risk adjusted net present value of the investment and the probability of this quantity being null. Oliver Acott meets the chief financial officer to find out what the initial investment amount and expected cash flows will be for the next 10 years. The CFO gives him the results shown in Table 2.46.

The uncertainty of cash flows is described by a standard deviation around the expected value, expressed as a percentage. For instance, the first year cash flow expected value is €0.5m, while its standard deviation is 30% of €0.5m, i.e. €150k.

Once he has collected financial data, Oliver Acott asks a geologist and technical services how much it would cost to get the plant back to work in the event of a serious earthquake.

Table 2.46 Cementware financial data

Initial investment	€7m
Annual return rate	10 %
Expected cash flow – year 1	€0.5m +/– 30 %
Expected cash flow – year 2	€1m +/– 30 %
Expected cash flow – year 3	€1.5m +/– 30 %
Expected cash flow – year 4	€1.5m +/– 30 %
Expected cash flow – year 5	€1.5m +/– 30 %
Expected cash flow – year 6	€1.5m +/– 30 %
Expected cash flow – year 7	€1.5m +/– 30 %
Expected cash flow – year 8	€1.5m +/– 30 %
Expected cash flow – year 9	€1.5m +/– 30 %
Expected cash flow – year 10	€1.5m +/– 30 %

From their analysis, almost 90 % of the factory would need to be replaced. Probability and severity of a serious earthquake are summarized in Table 2.47.

Model

The objective set is that the expected net present value (NPV) is positive.

$$E\,(NPV) \geq 0$$

The risk measurement required by the board of directors is the probability of the net present value being negative.

$$P\,(NPV) \leq 0$$

In addition, the board requires also the evaluation that the initial investment would be totally lost – i.e. generate no cash flow at all.

$$P\,(PV) \leq 0$$

To calculate the risk adjusted net present value, we must take into account the potential losses each year:

$$NPV = \frac{C_1 - E_1.L_1}{(1+r)} + \frac{C_2 - E_2.L_2}{(1+r)^2} + \cdots + \frac{C_n - E_n.L_n}{(1+r)^n} - I$$

The earthquake event E_i is a binary random variable whose value is 1 with probability 1/250 and 0 otherwise. The loss given event L_i is a constant equal to €6.3m.

Each C_i is modelled by a normal random variable according to the Table 2.46.

The risk adjusted NPV model can be represented as a causal graph, Figure 2.38.

Table 2.47 Earthquake probability and severity

Annual probability	1/250
Severity	€6.3m

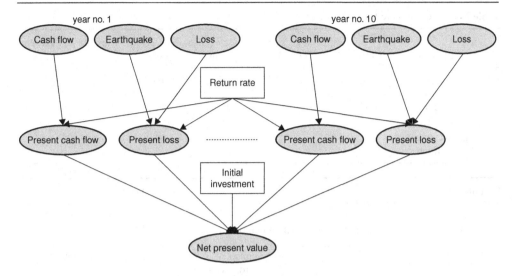

Figure 2.38 Cementware risk adjusted NPV model

Root variables are "Return rate", annual "Cash flows", "Earthquake" event and "Loss" given earthquake event. Return rate is a constant, annual cash flows and loss are random variables. Present cash flow depends on return rate and annual cash flow through a formula-type relation, as present loss depends on earthquake event and loss.

The outcome of the graph is the net present value which is calculated from annual present cash flows and loss through a formula. Its distribution is used (1) to calculate its expected value, and (2) to calculate the probability that the net present value is negative.

The computation process can be implemented within an Excel spreadsheet, as shown in Table 2.48.

Monte Carlo simulation

For this example again, it is more convenient to implement a worksheet so that each scenario is computed on one row.

The first objective of Oliver Acott (computing the net present value expected value) does not require any simulation. The analytical calculation is straightforward:

$$E\,(NPV) = E\left(\frac{C_1 - E_1.L_1}{(1+r)}\right) + E\left(\frac{C_2 - E_2.L_2}{(1+r)^2}\right) + \cdots + E\left(\frac{C_n - E_n.L_n}{(1+r)^n}\right) - E\,(I)$$

and yields:

$$E\,(NPV) = \frac{0.5 - 0.004 \times 6.3}{1.1} + \frac{1 - 0.004 \times 6.3}{1.1^2} + \cdots + \frac{1.5 - 0.004 \times 6.3}{1.1^2} - 7$$

and finally:

$$E\,(NPV) = €0.74m$$

The expected net present value is positive: the first condition required by the board is satisfied. In order to compute the probability that their investment is totally lost, we can not use this

Table 2.48 Cementware Excel formulas

Year	RAND()	Cash flow	RAND()	Earthquake	Loss	Present cash flow	Present loss
1	u1	C1	v1	E1	L1	PC1	PL1
...							
10	u10	C10	v10	E10	L10	PC10	PL10
Net Present Value				*SUM (PL1:PL10) − I*			
Initial Investment				I			
Return Rate				R			

Column	Code	Description	Formula
Year	Y	Integer	
RAND()	u	Uniform random number Range [0,1]	RAND()
Cash flow	C	Gaussian random number Mean mC and standard deviation sC specified in Table 2.46	NORMINV(u,mC,sC)
RAND()	v	Uniform random number Range [0,1]	RAND()
Earthquake	E	Binary random number 1 with probability 1/250, 0 otherwise	IF v < 1/250 THEN E = 1 ELSE E = 0
Loss	L	A fraction of initial investment	L = 0.9∗7
Present cash flow	PC	Discounted cash flow	$PC = C/(1 + 10\%)^Y$
Present loss	PL	Discounted loss	$PL = L/(1 + 10\%)^Y$

formula. We have to estimate the distribution of the risk adjusted net present value. Here we need Monte Carlo simulation.

Since the theoretical value of the expected NPV can be calculated analytically, Oliver Acott finds it interesting to evaluate the accuracy of the Monte Carlo simulation on this simple example. He plays 100 scenarios with his spreadsheet and gets an expected NPV of €0.80m. Trying 100 more scenarios, he gets €0.704m. This variability makes him uncomfortable with the robustness of his estimation. He decides to get a deeper insight on robustness issues before writing down his conclusions.

First, he plays 100 scenarios 100 times and calculates the standard deviation on the *estimation of the expected NPV*. Then he does the same thing with 1000 scenarios and 10 000 scenarios (i.e. he launches 100 batches of 1000 runs each and then 100 batches of 10 000 runs each). He gets the results shown in Table 2.49.

Table 2.49 Variability of estimation as a function of sample size

Sample size (*N*)	Standard deviation of estimation of expected NPV (€m)
100	0.073
1000	0.020
10 000	0.008

Table 2.50 Simulation
results

E (NPV)	€0.73 m
P (NPV) ≤ 0	16.4 %
P (PV) ≤ 0	0.01 %

Oliver notices that the standard deviation of the estimation of the expected NPV decreases as the number of simulations increases. For a 10 000 scenarios run, the standard deviation is about €0.008m, i.e. 1 % of the expected NPV. This uncertainty on estimation seems acceptable to him. He decides to run a 10 000 scenarios simulation to get a robust estimation of the distribution of the risk adjusted net present value. He gets the results shown in Table 2.50.

Using Monte Carlo simulation, i.e. sampling a large number of possible scenarios in the next 10 years, Oliver Acott was able to show the distribution of Cementware plant possible futures. The probability of ending up with a negative net present value is significant (16.4 %), while the probability of losing the whole initial investment is very low (0.01 %). When these figures are reported to the board of directors, the board would probably be worried about the likelihood of missing their return objectives. In order to analyze their risk in mode detail, they could focus on the distribution of their time adjusted rate of return.

Conclusion

Oliver Acott has used Monte Carlo simulation to evaluate the distribution of the risk adjusted net present value of his firm's investment. Oliver was also able to evaluate how the robustness of the simulation improves, as the number of runs increases. The model used was quite simple, but required several contributors to establish the individual parameters or distributions.

A bit of theory

We hope the examples presented above give an intuitive feeling of the benefits of Monte Carlo simulation. Theoretical foundations of Monte Carlo simulation are beyond the scope of this book but in this section we will try to present a brief overview of Monte Carlo history and theoretical aspects, returning to some issues raised by the examples.

Introduction

The actual use of Monte Carlo simulation methods stems from the work of a mathematician, Stanislaw Ulam, who was involved in the Manhattan Project at Los Alamos National Laboratory, to simulate the behaviour of nuclear reactions before testing the A nuclear bomb during the Second World War. Scientists had a good understanding of plutonium atom behaviour but it was impossible to model each of them and the way they interact together. At first Ulam set the equations which governed the reaction and modelled the atom behaviour with random variables. These simulations were given the code name "Monte Carlo" by John von Neumann and Stanislaw Ulam, after the famous gambling city close to the French Riviera.

The problem of Ulam and his colleagues sets the main features that can be addressed by Monte Carlo simulation:

- *The system being modelled is complex.* Monte Carlo simulation can be used for easy to solve problems, but generally, standard numerical methods are more efficient and should be preferred. Monte Carlo simulation is especially suited for complex real-world problems.
- *The system being modelled involves several random processes*, usually intricated with decision rules. The randomness of some system subprocesses is the main feature that justifies the use of Monte Carlo simulation. As soon as part of the system is random, it is impossible to predict its behaviour with certainty. Instead, you must take into account *the distribution of possible behaviours of the system* and Monte Carlo simulation is the appropriate tool.
- *It is impossible to perform actual experiments for this system.* When the system doesn't exist yet (this was the case for A-bomb before it was designed), or when the system cannot be tested, as for oceans or atmosphere, experiments can only rely on simulation models. Here again Monte Carlo simulation is required.
- *Actual experiments are time consuming, very expensive, or dangerous.* Even if model building cost cannot be neglected, simulations are generally low cost compared to actual experiments. Furthermore simulations are not destructive as experiments may be. Depending on the system, the power of computers allows millions of simulations to be run in less time than would be needed to run only one actual experiment. Finally, dangerous experiments cannot be conducted before their effects are forecast and appropriate protection built.
- *Various assumptions and alternatives need to be evaluated.* Changing some parameters on a given system may be difficult or prohibited because of the possible consequences. Simulation is a good method to change every parameter without affecting the actual system.

Definition

As discussed above, Monte Carlo methods are designed to simulate a complex system with random subparts. They offer a way to analyze and understand the possible behaviour of such a system. Let us assume that we want to measure a given characteristic of the system under observation. This quantity will be denoted Y. For example, we could try to measure the wind velocity in a given area during a hurricane. Although many variables could be measured on a given system, we will limit ourselves to the case of one variable Y whose values are continuously distributed and for which the expected value $E(Y)$ is defined. Since the system involves random subsystems, Y is a random variable and depends on the subsystems' states.

> The Monte Carlo method aims at estimating $E(Y)$ by generating a large number of *independent* samples of Y values with a simulation model.

This definition specifies both the objective and the method. More detailed mathematical definitions can be found in the literature, but will not be described here.

Is that objective – *estimating the expected value of Y* – too restrictive? For instance, can we estimate in the same way the cumulative probability distribution of Y, $P(Y \leq y)$? This can be done easily if we introduce the variable Z defined as follows:

$$\text{if } Y \leq y, \text{ then } Z = 1 \text{ else } Z = 0$$

Z expected value is exactly $P(Y \le y)$. Indeed since Z is conditioned by Y, we can write:

$$E(Z) = E(Z \,|\, Y \le y) \cdot P(Y \le y) + E(Z \,|\, Y > y) \cdot P(Y > y)$$

From the Z the definition, $E(Z \,|\, Y > y) = 0$ and $E(Z \,|\, Y \le y) = 1$. Hence, $E(Z) = P(Y \le y)$.

To sample Z, we simply have to sample Y and then apply the transformation defined above: the simulation process does not change. In other words, if we have at hand a method to evaluate the expected value of any random variable of the process, we can also estimate the full distribution of this variable – at least in a discrete fashion.

Generated samples are required to be independent. This requires that the simulation process is designed in such a way that, once a run has been processed, the model does not keep any data in memory.

Now let us address three important questions:

1. How is the approximation of $E(Y)$ produced by the Monte Carlo simulation defined?
2. How good is this approximation, and can we improve it?
3. How do we sample the random processes of the system?

Estimation according to Monte Carlo simulation

One particular *estimation* (approximation) of $E(Y)$ is calculated by running the simulation process n times and calculating the average of the n generated samples for Y, i.e. $y_1, \ldots, y_n$:

$$m = \frac{(y_1 + y_2 + \cdots + y_n)}{n}$$

For a given number of simulations, this estimation depends on the generated sample. Let us denote Y_1 the random variable Y for the first simulation, Y_2 for the second simulation, etc. These random variables are distributed as Y and are independent from each other. The $E(Y)$ *estimator*, denoted M, is defined as the average of Y_1 to Y_n.

$$M = \frac{(Y_1 + Y_2 + \cdots + Y_n)}{n}$$

M is the n sample-based estimator. As an average of random variables, M is also a random variable. This means that our estimation can be considered as one single outcome of M: the *estimation m* is a single outcome of the *estimator M*. We can build such an estimator for each desired sample size. Mathematically, we can prove that *this estimator is not biased*. This means that even if any specific estimation would be different from $E(Y)$, the expected value of this estimator is equal to $E(Y)$:

$$E(M) = E(Y)$$

This is straightforward from the definition of M and from the fact that $E(Y_1) = E(Y_2) = \cdots = E(Y_n) = E(Y)$. Moreover, as the sample size increases, the difference between M and $E(Y)$ gets closer to 0. This means that, taking into account practical time constraints, we should generate as many samples as possible to get a good estimation of $E(Y)$. Clearly, since M is a random variable, even with millions of simulations, it remains a nonzero probability that M is significantly different from $E(Y)$. As a consequence, the convergence of M towards $E(Y)$ as the sample size increases should be considered as a *convergence in probability*.

Can we evaluate the error of the estimator? To answer this question, we shall assume that the Y standard deviation (or variance) is finite. Let us remind oneselves that the variance of Y is the expected value of the squared distance between Y and $E(Y)$. The standard deviation, denoted σ, is defined as the square root of the variance:

$$\sigma^2 = E\left((Y - E(Y))^2\right)$$

Under this assumption, as soon as the sample size is large enough, the estimation error, $M - E(Y)$, is normally distributed with mean 0 and variance σ^2/n: this is an application of the central limit theorem mentioned above.

Since σ^2/n is the average square distance between M and $E(Y)$ its squared root $\sigma/\sqrt{n}$ is representative of the "standard estimation error". If n increases, or if the standard deviation of Y decreases, then the standard estimation error decreases.

Here we can get some help from the central limit theorem. This theorem tells us that the distribution of the estimation error converges to a normal distribution, when n increases. If we assume that we are close enough to a normal distribution, we can evaluate the probability that the distance between M and $E(Y)$ is greater than $\sigma/\sqrt{n}$. This probability is 31.7 % for a normal distribution. In other words, and in practice, once you have calculated an estimation, there is about a 30 % chance that this estimation is outside the interval $[E(Y) - \sigma/\sqrt{n}, E(Y) + \sigma/\sqrt{n}]$. The larger this interval, the less confident you can be in your estimation.

There are two ways to reduce the estimation error: either increasing the number of simulations or reducing the standard deviation of the random variable being estimated.

Now remember that we try to estimate $E(Y)$ and that it is very unlikely we have a prior evaluation of Y standard deviation. The first thing to do before setting the number of simulations is to estimate Y standard deviation. This could be done from the sample estimator:

$$s^2 = \frac{\left((y_1 - m)^2 + (y_2 - m)^2 + \cdots + (y_n - m)^2\right)}{n}$$

From the standard deviation, you can evaluate the number of simulations required to get an error less than a target value. If, for instance, the order of magnitude of Y standard deviation is 100, the number of simulations required to get a standard estimation error of 1 is such that:

$$\sigma^2/n \leq 1$$

i.e.:

$$n \geq 10\,000$$

Or, you have to run 10 000 simulations to reach a standard estimation error of 1 % of the variable standard deviation.

Random variable generation

Sampling random numbers is crucial in Monte Carlo simulation. We will present two common methods to sample a random variable:

- Inverse transform method
- Acceptance rejection method

We assume that we already have a uniform random number sampler at hand, which we will denote by U.

The *inverse transform method* provides a way of generating random numbers for which the cumulative distribution function (CDF) is known and can be inverted. This method has already been introduced in the first example.

Theorem

If X is a random variable, whose probability density function (PDF) is f, and whose cumulative distribution function is F, i.e. $F(x) = P(X \leq x)$, and if F^{-1} exists, and if u is uniformly distributed between 0 and 1, then

$$x = F^{-1}(u) \text{ is distributed according to } f$$

When the target distribution is complex and cannot be inverted, the *inverse transform method* cannot be used for random number generation.

To overcome this issue, the *acceptance rejection method* was introduced. Here, the idea is to sample using a simpler distribution, and to reject some of the samples.

More precisely let f denote the distribution function we want to sample. Let g denote a distribution that *dominates* f, which means that for any x, $f(x) \leq cg(x)$ (c is a fixed constant independent of x).

The *acceptance rejection method* to sample according to f is then as follows:

1. Sample x according to g distribution.
2. Sample u uniformly between 0 and 1.
3. If $u < f(x)/(cg(x))$ then accept x otherwise reject x and return to step 1.

It can be shown that the distribution of samples according to this algorithm is f.

Variance reduction

We have already mentioned the need to control the Monte Carlo estimation error.

The estimation error is $\sigma/\sqrt{n}$ where n is the sample size and σ is the target random variable standard deviation. We have two ways to improve the estimation error: either to increase the sample size or to reduce the variable standard deviation.

In the next paragraph, we will introduce some of the most usual techniques used to reduce estimator variance:

- Control variable technique
- Antithetic variable technique
- Stratification technique

All these methods either replace the target random variable by a new one or use alternative estimators. The main idea at the basis of these techniques is to use some sort of knowledge to reduce variance.

Using a control variable   The *control variable technique* requires finding an intermediate variable correlated with the target variable, and for which we can easily compute the expected value. If we can do so, we are able to build a new estimator whose variance is lower than the variance of the original estimator.

Let Y denote the target variable. Let X denote the intermediate variable. We define $Y(b)$ as:

$$Y(b) = Y + b \cdot (X - E(X))$$

The expected value of $(X - E(X))$ is 0. The new variable has the same expected value than Y. In order to estimate Y expected value, we can sample $Y(b)$ instead of Y.

Since $Y(b)$ is computationally more complex than Y, we should expect significant variance reduction to move to $Y(b)$ sampling.

The question is: Is the variance of $Y(b)$ lower than Y variance? The answer is yes.

If X and Y are correlated, it is possible to define b in such a way that the variance of the $Y(b)$ estimator is lower than that of the Y estimator. The variance reduction ratio directly depends on the correlation between X and Y.

Using antithetic variable sampling   Here we depart from the initial assumption that samples should be independent. Rather, we introduce some negative dependencies between samples of the target variable.

To introduce this technique, let us assume first that Y is a linear process of one input variable U uniformly distributed:

$$Y = f(U) = \lambda \cdot U$$

We can estimate Y expected value by sampling U and averaging the output values as usual. But if we notice that $1 - U$ is distributed as U, we could also estimate Y by sampling $1 - U$. We could also combine the two processes in order to sample Y.

If we sample U, calculate $1 - U$, and sum the resulting Y values we will always obtain the same value since f is linear:

$$f(U) + f(1 - U) = \lambda$$

This will obviously reduce the overall variance of the process since the two subsamples have a null variance. As a consequence, for a linear process, the antithetic variable technique will always yield a reduced variance estimator.

In the general case where the target process is not linear, we would rather divide it into a symmetric and an antisymmetric part:

$$f(U) = f_s(U) + f_a(U)$$

where:

$$f_s(U) = \frac{f(U) + f(1 - U)}{2}$$

and:

$$f_s(U) = \frac{f(U) - f(1 - U)}{2}$$

The symmetric part $f_s(U)$ is such that $f_s(U) = f_s(1 - U)$, whereas the antisymmetric part verifies $f_a(1 - U) = -f_a(U)$.

The antisymmetric part is similar to the linear process we have just discussed above.

By introducing a new estimator of Y expected value obtained by averaging the samples for $f(U)$ and $f(1 - U)$, we eliminate the variance due to the linear part of the process.

This technique is not specific and could be always applied but it is particularly efficient when the process is close to linear. If we know that the process is highly nonlinear, this method should not be used because the computation times needed for sampling negatively dependent input variables will not be balanced by variance reduction.

Using stratified sampling   If we know that the target variable can be partitioned into several subsets called *strata* and we are able to sample Y in each of these strata, we can build an estimator of Y expectation whose variance is lower than that of the standard estimator.

To illustrate this idea, let us consider the case of Y being a uniform random variable defined over [0,1]. In this case, we know that the Y domain can be partitioned into 10 equal size subintervals [0,0.1], [0.1,0.2], etc. and that each of these intervals has the same probability 0.1. To estimate Y expected value, we could use the standard expectation estimator:

$$M = \frac{(Y_1 + Y_2 + \cdots + Y_n)}{n}$$

But we could also draw 10 % of the samples in the [0,0.1] interval, 10 % in the [0.1,0.2] interval and average all of them.

It is easy to understand why we have reduced variance. Standard deviation of the standard estimator is $\sigma/\sqrt{n}$.

The stratified estimator can be expressed as the average of 10 independent estimators, each estimating the expectation of the uniform distribution over [0, 0.1], [0.1, 0.2], etc., and thus having a standard deviation equal to $(\sigma/10)/\sqrt{m/10}$. The variance of the stratified estimator is thus equal to $\sigma/10.\sqrt{n}$, i.e. is 10 times lower than the standard deviation of the standard estimator.

This estimator should converge 10 times faster than the standard estimator. A very important generalization of the basic stratification technique is that you can stratify the target variable Y with respect to another variable X, given Y depends on X. More precisely, if Y depends on X and if the conditional distribution of Y given X is known, and if we are able to stratify X, we can build a stratified estimator whose variance is lower than that of the standard estimator.

This generalization is of special interest in the field of risk quantification: it expresses the fact that some knowledge about process dependencies can directly be used to reduce the uncertainty of loss distribution.

For example, let us consider the number of casualties due to an earthquake. This number would obviously depend on the population density in the earthquake area. If our model can describe the conditional distribution of the number of casualties as a function of the population density, and if we have identified three main types of zones – low, medium or high density – we can use the stratification to evaluate the expected number of casualties. We only need to sample the zone type according to its distribution and then sample the number of casualties according to its conditional distribution.

The knowledge-based approach we promote in this book makes the stratification technique a natural method to reduce the standard deviation in risk quantification problems.

Latin hypercube sampling   Latin hypercube sampling is a special case of stratification technique for high-dimensional input variables. This is a rather complex technique, so in order to simplify the discussion, we will assume that the process has d input variables that are uniformly distributed between 0 and 1. We will assume further that all input variables can be stratified into p equally sized intervals. Stratifying input space requires p^d strata and thus involves at least p^d samples to ensure that each strata is correctly represented. This is infeasible in practice as soon as d becomes large.

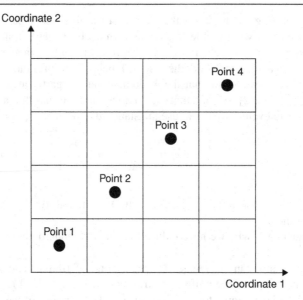

Figure 2.39 First step of the LHS process for a two dimensional process with four strata ($d = 2$ and $p = 4$)

Full stratification of a high-dimensional space is impossible. Nevertheless it is possible to ensure both stratification of each input variable and uniform sampling over the entire input space: this is the purpose of the latin hypercube sampling (LHS) method.

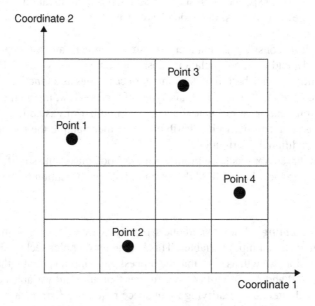

Figure 2.40 Second step of the LHS process for a two dimensional process with four strata ($d = 2$ and $p = 4$)

Initially LHS samples p points in d dimensional space, with the following coordinates:

Point 1: $(U_1 (1), U_2 (1), \ldots, U_d (1))$
Point 2: $(U_1 (2), U_2 (2), \ldots, U_d (2))$
. . .
Point p: $(U_1 (p), U_2 (p), \ldots, U_d (p))$

where $U_i (j) U_i(j)$ is a sampler of the jth strata for ith coordinate. First point coordinates stand in the first strata, second point coordinates stand in the second strata and so on. The p points stand in the diagonal stratum, Figure 2.39.

At the end of the first step, the stratification of each coordinate is fine, but the sampling process does not cover the overall hypercube. To meet this objective, the second step applies a random permutation to each column of the coordinates array to produce p new points:

Point 1: $(U_1 (\pi_1 (1)), U_2 (\pi_2 (1)), \ldots, U_d (\pi_d (1)))$
Point 2: $(U_1 (\pi_1 (2)), U_2 (\pi_2 (2)), \ldots, U_d (\pi_d (2)))$
. . .
Point p: $(U_1 (\pi_1 (p)), U_2 (\pi_2 (p)), \ldots, U_d (\pi_d (p)))$

π_i is the permutation applied to the ith column of the array. The permutations are chosen among the p possible permutations over $\{1, \ldots, p\}$. The effect of the permutation is that the new points do not stand necessarily on the diagonal stratum of the hypercube. They can stand anywhere in the hypercube, although there is exactly one point in each one-dimensional section: our objective is met, Figure 2.40!

When the target process is high dimensional and if stratification of individual inputs is possible, the latin hypercube sampling is the appropriate method.

Software tools

Several software tools can be used for quantitative risk modelling. Our intention is not to provide a catalogue of such tools, or a user manual for some of them.

We simply list here the tools we used to implement some of the examples throughout the book:

- Microsoft Excel is generally a good start for the nonexpert to model distributions, perform sampling, etc.
- Hugin (www.hugin.com) and Netica (www.norsys.com) are the Bayesian network tools we would recommend for risk analysis and modelling.
- @Risk (www.palisade.com) is a nice and easy-to-use Excel add-in to implement powerful and sophisticated Monte Carlo simulations.

3
Quantitative Risk Assessment:
A Knowledge Modelling Process

INTRODUCTION

Quantification significantly increases the benefits of risk assessment. Indeed, a qualitative risk evaluation is not always a strong enough selling point to convince the top management to invest in a risk control programme. A quantitative evaluation of the risk – a million euro figure – is more likely to be such a selling point.

Quantitative risk assessment increases the risk awareness within the organization.

The Basel II framework will be used as a reference example throughout this chapter, as the banking regulator has set a high standard for operational risk management: hedging 99.9 % of one-year-ahead possible futures.

This objective is quite simple to formulate, but has profound implications for risk assessment and management approach. It requires the implementation of a smooth knowledge elicitation and transformation process, from identification and mapping of loss exposures down to the evaluation of the overall distribution of costs.

This chapter is structured as follows.

First, we discuss the general contribution and issues of risk quantification. Second, we introduce the Basel II requirements for operational risk management. Third, we describe a qualitative risk assessment methodology, inspired by ARM, and its customization for operational risk. Fourth, we elaborate the quantification approach introduced in Chapter 1, down to the evaluation of the global risks distribution.

Although the Basel II framework and requirements are specific to the banking sector, we believe it is likely to inspire future standards in other sectors.

Increasing awareness of exposures and stakes

The analysis of recent major catastrophes outlines three important features of risk assessment. First, major catastrophes always hit where and when no one expects them. Second, it is often inaccurate to consider they were fully unexpected, but rather that they were not considered. Third, the general tendency to fight against risks which have already occurred leaves us unprepared for major catastrophes.

CIA reports on the 9/11 terrorist attacks against the US, US reports on major environmental risks pointing out hurricanes in Florida as one major risk scenario, and the existence of the reports becoming public only after Katrina confirm this analysis.

A sound risk assessment process should not neglect any of these points. What has already happened could strike again; and it is essential to remain vigilant. What has never happened may happen in the future, and therefore we must analyze potential scenarios with all available knowledge.

The Bayesian approach to probabilities can bring an interesting contribution to this problem. The major contribution of Thomas Bayes to scientific rationality was to clearly express that *uncertainty is conditioned to available information*. In other words, risk perception is conditioned by someone's knowledge.

Using the Bayesian approach, a probability (i.e. a quantification of uncertainty) cannot be defined outside an information context. Roughly speaking, "what can happen" is meaningless. I can only assess what I believe is possible. And what I believe possible is conditioned by what I know. This view is perfectly in line with an open approach to risk management. The future is "what I believe is possible". And "what I know" is not only what has already happened but also all available knowledge about organizations and their risk exposure. Risk management starts with knowledge management.

In the banking sector, the regulation authorities, willing to secure the stability of the banking system, introduced a regulatory capital charge for operational risks. Four sources of knowledge are identified by the Basel II agreement, which are all mandatory for risk assessment and measurement of the capital charge: internal loss events, external loss events, self-assessment of risks, and scenario analysis. This approach of the risks is consistent with a knowledge-based approach. It should guarantee that the risk assessment of a financial institution is not only based on internal losses, but also does not miss any known scenario.

But the requirements go further. According to the Basel II agreement, any event or combination of events which could happen in the next year with a probability valued above 0.1 % must be hedged by a capital charge. Here, risk identification and even qualitative assessment are not enough. An accurate (or at least fair) quantification of event probability and severity is mandatory to calculate the capital which can *hedge 99.9 % of all possible one-year-ahead futures*.

The guidelines set by the regulation authorities of the banking sector could be an inspiration for the future of risk management. For a general organization, the aim of risk assessment is to bring potential loss exposures to the "consciousness of an organization". In the long term, this effort will be the most important contributor to risk reduction, through the development of an internal culture of the risk. As already discussed in Chapter 1, once an exposure is recognized, uncertainty is somewhat reduced to a problem which, once identified, can lead to identify some kind of solution. The "hidden exposure" is always more threatening as, evidently, when it strikes there is no plan to cope with it.

Risk identification tools have already been mentioned in Chapter 1. They can be classified in categories, depending on whether they are based on self-assessment (internal experts, questionnaires), external assessment (audit and control, external experts), internal historical data (balance sheets, case analysis), or external historical data.

Now the question is whether risk assessment is sufficient to actually bring the organization exposures to consciousness. We argue that this could not be the case, in particular if the assessment is limited to a qualitative mapping. In practice, a lot of organizations have undertaken a risk mapping effort, often limited to hiring a consultancy firm. Identifying potential failures on a process diagram, providing a frequency and severity mark for a scenario, is far less a commitment than unfolding a scenario down to the distribution of potential losses.

Objectives of risk assessment

Risk assessment may target three objectives evaluation, forecast and understanding, the third one being the most demanding.

The first objective is to quantify the risks the company is exposed to. This objective assumes at least that a risk quantification measure has been precisely defined. For instance, the quantification of operational risks is defined as the 99.9 % percentile of the distribution of total losses (i.e. the total loss that would be exceeded in only 0.1 % of possible situations).

This figure must be clearly justified and the underlying assumption identified. Of course, risk evaluation is important but should be considered as a by-product rather the sole objective of this process.

The second objective is to forecast potential losses. Social, economic, regulatory, and climatic contexts are changing over the years, so do strategic and commercial objectives. As a consequence, risks are also changing over time. Past years' exposures or losses are not always representative of upcoming years' losses. The influence of a change in context or objectives should be quantifiable.

The third and most demanding objective is to understand why potential losses could occur and why historical losses have actually occurred. Identifying processes at risk, loss reduction or protection factors, and evaluating risk correlations are the main steps for risk control. Thus, risk assessment models are required to integrate this knowledge in order to help define the risk control actions.

Issues in risk quantification

Quantifying all loss exposures of a large organization in a consistent way is a very difficult task.

When dealing with quantification, it is rational to consider the quantitative piece of information immediately at hand, i.e. the historical loss data. This was the approach encouraged in the early years of operational risk quantification for banks. An approach called LDA (for Loss Distribution Approach) was proposed. The rationale of LDA is first to assume that, on average, and for a given type of risk, the number of losses observed over one year will remain stable, and, second, to adjust a theoretical distribution on observed loss data. Strictly considered, the implicit assumption of this approach is that the only random part of the risks is the number of losses, and their combination: a bad year could incur more losses than usual, several of them being serious losses (i.e. "tail" events).

We believe this approach misses the main point of risk quantification, i.e. the causal assessment of scenarios. A tsunami is not an unexpectedly strong wave. Even if adjusting a theoretical distribution on historical wave height or strength makes it possible to calculate the probability of a 30 metre-high wave striking the shore, this would ignore the essential nature of the phenomenon: tsunamis are not caused by the same process as waves.

Risk quantification cannot be addressed merely through statistical modelling of historical loss data. Even if the so-called LDA approach was relevant, historical loss data might be simply nonrepresentative. On the one hand, and fortunately, severity risks are not represented in historical loss data. On the other hand, for frequency risks, even if loss data are available, they only reflects the past and do not integrate changes in the context or in the firm objectives or in the risk control actions that have been applied. A loss distribution approach model is not a risk model but a loss model.

Thus, expert knowledge is mandatory for any type of risk: obviously for severity risks as no loss data are available, but also for frequency risks when part of the context is changing. Loss data must only be considered as part of the available knowledge, the main source being human expertise.

Risk quantification builds on knowledge elicitation rather than on data collection!

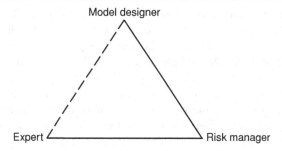

Figure 3.1   The actors of quantitative risk assessment

Risk quantification: a knowledge management process

Risk quantification, at the diagnostic stage, must be considered as a knowledge management process which transforms human expertise into a probabilistic model. This model is required to calculate potential loss distribution, identify risk control levers and analyze risk sensitivity to change of context, strategy, or commercial objectives.

This process should be continuous in order to avoid inconsistency between human expertise and models. The process must overcome the danger of creating a black box model that would be understood only by a few mathematicians. Models must be understandable, open to internal or external expert criticism, or auditable by regulatory authorities. To make this process as transparent as possible, each step must be fully documented.

This process has precisely two main steps: scenario identification and scenario quantification. The process involves three actors, the expert, the risk manager, and the model designer Fig 3.1. The expert has technical knowledge about a specific business or process. For instance, in the context of operational risk quantification, the contribution of credit card fraud experts, information networks specialists, jurists, etc. would be required. The expert is not necessarily aware of risk management issues. The risk manager must at the same time be aware of the processes being analyzed, and be trained in risk management. He is in charge of identifying scenarios and has to interact with all experts in order to select relevant risks. The risk manager is the pivot of the risk assessment process. The model builder is in charge of quantifying the scenarios. Even if his main skill is knowledge modelling, it would be unrealistic to entrust this project to somebody without any background in targeted business and a deep understanding of risk management issues.

The first step of the process – scenario identification – involves the risk manager and the experts, whereas the second step – scenario quantification – mainly involves the risk manager and the model designer and sometimes the expert when difficult issues arise.

Collaborative work and overlap of skills ensure the robustness and consistency of the process.

THE BASEL II FRAMEWORK FOR OPERATIONAL RISK

David Breden, Director, HSBC Operational Risk Consultancy

Note: The views expressed in this article are the author's personal views and do not necessarily represent the views of the HSBC Group.

Introduction

The concept of quantifying operational risk for the purpose of setting acceptable levels of minimum regulatory capital for internationally active banks was unleashed upon the banking community in January 2001 with the first Basel II Consultative paper. Since that time further Consultative papers and quantitative impact studies have been conducted in order to carry us forward to the publication of the "International Convergence of Capital Measurement and Capital Standards, a Revised Framework" in June 2004.[1] This final document now forms the basis upon which those national regulatory authorities that choose to do so will prepare new local banking regulation.

The Basel II regulations have the force of guidelines for internationally active banks, but when adopted by local regulatory authorities, they may acquire wider application, as it is the case in the European Union where regulations based on Basel II principles will apply to all financial institutions.[2]

The Basel II guidelines replace the Basel I regulations for capital adequacy. Originally introduced in 1988, these guidelines sought to establish a simple set of rules to govern the minimum amount of regulatory capital that should be held by internationally active banks. At that time, only credit risk was considered from a capital adequacy perspective, and capital at a level of 8 % of the funds being lent was considered appropriate. Subsequently market risk was introduced into the capital adequacy equation, making it necessary for firms to calculate market risk exposures and hold capital to cover for these risks. Basel II introduces the concept that capital should also be held for operational risk.

The other major objective of Basel II is to introduce a risk-sensitive approach to the calculation of minimum regulatory capital. The Basel I approach was based on a "one-size-fits-all" assessment, but Basel II aims to reward the quality of risk exposures and of risk management processes and procedures with a lower minimum regulatory capital charge. Such an objective brings about the need to establish a qualitative framework to work in parallel with the quantitative formulae necessary for capital calculation.

The three pillars

A basic element of the Basel II structure for calculating minimum regulatory capital for all risks is the three pillar framework.

Pillar One describes the basic formulae needed to calculate the minimum regulatory capital figure applicable to each class of risk. It also contains descriptions of different methodologies for calculating this capital. Methodologies are intended to demonstrate increasing levels of sophistication in risk management techniques and are recognized in theory by a lower capital charge.

Pillar Two deals with the supervisory review process. This is "intended not only to ensure that banks have adequate capital to support all the risks in their business, but also to encourage banks to develop and use better risk management techniques in monitoring and managing their risks."[3]

---

[1] International Convergence of Capital Measurement and Capital Standards, a Revised Framework. The Basel Committee on Banking Supervision. The Bank for International Settlements, June 2004.

[2] European Union Consolidated Banking Directive 2000/12/EEC and European Union Capital Adequacy Directive 93/6/EEC passim.

[3] International Convergence of Capital Measurement and Capital Standards, a Revised Framework. The Basel Committee on Banking Supervision. The Bank for International Settlements, June 2004, para. 720.

The section outlines the key principles of supervisory review and considers options for addressing increased risks or shortcomings. These options may include a requirement to hold capital in excess of the minimum figure calculated under Pillar One rules.

Pillar Three deals with market discipline, and outlines the standards of disclosure that financial institutions will be required to meet. The intention is to develop a set of reporting requirements that will give market participants sufficient information to judge the capital adequacy of the institution and hence its suitability as a counterpart or as a suitable place for the investment of funds.

The three pillar structure is applicable to all risks, including operational risks.

Operational risk

The Pillar One documentation that relates specifically to operational risk contains a basic definition of operational risk as follows:

> Operational risk is defined as the risk of loss resulting from inadequate or failed internal processes, people and systems or from external events. This definition includes legal risk, but excludes strategic and reputational risk.

As with credit risk, a series of methodologies are proposed to enable institutions to quantify their minimum operational risk regulatory capital figure. These methodologies increase in sophistication and impose increasingly stringent qualitative standards for the underlying risk framework. The intention is that banks will select an approach that is appropriate for their risk profile, and will move along the spectrum of approaches with time. It is not, therefore, the intention that a major internationally active bank, or an institution with significant exposures, will elect to use the most basic approach.

The basic indicator approach

The entry-level methodology for calculating minimum levels of operational risk regulatory capital is simple. All that is required is for the institution to hold capital for operational risk equivalent to a fixed percentage (the alpha factor) of a three year average of positive annual gross income. If gross income is negative in any year, then those figures must be excluded.

The alpha factor is set at 15 % by the committee and is intended to equate to the industry-wide level of required capital. The calculation assumes the existence of direct correlation between income and levels of operational risk and any specific shortcomings in risk management or heightened risk levels linked to the specifics of the business will have to be addressed by the regulator under a Pillar two review.

Gross income is defined as net interest income plus net noninterest income, gross of any provisions, operating expenses (including fees paid to outsourcing service providers), and should exclude realized profits or losses from sale of securities in the banking book, extraordinary items, and income derived from insurance.

As the basic indicator approach is intended to be an entry-level approach, there are no specific qualitative requirements for using it. However, firms that choose to use the approach are "encouraged" to comply with the guidance contained in the paper entitled "Sound Practices for the Management and Supervision of Operational Risk."[4]

---

[4] Sound Practices for the Management and Supervision of Operational Risk. Basel Committee on Banking Supervision – Bank for International Settlements, February 2003.

The sound practices Paper

On the basis that the qualitative requirements are based on the assumption that firms will have complied with the basic principles of operational risk management contained in the sound practices paper, it is worth including a brief summary of its content at this point.

The document is built around 10 principles that describe the basic skeleton of an operational risk management framework in a useful manner. Out of the 10 principles, the first three relate to the creation of a suitable operational risk management environment.

These principles highlight the responsibilities of the board of directors and of senior management. It is the intention that the board should be aware of the major elements of the bank's exposure to operational risk and should approve and review the framework for identifying, assessing, monitoring, and controlling or mitigating these risks. They should ensure that the framework is subject to independent audit.

Senior management is then responsible for implementing the framework that the board has approved throughout the organization. The ultimate goal is that all staff should clearly understand their responsibilities in the management of operational risk. The senior management team is also to be held responsible for developing the policies, processes and procedures that will be used to manage operational risk in all of the products, systems, and processes throughout the bank.

A further set of four principles deals with the key elements of the implementation of the framework. The principles cover the following required features of the framework:

- Risks must be identified and assessed in all material areas of the institution and a similar exercise should cover all new products, processes and systems before they are introduced. The aim, of course, is to ensure that banks fully understand the risks they face (or are about to face from new activities) and are therefore able to make reasoned decisions about the management of the risks.
- A process to monitor evolving risk profiles and exposure to losses is required. Information on losses and profiles should be reported to the board to support the proactive management of operational risk. This will oblige organizations to gather operational loss data and to consider introducing measures, such as key risk indicators, to signal changes in underlying risk profiles.
- Once risks have been identified and assessed, there should be policies and procedures in place to control and mitigate operational risk. These decisions should be taken in the context of guidance from the board and senior management as to the desired level of risk acceptable to the organization.
- Finally business continuity and contingency plans should be in place to ensure that business activities can continue in the event of serious business disruption.

Guidance is then provided to the supervisors as to the requirements needed to effectively oversee the activities of the banks under review. The final principle reminds the banks of the need to make suitable disclosure to the market to allow external assessment of the operational risk management framework.

The standardized approach

The standardised approach to operational risk aims to link the calculation of required levels of minimum operational risk regulatory capital more closely with the risk profile of the concerned

Table 3.1   Business lines and beta factors according to Basel II

Business lines	Beta factors
Corporate finance	18 %
Trading and sales	18 %
Retail banking	12 %
Commercial banking	15 %
Payment and settlement	18 %
Agency services	15 %
Asset management	12 %
Retail brokerage	12 %

bank. To do this, bank activities are divided into eight business lines and a beta factor is assigned to each business line that is designed to reflect the level of risk inherent in each business line.

The list of business lines and beta factors is as shown in Table 3.1.

Gross income continues to be used as a proxy for exposure levels to likely levels of exposure to operational risk, but by requiring banks to split gross income between the different business lines, the intention is that the capital figure will more closely reflect the risk profile of the business.

To calculate the minimum capital charge, therefore, banks will take the gross income for a business line in a given year and multiply that figure by the beta factor. The total capital charge will be calculated by finding the three year average of the simple sum of the regulatory capital charges across each business line in each year.

The total capital charge will therefore be linked to the split of the business between the different business lines. This means that a business skewed towards higher risk activities such as corporate finance, trading and sales or payment and settlement will see its capital charge increase if it decides to move away from the basic indicator approach. On the other hand, firms with activities centred on asset management, retail brokerage or retail banking will be able to reduce their capital charges.

To move over to the standardized approach, banks will need to meet certain qualifying criteria, and will need to demonstrate that they have done so to their regulator. Minimum standards to be met include:

- Active involvement of the board and senior management in the enforcement of the operational risk management framework.
- An operational risk management system in place that is sound and implemented with integrity.
- Sufficient resources dedicated to operational risk management in the business lines and in the control and audit areas.
- Policies and criteria must be drawn up to map gross income to the business line framework.

Internationally active banks using the standardized approach must also:

- Have a system with clear responsibilities assigned to an operational risk management function. This function has responsibility for developing and implementing processes to identify and assess, monitor, and control or mitigate operational risk. It should also draw up policies and procedures and create a risk reporting structure.

- Systematically track operational risk data, especially material losses by business line.
- Integrate the assessment process into the operational risk management processes of the bank and create incentives to improve operational risk management throughout the firm.
- Regularly report operational risk exposures including material losses to the board, senior management and business unit management. The bank must have procedures to take action on the basis of these reports.
- The operational risk management system must be well documented. A system must be in place to ensure compliance with policies and procedures connected with the management of operational risk and to deal with issues of noncompliance.
- The system must be subject to regular validation and independent review.
- The system must be subject to regular review by external auditors and supervisors.

The alternative standardized approach

National regulatory authorities may make an alternative standardized approach available. This approach is identical to the standardized approach except for the retail banking and commercial banking business lines. Here the total outstanding loans and advances (gross of provisions) are averaged over three years in the business line and use gross income as the proxy for risk exposure. These figures are then multiplied by a fixed factor of 0.035.

The capital charge is found by multiplying the result of this calculation by the beta factor for the business line. The result is then added to the total of the other business lines calculated under the standardized approach to find the overall capital charge.

The advanced measurement approaches (AMA)

The advanced measurement approaches represent the most advanced methodology for calculating minimum regulatory capital for operational risk. The aim of this approach is to encourage banks to develop a methodology to calculate the capital that relies on their experience as to how such exposures can be quantified. According to the Basel II papers:

Under the AMA the regulatory capital requirement will equal the risk measure generated by the bank's internal operational risk measurement system using the quantitative and qualitative criteria for the AMA...Use of the AMA is subject to supervisory approval.[5]

This essentially leaves it to the banks to develop their own quantification methodology and to then agree with their supervisor that the methodology adequately reflects their risk profile and complies with the guidelines outlined in the AMA.

There is a requirement that the bank should also calculate its capital requirement in accordance with the 1988 Accord for comparison purposes.

It should be noted that there is no prescribed methodology for calculating capital, but there is a lengthy list of qualitative and quantitative requirements that must be met.

General standards are similar to those for the standardized approach and require:

- Active involvement of the board and senior management in the oversight of the operational risk management framework.
- A sound operational risk management system in place implemented with integrity.

---

[5] International Convergence of Capital Measurement and Capital Standards, a Revised Framework. The Basel Committee on Banking Supervision. The Bank for International Settlements, June 2004, para. 655.

- Sufficient resources dedicated to operational risk management in the business lines and in the control and audit areas.

There are also specific qualitative standards that must be met before an AMA may be used. These are:

- An independent operational risk management function responsible for designing the framework, creating policies and reporting procedures for operational risk management and for identifying, assessing, monitoring, controlling and mitigating the operational risk.
- The operational risk measurement system must be integrated into the process for managing operational risk. Procedures must exist to allocate operational risk capital to business lines and to incentivize improving operational risk management.
- Operational risk losses and profiles must be reported to the board and procedures must exist so that actions can be taken in view of the reports.
- The system must be well documented and must include procedures to ensure compliance with the policies and to deal with noncompliance with procedures.
- Internal and external auditors must perform regular reviews of the processes and measurement systems.
- External auditors and supervisors must verify that internal validation processes are adhered to and that data flows connected to the measurement system are transparent and accessible.

It can be seen that these qualitative standards are close to those marked out by an internationally active bank for the use of the standardized approach.

A considerable difference can be seen when we turn to the quantitative standards for the AMA. While no detailed specific approach exists, banks are required to develop an approach that captures potential tail events. The specific requirement is that the bank must demonstrate that its operational risk measure meets a soundness standard comparable to a one year holding period and a 99.9 % confidence level. The practical difficulty of meeting this requirement for a portfolio of risk with no known upper limit is left to individual banks to resolve. The Committee for Banking Supervision reserves the right to review its requirements to itself in the light of evolving industry practice.

Detailed quantitative criteria are:

- The AMA measure must be consistent with the Basel definition of operational risk and cover the defined loss types.
- The AMA calculation should be based upon the sum of expected and unexpected loss unless it can show that expected loss is being captured elsewhere in its business practices (i.e. general provision is raised for such losses).
- The measure must be able to capture key loss drivers to enable the bank to gauge the impact of those factors that will influence the tail of the loss distribution.
- Risk measures for the operational risk estimates must be added together to reach the regulatory capital requirement unless it can satisfy its local regulatory authority with a sound methodology to take into account correlation between losses.
- The operational risk measurement system must use internal data, relevant external data, scenario analysis and factors reflecting business environment and internal control systems. There must be a sound and documented procedure for weighing these elements.

When we focus upon the different data types that we are required to use, further guidance is provided to ensure that the AMA developed in the banks is sound.

Internal data is seen as an "essential prerequisite"[6] to the development of the AMA. However, the Basel II guidance is not prescriptive, allowing this data to be used as a basis for risk estimates or as a means to validate the output of the system.

Internal data needs to be relevant to the organization and should be linked to current activities. On a simple basis, this would suggest that data related to a discontinued business should be excluded from the model, but also requires that the methodology includes a procedure whereby losses can be adjusted to reflect growth, decline, or other changes in the underlying business.

Data should be collected over a minimum five year observation period (reduced to three years when the bank first moves to AMA) and should be mapped to relevant supervisory categories. Data must be comprehensive and should capture all material exposures worldwide above a gross loss threshold. The data should include information on the date of the event, on recovered amounts and descriptive information on the drivers or causes of the event.

Banks must develop methodologies for assigning losses in a centralized function (such as IT, for example) to the defined business lines in the event that the incident affects more than one business line. It will be up to the bank to develop such policies and to approve the procedures in agreement with their regulatory authority.

Operational losses formerly included in credit risk capital calculations (i.e. flawed security documentation) must continue to be included in credit risk capital calculations, but must be managed consistently with other operational losses. On the contrary, operational risks associated with market risk will be treated in the same fashion as all other operational losses.

When banks look at the output of their internal loss database, it is likely that they will see gaps in their loss exposures, both in terms of the population of certain loss categories and in terms of the presence of extreme events. To populate these areas, other data sources must be used to complement internal data.

External data are the first source of additional information that must be used, and these can be extracted from public data, from pooled data, or from commercially available databases. Such data must, however, be relevant to the bank, and the information source therefore must provide sufficient information to allow the bank to judge it. It is evident that a loss caused by an automated reconciliation system failure will be irrelevant to a firm that performs manual reconciliations and does not use an automated system. The source of information needs to be sufficiently detailed for such judgements to be made.

Other pieces of information that must be gathered from external data include loss amount, the causes and background of the loss, and the scale of the underlying operations. The bank must then create its own documented procedures for incorporating these data into the overall capital calculation. Again no specific prescriptive guidelines are provided, so the bank can develop its own procedures, subject always to regulatory approval.

Scenario analysis must also be used to complement the database. Such scenario analysis is based on the expert knowledge of the business managers. It can be created on the basis of internal or external loss events or draw on identified weaknesses in the firm's processes, products, systems, procedures, or control structures to create realistic scenarios capable of exploring exposures to tail events or to a combination of events producing an extreme scenario. Scenarios can be developed from risk workshops or from the output of risk self-assessment exercises, but must be re-examined in the light of the experience to ensure that scenarios continue to reflect the reality of the firm's risk exposures.

---

[6] International Convergence of Capital Measurement and Capital Standards, a Revised Framework. The Basel Committee on Banking Supervision. The Bank for International Settlements, June 2004, para. 670.

In order to open the measurement system to future changes, factors related to the business environment or to internal control factors must also be included. Once the key drivers of risk are understood, variations in these drivers should point to future trends in risk exposures. To use a simple example, if we believe that the number of transactions drives the frequency of loss, and changes in the environment lead to a sizeable increase in volumes, then this will lead to increased frequency of loss. The Basel II principles suggest that this should be factored into the model to reflect a potentially increasing exposure.

Before a factor can be selected, however, the bank must be sure that it is a meaningful risk driver – basing this decision on the experience or on an expert opinion. The weighing of such factors must be documented and subject to review. Use of these factors must be validated against the experience and adjusted in the light of ongoing events.

Risk mitigation

Financial institutions may acquire insurance policies to cover many of the operational risks included within the Basel II definition. This mitigation is specifically recognized for the banks using an AMA approach (we are told that the presence of an adequate insurance cover is assumed in the setting of the alpha and beta factors under the basic indicator and standardized approaches).

AMA banks can recognize the risk mitigating effect of insurance by reducing their capital requirement by a maximum of 20 % of the total capital charge calculated under the AMA. Recognition of such mitigation is, however, subject to the specific approval of the local supervisor who will make sure that the insurance policy offers prompt and guaranteed payment of claims if it is to equate to available capital. A further concern might be the comprehensiveness of cover when compared to the Basel II loss categories.

Limited guidance is provided to assist in the assessment of the policies and must:

- Be provided by an insurer with a minimum A-rating to minimize the impact of a potential credit risk on the insurer.
- Have an initial term of no less than one year. As the maturity of the policy approaches, haircuts must be applied to reflect the expiring term with a 100 % haircut applied for policies with a residual term of 90 days or less.
- Have a minimum 90 day period for advanced notice of cancellation.
- Have no exclusions or limitations that are triggered by a supervisory action or that preclude a liquidator from recovering under a claim if the bank has failed.
- Be specifically mapped to the underlying exposure calculations of the likelihood and the impact contained in the determination of capital and its mitigation.
- Be provided by a third party entity. If risk is retained in a captive, it must be laid off into the market through a reinsurance contract provided by a third party that meets eligibility criteria.
- The framework for recognizing insurance must be well documented.
- The basis for mitigation must be disclosed.

Partial use

Basel II recognizes that banks may wish to use AMA for parts of its operations and one of the simpler approaches for other areas. This is permitted if all global risks are captured and all relevant qualifying criteria for the approach being used are complied with.

In addition a significant proportion of the organization must be using AMA and a timetable for full AMA rollout must be agreed with the relevant supervisory authority.

Conclusion

Basel II provides a framework for operational risk that ranges from a very simple calculation based on a broad proxy for risk exposures to a complex, custom-built structure that will form the basis for the discussion contained in the remainder of this chapter.

IDENTIFICATION AND MAPPING OF LOSS EXPOSURES

In Chapter 1, we proposed a consistent model for developing an exposure diagnostic giving the details for the different steps: identification, analysis, and assessment. This approach must be coupled with the split of the organization in as many of the "risk centres" (service, department, process, etc.) as needed to make the persons in charge of the centres accountable for the diagnostic and the control of the risk that may affect the centres. The systematic investigation of the risks to which an organization may be confronted leads to a consolidation of the risk register in which all founding and future actions are documented so that each level in the organization can be made accountable to the risk under their direct responsibility. Indeed, in that framework, provided it clearly establishes the risk management policy and communicates to all the appetite for risk, the board of directors will have to be challenged only on those exposures, threats, and opportunities of "potentially strategic" consequences. This process is similar to the principle of subsidiarity applied in the management of the EU: only those decisions that cannot be taken at a lower echelon are brought to the attention of the upper echelon.

The general model described in Chapter 1 can be used efficiently for diagnosing operational risk in banks in a manner compatible with the Basel II agreements requirements but leading to a wealth of additional information and knowledge about the complete risk profile of the bank.

The limitation of the 56 cell report mandated by the Basel II agreements illustrated in Table 3.2 is clearly evidenced when one considers that the eight business lines are some of the "risk centres" that could be identified in any bank – there are more – and that the event types are either causes, hazards or perils, or impact. In any case they do not represent the complete picture that the ARM approach could bring. However, as evidenced by the mark in each of the cells, the complete approach is compatible with the Basel II requirements, as these appear as a subset of the total picture.

To each of the risk centres, or processes, or services identified in the table developed under the Basel II framework, rather than sticking to the elements on the horizontal axis, we could then apply the identification matrix already mentioned in Chapter 1 with the five classes of resources, plus the "free resources" and go through the list of the perils to verify which should apply. This would lead to a much more thorough analysis of all the possibilities of loss stemming from operational risks for a given operation.

As an illustration we could take retail banking as probably one of the most complete "centres" as it requires all five classes of resource even at the branch level.

Therefore the first step is to list all the resources needed for a branch to deliver the services expected by the clients.

Table 3.2   Basel II reporting matrix (business line and loss event)(P = peril, R = resource, I = impact)

Event type Business line	Internal fraud	External fraud	Employment practices and workplace safety	Clients, products and business services	Damage to physical assets	Business disruption and system failures	Execution delivery and process management
Corporate finance	P	P	R	R	I	I	R
Trading and sales	P	P	R	R	I	I	R
Retail banking	P	P	R	R	I	I	R
Commercial banking	P	P	R	R	I	I	R
Payment and settlement	P	P	R	R	I	I	R
Agency and custody services	P	P	R	R	I	I	R
Asset management	P	P	R	R	I	I	R
Retail brokerage	P	P	R	R	I	I	R

The following list does not pretend to be exhaustive but offers the essentials for branch operations:

1. *Human resources*: all branches need a manager and a staff whose competencies are identified according to their contribution to the smooth operation of the branch.
2. *Technical resources*: each branch has not only premises, easily reachable, and depending on the country, some "drive-in facilities", but also furniture, electronic equipment, etc.
3. *Informational resources*: the branch must be easily identifiable (logo, colours, etc.) and have access to all the information concerning its clients and the product they are suppose to market.
4. *Partners' resources*: the branch needs access through external providers to the minimum utilities (electricity, water, sewage, waste management, etc.) and it also needs a pool of clients and prospects.
5. *Financial resources*: the branch needs to pay its employees and management, its providers, etc.
6. *Free resources*: access to the branch must be clear at all time during opening hours (streets, bridges, public parking lot, etc.), their employees must be able to breathe (air quality), etc.

The second step is to envision all of the perils listed in Chapter 1 as they may impact the resources above.

As an illustration, as far as the technical resources are concerned we can investigate the perils, and remember, for each one of them, to question whether they are "endogenous" or "exogenous":

1. Economic: sudden change in consumer's taste and shift to online banking makes the branches obsolete or redundant.
2. Natural: is the location prone to hurricane, earthquake, flood, and extreme temperatures (cold or hot)?

3. Industrial: is the building subject to fire, water damage? Are the equipments likely to suffer a breakdown? What about the boiler, if any, for heating the building? etc.
4. Human
   - Nonvoluntary: can an error occur in a client's account? Could one of our loan officers make a mistake in granting a loan to an unreliable client, by not following the normal procedure or making a calculation error, etc.?
   - Voluntary
     - "Wise guy": has a local "computer wizard" tampered with our programs to "improve them" and not documented the modification or not sought approval from IT staff?
     - "Criminal"
       ◇ For profit: is it possible that a burglary occurs in the branch? Is an armed robbery possible?
       ◇ Not for profit: could vandals invade the branch and ruin the equipment?

Clearly, behind this one cell in the framework "damage to physical assets" in "retail banking" there is a host of questions to ask and they are easily identifiable through the ARM methods suggested in Chapter 1. This systematic approach provides the causes that may result in damages to physical assets thus allowing for tapping much more efficiently into the pool of knowledge accumulated in the organization.

But the same vectors resource and peril mentioned above could also result in "business disruption and systems failures" and the same expert knowledge and scenarios could be used as part of the approach to the next cell.

It could be cumbersome for the reader to go through all of the 56 cells of the Basel II framework on operational risks, the example here above should be enough to convince any practitioner that the "cells" approach would not allow for a reasonably reliable funding of the operational risks through a reliable measure of possible losses in the next 12 months with a high level of confidence.

However, it is important to notice that the proposed ARM framework is entirely compatible with the Basel II framework and will allow for a sound measurement of the risks involved and the capital requirements to meet these risks.

The result can be represented in a matrix where all exposures are measured in frequency and severity and thus can be prioritized in terms of treatment allocation. However, rather than a two by two matrix, it will be necessary to have more choices by a four by four, four by six, six by four, and a maximum suggested of six by six matrix. This means that frequency would be split in four or six categories and severity as well.

Let us stress the fact that each category must be defined so as to have a meaning for the decider.

For illustration purposes, we could imagine such scales like:

- For likelihood (frequency): "once a day", "once a week", "one a month", "once every 10 years", "once a century", "once in a millennium".
- For impact (severity): "1 % of annual profits", "10 % of annual cash flow", "20 % of annual turnover", "50 % of net book value".

And we could draw a frontier of acceptable risk by interviewing with the members of the board of executives or directors.

QUANTIFICATION OF LOSS EXPOSURES

The candidate scenarios for quantitative risk assessment

The approach to risk assessment we will describe in this chapter and which has been implemented in a banking group is based on Bayesian networks and Monte Carlo simulation.

Quantification, as defined in this book, assumes that a knowledge-based approach has been carried out to identify, analyze and assess every loss exposure, and to investigate every scenario which could cause some loss for the company.

Our doctrine for a large company quantitative risk assessment can be easily summarized as follows:

Damages or losses that have already occurred will occur again in the same conditions, if no appropriate prevention action is taken. For potential or rare damages, we must understand why and how they could occur and if they can cause serious losses without any appropriate protection.

We can express this doctrine in the two-dimensional plan for risks, where the horizontal axis measures loss impact or severity and the vertical axis measures loss frequency or probability, Figure 3.2.

Potential losses due to high-severity and low-frequency risks are handled by building causal models based on probability scenarios. This method is also applied to high-frequency risks where the cumulative impact is important – credit card fraud risks are examples of this kind of risk – since an in-depth understanding of possible evolutions of these risks is necessary if we want to define appropriate prevention and protection actions.

Potential losses due to low-severity and high- or medium-frequency risks are handled with the Loss Distribution Approach (LDA). The LDA principle is to model actual loss data with a statistical law and to infer potential loss by extrapolation. In this book we are not interested in loss data modelling; literature on LDA and on data modelling is extensive and the reader can refer to the Bibliography for that purpose.

We hereafter present this risk quantification approach without further investigating risks, which could be modelled by the Loss Distribution Approach.

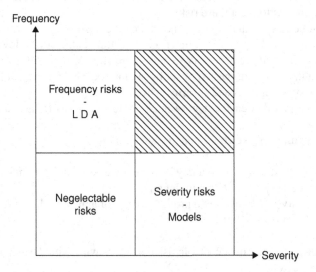

Figure 3.2   Selection of vulnerabilities for scenario modelling

The exposure, occurrence, impact (XOI) model

We will go back to the foundations of our approach, i.e. the – exposure, occurrence, impact – model. We already introduced this model in Chapter 1, and we discussed a simple example in Chapter 2 (the road accident risk for a truck fleet). From an intuitive point of view, this model really tries to capture the three dimensions of the risk variability and, not surprisingly, matches the three dimensions of the loss exposure defined in the qualitative assessment of risks, and also the main approaches to risk control.

Exposure is a quantitative measurement of the volume of activities at risk. This simply implies that if you increase your exposure to a given risk, your risk is also increased. More precisely, we define exposure as the number of independent objects exposed to a given hazard during one period (this period would be typically one year, e.g. for operational risks). Exposure is a random variable that you can partially control or forecast.

Occurrence is generally a binomial random variable which represents the occurrence of the considered hazard striking one exposed object during one period. This occurrence is quantified by its probability.

Impact is the measurement of the severity of one particular accident. In the framework of operational risks, this would be the cost of an accident in a given currency.

The (exposure, occurrence, impact) triplet is the quantified transposition of the (object, peril, consequence) triplet which defines a loss exposure. This consistency is an important feature of our model since it guarantees a smooth transition from qualitative to quantitative risk assessment: the XOI model is nothing but the quantitative version of the loss exposure identified during the mapping process.

Modelling and conditioning exposure at peril

Exposure at peril is defined as the number of *objects independently exposed to the considered peril* for the next considered period. We have already mentioned the importance of this notion of independence in Chapter 1. From a probabilistic point of view, two events are independent if the occurrence of one of them would not increase the occurrence probability of the other. From a risk management point of view, this means that a peril striking one exposed object would have no impact on other instances of the object – i.e. would not increase or decrease the probability of any other instance being hit by the peril.

In most cases, and if the considered time period is significant – usually one year – a perfect independence is impossible, for a very simple reason: the occurrence of a loss for a peril considered rare in an organization will increase the focus on this risk, and would normally reduce the probability of subsequent losses for the other instances of the object being considered. For instance, a significant fraud will probably increase fraud control, and reduce the probability for other frauds in the next few months. But this could have the opposite effect if the fraud remains undetected.

Although one can always argue that objects can never be considered to be completely exposed independently a posteriori, the minimum effort required when trying to define exposure to a given peril is to make sure that there is no obvious dependence a priori.

For instance, trading orders can be reasonably considered as independent as far as the human error peril is analyzed ("fat finger" error). A typo in a trading order is not expected to increase or decrease the probability of future errors. This could be the case if the consequences of this typo were dramatic, and were contributing to the implementation of additional controls – and

Table 3.3 Measurements for exposure to different types of risk

Nature of peril (Basel loss event)	General measurement for exposure at peril
Internal fraud	Employees
External fraud	Market share
Employment practices and workplace safety	Employees
Clients, products and business practice	Clients, contracts, products being designed
Damage to physical assets	Assets (buildings, etc.)
Business disruption and system failures	Periods of activities × systems
Execution, delivery, and process management	Employees, trades, clients, contracts, counterparts, etc.

we already mentioned this a posteriori dependency through risk control. But individual trading orders cannot be considered independent, even a priori, if we analyse the possible failure of the computerized routing system. If such a failure occurred, a significant number of orders would be lost simultaneously. In that case, an appropriate measurement of exposures could be periods of trading activity, say hours. Each hour of trading activity would be considered exposed independently to that risk.

In Table 3.3 we suggest typical measurements for exposure to different types of risk (Basel II classification of loss events).

These measurements are proposed here as general indications and need to be considered very carefully when analyzing specific scenarios. Let us consider for instance the "internal fraud" risk. If the scenario being analyzed requires no collusion, any employee with the appropriate level of authorization can commit the fraud. In this case, the number of employees could be the appropriate measurement of exposure at peril. On the other hand, if the scenario requires the collusion between two or more people, the exposure would no longer be measured as the number of employees.

Considering the "Execution, delivery, and process management" loss event, the nature of underlying scenarios is very different and could require similarly different measurements of exposure. Again, if we consider the "fat finger" scenario, the "number of trades" is an acceptable measurement. If we considerer the "Failed mandatory reporting obligation", we may think of measuring the exposition through the "number of mandatory reports".

Why is exposure a random variable? Simply because risk management is a prospective activity, and that, even if you can easily define the appropriate exposure measurement, and observe it for the past or current period, you will have to forecast this exposure for the next period you need to consider.

Summary

In most cases, the exposure at peril would be defined by some measurement of the activity of the organization (employees, clients, contracts, facilities, etc.). The evolution of this activity may depend on external factors, or on internal strategic decisions. The general conditional model for exposure is therefore as shown in Figure 3.3.

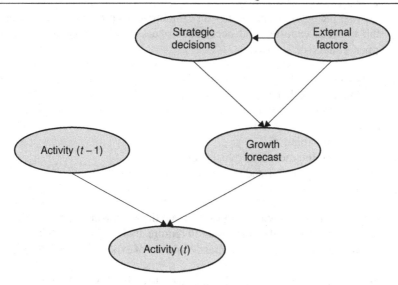

Figure 3.3 Typical conditioning of exposure

At this stage it is important to note that:

- Strategic decisions may depend on external factors. However, since we generally consider initial decisions and their consequences throughout the considered period, the causal link from external factors to strategic decisions will generally not be present.
- Beliefs can be set at any level, depending on the quality of the models available for the considered activity. For instance, if the activity is directly dependent on general economy growth, external economic models can be used to condition the growth forecast. On the other hand, if the activity is very specific, the probability distribution of growth can be set from experts' opinion, typically using three forecast scenarios: low, medium, high.
- Activity growths are not independent of each other. This point is crucial and will have to be kept in mind when merging scenarios.

Modelling and conditioning occurrence

Modelling occurrence is generally the most difficult task. To be consistent with the definition of exposure, the occurrence must be defined as the following random variable: " The peril hits one exposed object during the next period of time." The occurrence of a peril is thus generally a binomial variable (i.e. with values of either "Yes" or "No"). We mentioned in Chapter 1 that occurrence should be in theory considered as a special case of "intensity". Indeed, for some perils, the occurrence may show several levels of intensity (e.g. fire or earthquakes).

Consistency of exposure and occurrence

Evaluating the distribution of occurrence consists, at the very least, in evaluating the probability that the considered peril would hit one of the exposed objects during the next period – one year for operational risk.

Before we discuss the possible approaches for evaluating this probability, we need to clarify the relationship between exposure and occurrence one step further. Let us examine some situations of operational risk, such as:

- A trading order is mistaken
- A client's credit card is stolen
- A class action is issued by customers
- A local branch is destroyed by fire
- An employee commits fraud
- A client is a victim of Internet fraud (phishing)
- A client is a victim of Internet fraud (sniffing)
- A server is infected by a virus

These scenarios are fictitious, although close to realistic ones. Not all of them are severity scenarios, but we consider that all of them should require attention and modelling.

All these scenarios lead to apparently natural definitions of exposure, occurrence, and impact Table 3.4.

Let us examine these scenarios in more detail, and try to define the probability of occurrence. The first three scenarios are quite straightforward. A trading order is or is not mistaken. A given credit card can only be stolen once. A class action would gather several customers against the bank. It is reasonable to consider that only one class action exists at one time. Several class actions (for instance, in different countries or states) could be merged in a single one of higher severity.

The next scenarios are more difficult to handle. For internal fraud, is the peril the fact that the employee becomes a fraudster, or that he specifically executes a fraudulent operation? If we select the first definition, the peril can hit only once a year. For the local branch destroyed

Table 3.4   A first attempt to define exposure, peril and impact for some scenarios

No.	Scenario	Object exposed	Peril	Impact
1	A trading order is erroneous	Trading order	Error	Cost of cancelling the order and issuing the correct one (market dependent)
2	A client's credit card is stolen	Credit card	External fraud	Cost of fraud
3	A class action is issued by customers	Products or services	Legal	Compensation
4	A local branch is destroyed by fire	Local branch	Fire	Cost of repair + induced costs
5	An employee commits a fraud	Employee	Internal fraud	Cost of fraud
6	A client is an Internet fraud victim (phishing)	Client	External fraud	Cost of fraudulent transfers
7	A client is an Internet fraud victim (sniffing)	Client	External fraud	Cost of fraudulent transfers
8	A server is infected by a virus	Server	System failure	Repair cost + induced costs

by fire, in theory this could happen twice – if the branch is repaired very shortly. In theory, a client may be victim of Internet phishing more than once in one year, but this is not realistic. Although it seems similar, the scenario of Internet fraud through packet sniffing is different. Each individual Internet banking *session* is exposed to fraud through packet sniffing. Finally, for the last scenario, it is clear that a server may fall down because of a virus infection several times in one year.

We recommend making sure that the definition of exposure makes it impossible – or at least unrealistic – that the peril would hit a given object more than once during the coming year.

The ideal situation is when dealing with transient objects, for which the occurrence of peril would be consubstantial with the object. Scenario 1 (trading order error) is such a case. As we mentioned already, the order is, or is not, mistaken, and disappears once issued.

Redefining exposure using transient objects is sometimes possible. For instance, if we select "Session" rather than "Client" as the exposure for scenario 7 (sniffing), it becomes clear that the capture of one *identified* session by hackers could only occur once. Now, the peril is attached to a transient object.

When this is not possible, one trick is to include time in the definition of exposure. If we use "Days of server activity" (typically 365 days times the number of servers at risk) as the exposure definition for scenario 6 (virus infection), each "day of activity" of a given server now is nearly a transient object. If we believe that significant losses can occur even if the server is down for less than one day, we may even use "Hours of server activity" (8760 times the number of servers) Table 3.5.

From a mathematician's point of view, the appropriate definition would be to consider an "instantaneous peril", and to define the probability of an object being hit by the peril during an *infinitesimal* duration or, in other words:

$$\frac{\mathrm{d}p}{\mathrm{d}t}$$

Table 3.5   Redefining exposure, peril, and impact for some scenarios

No.	Scenario	Object exposed	Peril	Impact
1	A trading order is erroneous	Trading order	Error	Cost of cancelling the order and issuing the correct one (market dependent)
2	A client's credit card is stolen	Credit card	External fraud	Cost of fraud
3	A class action is issued by customers	Products or services	Legal	Compensation
4	A local branch is destroyed by fire	Local branch	Fire	Cost of repair + induced costs
5	An employee commits a fraud	Employee	Internal fraud	Cost of fraud
6	A client is an Internet fraud victim (phishing)	Client	External fraud	Cost of fraudulent transfers
7	A client is an Internet fraud victim (sniffing)	*Session*	External fraud	Cost of fraudulent transfers
8	A server is infected by a virus	*Hours of server activity*	System failure	Repair cost + induced costs

In practice, we simply suggest excluding obvious contradictions of the principle "an object can only be hit once", this exclusion being guaranteed either through the definition of the object itself or through empirical reasons (i.e. a local branch being destroyed twice in one year is not realistic). Keep in mind that a sound definition for exposure also needs to be understood by business experts.

Evaluating the probability of occurrence

Assuming we have come out with an appropriate definition of the exposure to peril, we now have (1) to assess the probability that the considered peril would hit one of the exposed objects during the coming year, and (2) to identify the drivers of this probability.

Three modes of evaluation are possible:

- The empirical evaluation is simply based on the number of observed losses.
- The theoretical evaluation is based on some sort of external assessment
- The subjective evaluation is based on an expert assessment.

The *empirical evaluation* is simply defined as

$$p = \frac{n_L}{X.d}$$

where:

- n_L is the number of losses observed during a time period of reference
- X is the average exposure during this time period of reference
- d is the duration of the time period, in years.

In other words, the empirical evaluation is defined as the *frequency* of losses for the peril being considered divided by the *exposure* to this peril. As we discussed already, this type of evaluation is valid only if some sort of stability is expected for conditions of occurrence of the peril. Obviously, some historical losses could be irrelevant, as they would reflect a period when fewer controls were in place, or, on the contrary, the peril was less salient (e.g. phishing, or other Internet frauds, terrorism, etc.).

When dealing with high-severity scenarios, usually, and fortunately, no recorded losses would be available within the organization. The empirical method per se is generally not applicable. When dealing with high-frequency scenarios with expected evolutions, the empirical frequency must be used with caution: if we are trying to analyze these scenarios more thoroughly, this is precisely because some change in nature is expected. Therefore, using the empirical probability only makes sense if one can justify that the foreseen evolution mainly concerns the exposure or the impact. Simply said, the empirical probability is generally not applicable for scenarios selected for quantitative modelling.

The *theoretical evaluation* of the probability of occurrence can be addressed in two ways. The simplest one is to rely on the external evaluation of probabilities. Possible sources of information could be:

- External experts, or insurance brokers (typically for natural perils).
- External frequency of losses: this type of evaluation is similar to empirical evaluation, with a larger exposed surface. In the Basel II framework, this type of information can be found in the QIS, or in external losses databases.

The other way to assess the probability of rare events is borrowed from safety engineering in industry, using the fault tree analysis approach. We typically recognize here that the occurrence of a high-severity scenario is only observed when several events happen simultaneously. A detailed analysis of the causes and an evaluation of the probability of each individual cause are required. Causes usually mix external events and internal failures. Each cause being individually more frequent, a probability assessment is possible and can be based on historical data, provided that information is recorded for these causes – or is available externally.

Fault tree analysis, a possible inspiration for rare event probability assessment

In the "fault tree analysis" technique, an undesired effect is considered as the root ("top event") of a tree. Then, each combination of the causes for that effect is added to the tree as a series of logic expressions. The tree is generally drawn using conventional logic- gate symbols.

When none of these methods is applicable, a *subjective evaluation*, i.e. a direct expert assessment, is the only option. Let us make one point clear: experts need to be involved in any of the above methods. When using empirical frequencies, experts need to assess the stability of the conditions, or the quality of the historical data. When using theoretical frequencies from external sources, experts need to assess the relevance of external data applied to the organization.

A direct expert assessment is used when the scenario is considered unique, or cannot be related to close enough scenarios, or cannot be easily decomposed. In that case, an expert is prompted to directly evaluate a *frequency*, using a scale, for instance: once every 10 years, once every 20 years, etc. This evaluation will be transformed into a probability using the current exposure.

In practice, our general recommendation would be as follows:

- Use an empirical evaluation when recorded data are available and when the conditions of occurrence can be considered stable.
- Otherwise, try to analyze the conditions of the occurrence to implement some kind of a fault tree model, even a very simplified one.
- Use a direct subjective assessment of the probability of the scenario occurrence when no other option is available.

The rationale of these recommendations is clear. The first two approaches are fully explicit, and at the same time would help you justify your assessment, and give you some deeper insight on the scenario. The last one is implicit – the expert does not justify his assessment. Simply said, the more explicit you can be about your risks, the better. This is fully in line with the general awareness objective.

In order to illustrate our discussion, let us return to the scenarios used as examples and introduced above, Table 3.6.

These recommendations can be justified as follows.

For scenario 1 (erroneous trading order), we recommend using an empirical probability. From experimental studies on human errors in various contexts, the probability of a human error can be considered stable, given the skill of the operators and the conditions of the operations. If these conditions (drivers) are stable over time within the organization, then an

Table 3.6 Recommended probability assessment for some scenarios

No.	Scenario	Recommended probability assessment
1	A trading order is erroneous	Empirical
2	A client's credit card is stolen	Empirical
3	A class action is issued by customers	Theoretical (fault tree type) or subjective.
4	A local branch is destroyed by fire	Theoretical – external data (typically insurance data)
5	An employee commits a fraud	Empirical
6	A client is an Internet fraud victim (phishing)	Theoretical – fault tree type
7	A client is an Internet fraud victim (sniffing)	Empirical
8	A server is infected by a virus	Theoretical – fault tree type

empirical assessment is valid. Otherwise, and under certain conditions, these parameters may serve as probability drivers (see below). Controls in place could be used to condition the impact.

For scenario 2 (credit card theft), and if we exclude theft over the Internet from this scenario, we may consider that the material conditions of a physical theft are stable. For this reason, the use of the empirical probability is acceptable. Considering this risk as a scenario is nevertheless relevant since significant evolutions of exposure or impact are possible.

For scenario 3 (class action), recorded cases would be generally very rare (at least internally). Using external probability would not reflect the specific efforts of the considered bank to reduce the likelihood of customers' action. Finally, a theoretical analysis of causes would be very difficult. Although the conditions of occurrence of a class action can be identified and listed, their individual probability may be very difficult to assess. In this case, a subjective evaluation may be the only acceptable solution. In practices, however, we would recommend assessing probabilities individually for each product being considered, and not globally.

For scenario 4 (fire), although some cases may be recorded, and would allow an empirical assessment, we would rather recommend that a global evaluation of the probability is obtained through insurers or insurance brokers. This is actually an empirical evaluation based on a larger exposure. Drivers of this probability (e.g. location) could also be obtained from the same source.

For scenario 5 (fraud), external experimental studies have been conducted on the individual conditions that would turn an employee into a fraudster. For instance, a study by KPMG in 2004 shows that gambling is among the main motivators for major frauds. These drivers cannot be assessed individually (see discussions on drivers below). For this reason, we would rather recommend an individual probability of fraud for an employee, assessed globally, or conditioned on objective factors – hierarchical position, salary, age, etc.

For scenario 6 (phishing), the detailed analysis of the causes is here relevant. A phishing requires the co-occurrence of at least three conditions: (1) the bank is victim of an attack – through massive emailing, for instance, (2) the client does not detect the fraud and follows the email instructions, and (3) the bank cannot stop the fraudulent site. The probability of each of these events can be assessed individually.

For scenario 7 (sniffing), different options could be selected, although we recommend an empirical approach. This type of fraud will generally be independent of the bank – actually, it would most probably be a random attempt to capture confidential data. Technical protections against this type of attack exist, but the bank cannot easily assess the level of its clients' protection.

Finally, for scenario 8 (server failure due to a virus), a detailed analysis of all events and failures that would make this scenario possible should be performed by the information system security officer. The probability of each of these events should be analyzed individually.

Conditioning the probability of occurrence

Two types of conditioning could be considered when assessing the probability of the occurrence of a scenario:

- A deterministic conditioning, when the probability of the occurrence is assessed through some type of fault tree causal model.
- A probabilistic conditioning, when the probability of the occurrence (or one of its determinist causes) depends on the object being exposed, or on external conditions of the occurrence.

These two modes of dependency are not exclusive. Let us discuss them on the "phishing scenario", and assume the following circumstances for this case:

- A massive emailing is sent to a large number of people, irrespective of their actual bank, prompting them to connect to a website. This emailing has the look and feel of the targeted bank.
- At the same time, a website is set up, again with the appropriate look and feel. People would enter their username and password, which is then captured.

A client of the target bank is phished if the three conditions below happen together:

- She receives the email (P_1).
- She does not receive a warning from the bank (P_2).
- She is naïve enough to connect to the website (P_3).

We assume that Internet providers can provide an estimation of the probability that a given person, identified through her email, receives at least one fraudulent email during a given period of time. Assuming that these fraudulent emails are sent at random, irrespectively of the recipient's bank, this probability is also that of a client of the targeted bank receiving such an email (P_1).

If the bank has set up a policy to contact its clients by email whenever such an attack is identified, the probability that a client is not warned by the bank can be considered equal to the proportion of clients the bank cannot reach through email (P_2).

Finally the proportion of clients that would be phished if not warned can be evaluated empirically – from past cases (P_3).

Now we can see that these probabilities can in turn depend on other factors. For instance, a client can only be warned by the bank if (1) she is reachable through email, and (2) the bank actually tries to reach her. Similarly, the proportion of clients who actually connect to the fraudulent website may depend on their age, considered as representative of their familiarity with the Internet technology. From this type of analysis, a conditional model of occurrence can be proposed, Figure 3.4.

The first (bottom) layer of dependencies depicted in this model is deterministic and can be considered as some kind of "fault tree" model. The second (top) layer of dependencies is probabilistic, and could be assessed either with the help of experts' opinions, or using observed data.

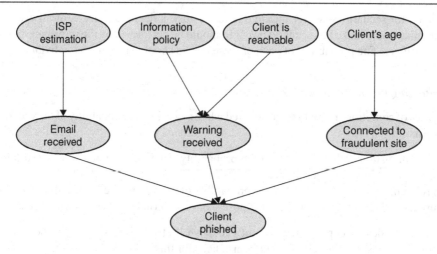

Figure 3.4   A causal model for "phishing" scenario

Summary

From this first discussion, we could suggest the general guidelines of a method for assessing the probability of the occurrence of rare events, Figure 3.5. This assessment can be addressed *recursively* as follows:

- First, one should try to decompose the occurrence of the event into "sub-events" through some type of fault tree dependency.
- If the fault tree decomposition is not applicable, one should try to identify some conditional drivers of the occurrence.

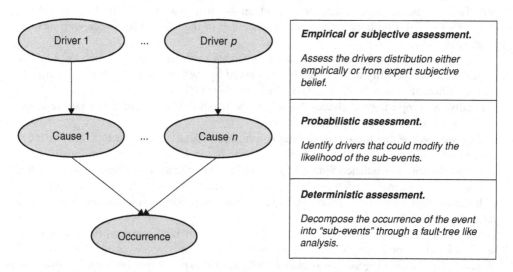

Figure 3.5   A typical three-layer model for occurrence conditioning

- If no relevant drivers can be identified, one should directly assess the probability of the considered event, either empirically, or with the help of expert subjective opinion.

Modelling and conditioning impact

When modelling the impact of a loss, the occurrence is no longer questioned. We consider the event has actually happened, and we try to quantify its consequences.

This process can be decomposed into three main steps:

- Define the impact equation.
- Define the distribution of the impact equation variables.
- Condition the impact equation variables.

Defining the impact equation

This equation expresses the cost of the considered loss as a function of several variables.

Consider the loss scenario introduced above: "A local branch is destroyed by fire". The resulting total loss is the sum of the partial rebuild cost and the refurbishing and furniture replacement costs. Rebuild cost will depend on the percentage that has been destroyed, and on the branch's type of building. We may consider, using a conservative approach, that total refurbishing and furniture replacement will always be needed, no matter the fire intensity. These costs increase linearly with the surface of the branch.

The loss impact will finally depend on the factors shown in Table 3.7.

Through the simple equation:

$$I = P \cdot S (C_1 + C_2)$$

The impact equation is a formal expression involving several variables. The fact that these variables are unknown, or may be difficult to assess, should not be an issue at this stage.

The main advantage of this approach is that the potential loss impact can be evaluated even if no historical data are available. If the distribution of individual variables can be assessed in some manner, it becomes possible to simulate potential losses.

When some variables are very difficult to assess, either by nature, or because the data which are needed would take very long to collect, one may consider simplifying the equation, using alternate variables, provided that the new model is more conservative.

Going back to the different scenarios introduced above, let us try to assess the different impact equations, and identify the different variables involved, Table 3.8.

Table 3.7   Symbol table for an impact equation

Symbol	Description
S	Branch surface
P	Percentage that has been destroyed
C_1	Rebuild cost/m^2
C_2	Refurbishing and furniture replacement cost/m^2

Table 3.8 Impact equations and variables for for different scenarios

No.	Scenario	Impact equation	Variables
1	A trading order is mistaken	Order amount × variation of market price during time elapsed before correction	Order amount Time elapsed before correction Variation of market price
2	A client's credit card is stolen	Total amount of fraudulent operations issued during time elapsed before card cancellation	Number of fraudulent operations Amount of a fraudulent operation Time elapsed before card cancellation
3	A class action is issued by customers	Analysis would depend on the product being considered	—
4	A local branch is destroyed by fire	Cost of branch × percentage destroyed	Cost of branch Percentage destroyed
5	An employee commits a fraud	Amount	—
6	A client is an Internet fraud victim (phishing)	Total amount of fraudulent transfers issued during time elapsed before account blocking	Number of fraudulent transfers Amount of a fraudulent transfer time elapsed before account blocking
7	A client is an Internet fraud victim (sniffing)	See 6	See 6
8	A server is infected by a virus	Analysis would depend on server considered	—

Defining the distributions of variables involved

Generally, the variables used in the equation would depend at least on the object hit by the peril. They are random variables.

It is now necessary to assess the distribution of each variable. Once again, one may use here three approaches for probability distribution assessment:

- Empirical, when observations are available for a given variable (e.g. surfaces of branches, amounts of trading orders, etc.).
- Theoretical, when a variable is known to follow a specific law (e.g. returns of financial assets are normally distributed).
- Subjective, i.e. using an expert's opinion, when no other option is available (e.g time elapsed before correction of mistaken order).

If we go back to the "local branch destroyed by fire" example, we can assess the distribution of the different variables as follows. The distribution of "Branch surface" would be computed empirically from actual surfaces of existing branches. The distribution of "Percentage destroyed" would be approached from insurer's data. Finally, the distribution of "Refurbishing and furniture replacement cost/m^2" or of "Rebuild cost/m^2" would be evaluated by experts – real estate

Table 3.9   Variable quantification method

Variable	Distribution assessment
Branch surface	Empirical
Percentage destroyed	Insurer's data
Rebuild cost/m^2	Expert
Refurbishing and furniture replacement cost/m^2	Expert

professionals, or architects. The surface distribution is empirical, and therefore adjusted from the actual surfaces of local branches of the bank, Table 3.9.

Identifying drivers

The variables involved in the impact equation are the drivers of a potential loss impact. This means that the distribution of the impact can be calculated from their distribution, as shown in Figure 3.6.

Now the question may be to identify the potential of these drivers. For instance, for an International bank, it may be clear that the rebuild and refurbishing costs would depend on the country. The percentage destroyed would depend on the fire protection equipment (sprinklers, etc.), which may well be country specific. Finally, the surface of the branches would also be country dependent, Figure 3.7.

A driver must be at least *observable*, i.e. one must be able to assess its distribution. Otherwise, this driver cannot be used in the distribution. For instance, one could rationally consider that the vigilance of the employees in a local branch would help to stop a fire before it has dramatic consequences. However, this vigilance cannot be measured and, therefore, should not be included in the model. Although some drivers may not be directly observable, it is nevertheless important to take them into account in the analysis process. For instance, it is reasonable to think that the level of vigilance would be increased through some training action, and would indeed reduce the risk.

In other words, our recommendation would be: when quantifying the risks, one should only use observable drivers. When reducing the risks, one should consider any driver that seems reasonably efficient. The quantification of risks is aimed at increasing the awareness of risks, not at limiting it through a dogmatic approach!

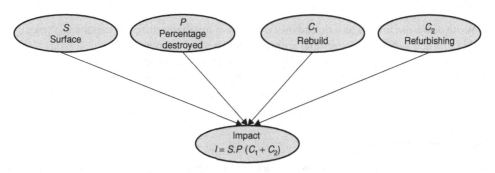

Figure 3.6   Impact equation graph

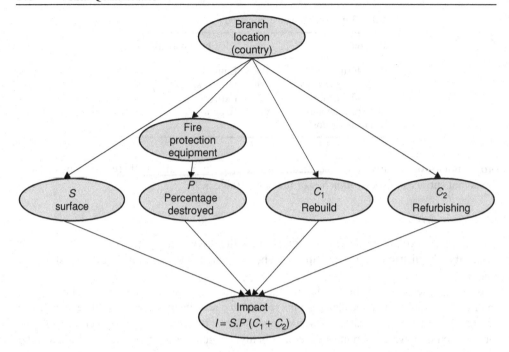

Figure 3.7 Impact equation graph including causal analysis

Among observable drivers, we would differentiate among two categories:

- *Controllable drivers* can be influenced by some decision. In our example, the rate of fire protection installations in local branches can be increased by a management decision.
- *Predictable drivers* cannot be really influenced by a decision, but their evolution can be predicted to some extent.

Summary

As for exposure or occurrence, we can now summarize the general guidelines for impact conditioning, Figure 3.8:

- Write down the impact as a deterministic equation involving different variables. Typically, this formula would require simple arithmetic and logical operators.
- Assess the distributions of the variables involved in the equation.
- Identify the observable drivers that could modify the distribution of the variables.
- Identify the non-observable drivers and keep this information for further actions.

Quantifying a single scenario

At this stage, we should have three models at hand, one for each of the three quantities involved in risk quantification: exposure, occurrence, and impact.

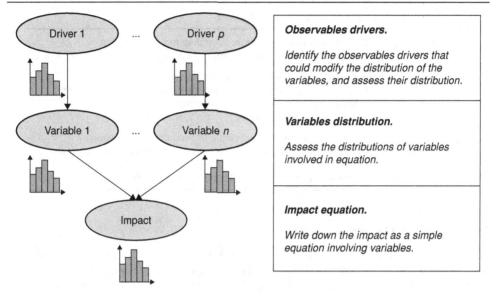

Figure 3.8   A typical three-layer model for impact conditioning

Each of these models is a Bayesian network. These networks may be interconnected. For instance, occurrence and impact may have common drivers. In Chapter 2, the road accident risk model showed an example of such a situation: higher speed increases both the probability of an accident, and the severity of its consequences.

In the Basel II framework, the "amount" of the object being exposed is usually a driver of both occurrence and severity. For instance, a high amount trading order would be usually double-checked, and the probability of an error reduced. On the other hand, an error on such an order would on average have more significant consequences.

Using these three networks, we now need to determine the potential distribution of losses for the scenario being considered.

This calculation will be performed using a Monte Carlo simulation. Here we will simulate thousands of possible configurations of losses for next year.

According to the XOI (exposure, occurrence, impact) model, the variability of next year potential losses has three sources:

- *The exposure may vary*: We may be more or less exposed to the scenario.
- *Each exposed object may be subject to loss*: each exposed object may or may not be hit by the peril, with a variable probability, depending of the characteristics of the object.
- *The impact of a loss may vary*: if a specific object is hit, the impact of the loss would depend on the object, and on other circumstances.

The Monte Carlo simulation of one "next year" instance will be performed according to the algorithm in Table 3.10.

We will now analyze an example in full detail.

Table 3.10   Monte Carlo simulation of an XOI model

Sample exposure	Draw each driver of exposure according to its distribution Once all drivers of exposure have been drawn, draw the exposure X itself
Sample occurrence	For each exposed object (repeat X times) Draw the drivers of occurrence until all causes of the occurrence are known, and finally draw the occurrence If the object incurs a loss
Sample impact	Draw the remaining drivers of the impact, until all variables involved in impact calculation are known, and finally compute the impact Cumulate all losses incurred for the current instance

An example – "fat fingers" scenario

This scenario has already been mentioned above. When issuing an order, an operator may mistype the amount, the direction (buy or sell), the currency, the recipient ID, or any other information. In some contexts, this error may have serious consequences (for instance, if a payment is made to the wrong person, it may happen that the money transferred by mistake will never be paid back). In most cases however, the only incurred loss would be due to the underlying market volatility: the wrong order will have to be cancelled, and the correct one issued again, one or two days later.

Modelling the exposure

Let us focus on the asset management activity. We consider the asset management team, and assume that all orders issued as part of this activity are exposed to a possible mistake.

According to the general exposure model proposed above, we need to evaluate:

- Today's activity (i.e. the number of orders issued as part of the asset management activity).
- The forecast growth.

By interviewing the sales manager, we can obtain the following information. The fund management activity has shown a steady 5 % yearly growth. Next year, a new range of products related to retirement plans could offer an additional 10 % growth. This new activity requires a new software implementation, which should be ready at the beginning of next year. However, the sales manager believes that there is only a 25 % chance that this new software will be ready on time. From past experience, he believes a more reasonable assumption would be that it will be ready at the beginning of Q2, or even of Q3, Table 3.11.

Table 3.11   Exposure

Activity today	100 000 orders a year		
Forecast growth	Assumptions	Forecast growth	Probability
	Software is ready on Q1	5% + 10 % = 15 %	25 %
	Software is ready on Q2	5 % + 10 %.75 % = 12.5 %	50 %
	Software is ready on Q3	5 % + 10 %.50 % = 10 %	25 %

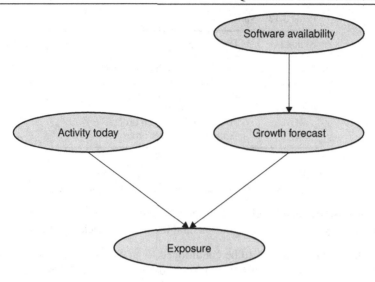

Figure 3.9   Exposure model

Modelling the occurrence

Each order is assumed to be independently exposed to a possible mistyping.

An analysis of the recorded losses shows an empirical 1/2000 probability.

After a series of discussions with asset managers, it turns out that a double-check procedure is in place for orders above €1 million. Indeed, no mistakes have been recorded for orders above this amount, although the people who were interviewed believe this would be possible, in particular in an overwork situation.

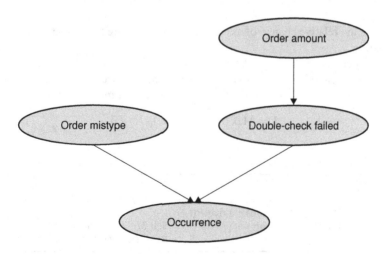

Figure 3.10   Occurrence model

Table 3.12 Variables

Symbol	Description
t	Date when mistaken order was issued
$t + d$	Date when order was corrected
$P(t)$	Price of asset at t
$P(t + d)$	Price of asset at $t + d$
M_1	Amount of mistaken order
M_2	Amount of correct order

For this analysis, it appears that the occurrence of the peril is possible if, and only if:

- The order is mistyped and is below €1 million.
- The order is mistyped, is above €1 million, and the double-check procedure fails.

The double-check failure appears to be conditioned to an overwork situation. However, this driver is not observable, and is not retained for modelling. After analyzing the double-check procedure, you finally come to the conclusion that if a large amount order is issued just before the close of day, it may very well go through without being actually double-checked. Analyzing the flow of orders during the day results in a double-check failure probability of about 1 %. This evaluation is accepted by experts, and a recommendation on how to improve the double-check procedure is proposed.

Modelling the impact

Now we are in the situation where a mistyping has actually happened. What would be the cost of this error?

Let us consider the variables in Tables 3.12 and 3.13.

The difference between the two situations is therefore:

$$I = (M_2 - M_1) \cdot \frac{P(t + d) - P(t)}{P(t)} = (M_2 - M_1) \cdot V(d)$$

where $V(d)$ is the relative change of asset price (return) during the period elapsed before the error is fixed.

Such an error can yield a profit (if the market has moved in a favourable direction). However, operational risk measurement excludes taking such profits into account, or to compensate losses and profits. Finally we can consider the following *impact equation*:

$$I = \text{Max}(0, (M_2 - M_1) \cdot V(d))$$

Table 3.13 Process details

Situation	T	$t + d$
No error	Buy $M_2/P(t)$ shares at price $P(t)$	—
Error	Buy $M_1/P(t)$ shares at price $P(t)$	Sell $M_1/P(t)$ shares at price $P(t + d)$
		Buy $M_2/P(t)$ shares at price $P(t + d)$

Table 3.14 Equation variables

Symbol	Description
M_1	Amount of mistaken order
M_2	Amount of correct order
d	Time elapsed before correction
$V(d)$	Asset return during d days

The *variables* involved in this equation are shown in Table 3.14.

Now we need to evaluate the distribution of these variables.

The first variable may seem very difficult to assess. How can we know the distribution of a mistaken order? Indeed, strictly speaking, we cannot. However, we can reasonably assume that this amount is distributed exactly the same way as correct orders are.

M_1 and M_2 are therefore two variables, identically distributed, but independent. Their distribution can be assessed empirically from actual orders issued this year, *assuming that this distribution is stable*.

According to the organization in place, a wrong order would be fixed usually the next working day. Assuming the asset managers are at work five days a week, and the markets are open six days a week, this would result in a one day delay if the order was issued on Monday to Thursday, and a three day delay for an order issued on Friday.

Finally, the assets returns are assumed to be normally distributed. We would consider three types of funds under management: stock market funds, fixed income funds, and money market funds.

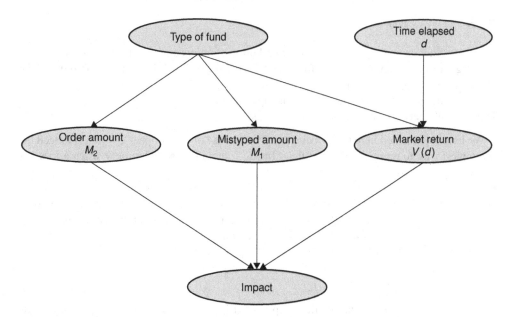

Figure 3.11   Impact model

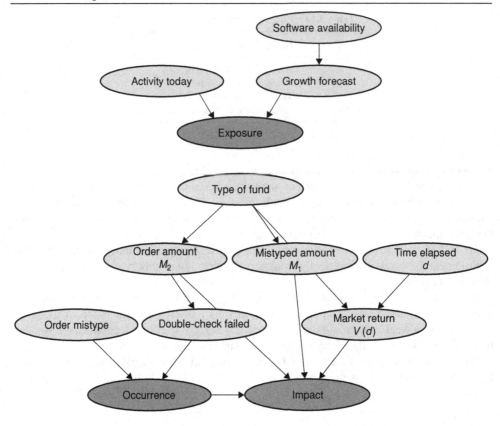

Figure 3.12   Global model

Now another dependency appears: the distribution of orders amounts is quite different when working on these different types of fund. The "Type of fund" will become a shared driver for M_1, M_2, and $V(d)$, Figure 3.11.

Finally, merging the three models yields Figure 3.12.

This "global" network requires some comments:

- We have represented here the "Occurrence" as a cause of the "Impact", which is indeed the simplest way to represent the fact that "Impact" should be sampled only when a loss has actually occurred.
- In this example, the "Exposure" network is completely separated from the "Occurrence/Impact" network. This is not necessarily always the case. For instance, one could consider that the new planned activity (retirement plan funds) could have a significant impact on the allocation of the funds under management. In other words, this would introduce a link between "Software availability" and "Type of funds".

Quantitative simulation

Now we will calculate the distribution of potential losses for this scenario. For this purpose we need to actually quantify all the variables used in the models. The values in Table 3.15 are fictitious but can be considered as being realistic.

Table 3.15   Quantification of a sample XOI model

Variable	Code	Usage	Distribution				Source
Activity today	X0	Exposure	Constant 100 000				Datawarehouse

			SW	Prob			
Software availability	SW	Exposure	Q1	25 %			Expert assessment
			Q2	50 %			
			Q3	25 %			

			AG \ SW	Q1	Q2	Q3	
Growth forecast	AG	Exposure	10 %	0	0	100 %	Arithmetic formula
			12.5 %	0	100 %	0	
			15 %	100 %	0	0	

			X \ AG	10 %	12.5 %	15 %	
Exposure	X	*Exposure*	110,0	100 %	0	0	*Arithmetic formula*
			112,5	0	100 %	0	
			115,0	0	0	100 %	

			FT	Prob			
Type of fund	FT	Occurrence Impact	Equity	45 %			Datawarehouse
			Fixed income	30 %			
			Money market	25 %			

			OR (€k) \ FT	Equity	Fixed income	Money market	
			[0,50]	30 %	1 %	0 %	
			[50,100]	40 %	4 %	0 %	
Order amount	M2	Occurrence Impact	[100,250]	25 %	35 %	0 %	Datawarehouse
			[250,500]	5 %	25 %	0 %	
			[500,750]	0 %	25 %	0 %	
			[750,1000]	0 %	10 %	40 %	
			[1000,1250]	0 %	4 %	30 %	
			[1250,1500]	0 %	1 %	20 %	

(*cont.*)

Table 3.15   *(continued)*

Variable	Code	Usage	Distribution	Source
Mistyped amount	M1	Occurrence Impact	Same distribution as M2	Datawarehouse

				OR		
Double-check failed	CF	Occurrence	CF	[0,1000]	[1000,1500]	Expert assessment
			Yes	100 %[a]	1%	
			No	0 %	99 %	

			MT	Prob	
Order mistype	MT	Occurrence	Yes	0.2 %	Expert assessment or Dataware-house
			No	99.8 %	

CF→		Yes		No		
MT→ O↓		Yes	No	Yes	No	
Occurrence (O) *Occurrence* Yes		100 %	0 %	0 %	0 %	*Logical formula*
No		0 %	100 %	100 %	100 %	

			d	Prob	
Time elapsed	d	Impact	1	80 %	Expert assessment
			3	20 %	

FT→	Equity		Fixed income		Money Market	
d→	1	3	1	3	1	3
MR(%)						
[−4,−3]	0%	2%	0%	0%	0%	0%
[−3,−2]	2%	7%	0%	0%	0%	0%
[−2,−1]	12%	15%	0%	4%	0%	0%
[−1,0]	34%	22%	48%	43%	16%	5%
[0,1]	36%	23%	51%	48%	84%	95%
[1,2]	14%	17%	0%	5%	0%	0%
[2,3]	2%	9%	0%	0%	0%	0%
[3,4]	0%	5%	0%	0%	0%	0%

Market return — Vd — *Impact*

This distribution is established assuming a normal distribution of each asset class. Average return and standard deviation are estimated from publicly available data.

Variable	Code	Usage	Distribution	Source
Impact	*I*	*Impact*	The conditional distribution table is not reproduced here because the impact node has three parents. This results in a large table. The conditional distribution can be calculated directly from the equation $I = \text{Max}(0, (M_2 - M_1).V(d))$	*Arithmetic Formula*

[a] Double-check is not implemented for orders below €1 million. This is expressed in the network by setting the probability of double-check failure to 100 % for such orders.

Table 3.16   Monte Carlo simulation of a sample XOI model

Sample Exposure	*Sample SW (software availability)* *Sample X conditionally to SW*
Sample Occurrence	*For each object of the X orders exposed to error* *Sample FT (type of fund)* *Sample M2 (order amount) conditionally to FT* *Sample MT (order mistype)* *Sample CF (double-check failed) conditionally to M2* *Sample occurrence conditionally to MT and CF* *If occurrence is "Yes"*
Sample Impact	*Sample M2 (order amount) conditionally to FT* *Sample d (time elapsed)* *Sample V(d) (market return) conditionally to d* *Sample Impact conditionally to M1, M2 and V(d)* *Cumulate all losses incurred for the current "next year" instance*

The calculation of the total loss distribution is obtained using a Monte Carlo simulation, according to the general algorithm described above, Table 3.16.

Direct calculation of the cumulated loss distribution is possible in some software tools, such as Hugin.

Merging scenarios

In the Basel II framework, we just described how to quantify all identified vulnerabilities. Frequency risks can be modelled using a typical Loss Distribution Approach (LDA).

Severity risks involve a specific causal model. More precisely, three causal models are required per scenario.

If we assume we have modelled all scenarios with this method, and if we now go back to the "Basel matrix", each cell of the matrix will contain, Figure 3.13:

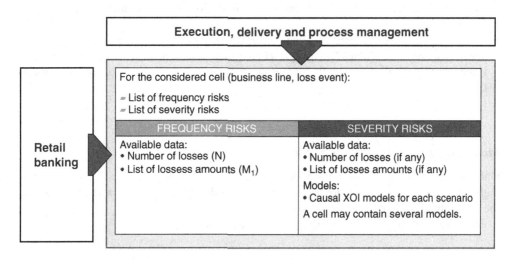

Figure 3.13   Available knowledge in a "Basel matrix" cell

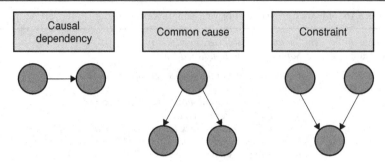

Figure 3.14 Type of indicator dependencies

- Historical data of observed operational losses.
- Scenarios and models.

Now we must merge all the pieces of information together to build a global distribution of potential losses. To do so, we first need to be able to merge individual scenarios. This requires identifing potential cross-scenario dependencies.

One important point is that some drivers may be shared among models. This would induce correlations between models. This further analysis is required to identify the "dependency model" of the global distribution of losses.

At least three types of dependency can be considered, Figure 3.14:

- *Causal dependency*: a driver is the cause of another driver. For instance, if a scenario exposure is conditioned by the number of clients, and another scenario exposure is conditioned by the number of credit cards, these two drivers are clearly related. More precisely, there should be a causal link from "Number of clients" to "Number of credit cards".
- *Common cause*: some drivers may have a common cause and may evolve simultaneously. For instance, both business lines, "Asset management" and "Agency and custody services", would show increased activity, and hence, increased exposure, if the stock markets are in a favourable trend.
- *Constraints*: in some situations, some indicators may be correlated through constraints. When resources are limited, a strategic choice may favour one activity against another. Exposures of activities sharing limited resources (people, for instance) cannot grow simultaneously.

Modelling the global distribution of losses

Once the dependency structure has been identified, the different models can be merged into a global distribution. This simply requires connecting the different indicators together, using the applicable type of dependency (above).

This gives a global operational risk model as shown in Figure 3.15.

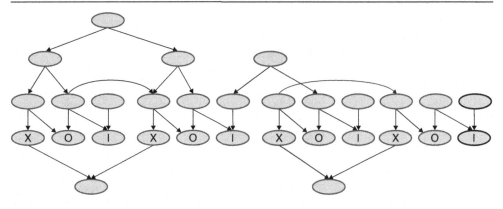

Figure 3.15   The global operational risk model

CONCLUSION

The Basel II regulation urges the banks to bridge the gap between risk assessment and quantifi-cation. It also provides a very concrete incentive for quantification: increased sophistication in risk modelling can reduce regulatory capital charges and free resources for new opportunities. From this point of view, we believe this example could be a methodological inspiration for enterprise-wide risk management in other industries. Quantitative risk modelling is a manda-tory step to prioritize risks and loss control actions. Quantitative models can be compared to prioritize risks and risk control actions. They can be merged to build an enterprise-wide risk model, and identify possible correlations. We will now examine how quantitative risk models can be used to identify risk control drivers.

4

Identifying Risk Control Drivers

INTRODUCTION

Reducing the risks is the ultimate objective of risk management, or should we say reducing *some* risks. Since risks cannot be totally suppressed – as a consequence of the intrinsic incompleteness of human knowledge, risk reduction is a trade-off.

Furthermore, even when knowledge is not the issue, it may not be "worth it" for an organization to attempt a loss reduction exercise, at least not beyond the point when the marginal costs and marginal benefits are equal. Beyond that point it becomes uneconomical to invest in loss control. Then two questions will have to be addressed:

- At the microeconomic level, how do we handle the residual risk, including the treatments through risk financing that will be discussed in Chapter 5?
- At the macroeconomic level, or should we say at the societal level, is there in the situation left by the individual organization some externalities, risks or cost to society not borne in the private transaction? In such a case the authorities may want to step in through legislation or regulation to "internalize" the costs so that the organization is forced to reconsider its initial position. A clear illustration is the environment issue: many governments and some international conventions have imposed drastic measures to clean the environment which have forced many private organizations to reconsider their pollution and waste risks.

Beyond the macro–micro distinction, there are individual variations on the perception of risk by each member of a given group, and the final decisions may rest heavily on the perception of risk by those in charge of the final arbitration. This should be kept in mind throughout this chapter. Why do people build in natural disaster-prone areas without really taking all the loss reduction measures into consideration while at the same time not understanding why the insurer will refuse to offer them the cover they want, or at premiums they refuse to pay?

Individuals build their own representation that dictates their perception of risks, and the structural invariants in their memory helps in understanding the decision they reach. Their reasoning is based on prototypes or schemes that will influence the decision they reach. In many instances, decisions are made on a thinking process based on analogies: they try to reminisce from previous situations analogous to the one they are confronted with. Therefore, organizing systematic feedback at the unit level and conducting local debriefing should lead to a better grasp of the local risks and a treatment more closely adapted to the reality of the risks to which people are exposed. This method should partially solve the paradox we have briefly described above, as the gradual construction of a reasonable perception of risk in all should lead to more rational decisions.[1]

There remains to take into account pre-crisis situations where the deciders are under pressure and where the time element is key to understanding sometimes disastrous decisions. Preparing everyone to operate under stress will therefore prove a key to the resilience of any organization.

---

[1] Bernstein, Peter L. 1996. Against the Gods. The remarkable story of Risk, John Wiley & Sons, New York.

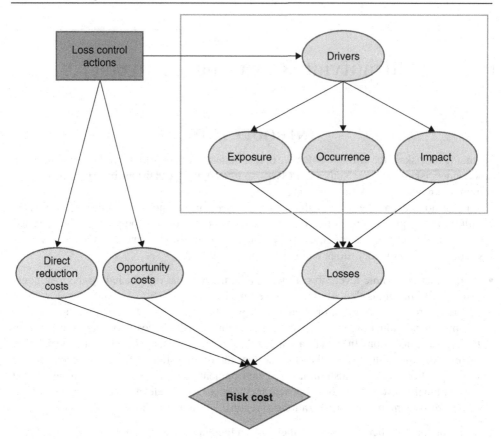

Figure 4.1   Optimizing the risk cost

From a quantitative point of view, and as we discussed in Chapter 1, the implementation of any risk control measure will:

- Change the distribution of some risk driver, either at the exposure, occurrence, or impact level.
- Have a direct cost, related to the implementation itself.
- Have an indirect or opportunity cost, related on the potential impact on the business.

Therefore, the cost of risks is the sum of three elements: accident losses, loss control cost, and opportunity cost.[2] These elements are of course interrelated. Reaching the best configuration of acceptable risks is therefore an optimization problem, under budget and other constraints. From a mathematical point of view, this is a well-defined problem, as introduced in Chapter 1.

As a *utility graph*, the model in Figure 4.1 can be read as "What are the loss controls that minimize the cost of risk?"

Of course, since loss control actions have an intrinsic cost, there is no way of reducing the cost of risks to 0. Sometimes, the loss control action is simply not worth implementing. The

---

[2] Kervern, Georges-Yves 1994. Latest advances in cindynics, Economica, Paris.

opportunity cost is also essential: ignoring this dimension of the loss control would often result in a very simple optimal solution: reducing the exposure to 0, or in other words, stopping the activity at risk! This loss control method is called avoidance, and will be discussed further.

As we will see, the quantitative approach to risks is a very helpful tool for selecting the appropriate loss control actions. But here we must be very careful. As introduced in Chapter 1, four categories of drivers can be identified:

- *Controllable drivers* can be influenced by some decision.
- *Predictable drivers* cannot really be influenced by a decision, but their evolution can be predicted to some extent.
- *Observable drivers* cannot be influenced, or predicted. They can only be observed after the facts, a posteriori. Observable drivers should not normally be included in a causal risk model, since they cannot be used in a prospective evaluation.
- *Hidden drivers* cannot be measured directly, not even a posteriori, but may be controlled to some extent.

When a first set of risk models is created during the risk assessment phase, observable and hidden drivers would generally be ignored, simply because they cannot be evaluated during the assessment phase.

For instance, when dealing with terrorist risks, the hostility of potential terrorists cannot be measured. When dealing with operational risks, the training level and the workload of the employees certainly impact the probability of a mistake. However, this dependency is very difficult to assess. But should these drivers be ignored in risk reduction? Should a state ignore the potential impact of sound diplomacy or communication to reduce terrorist exposure? Should a bank neglect to train its employees to improve the quality of service and reduce the probability of errors?

Simply said, we must recognize that causal models of risks are partial. And, although using this type of model is a significant improvement when dealing with risk assessment, they should only be considered as a contribution when dealing with risk reduction.

For this reason, we will first analyze the qualitative approach to risk reduction in detail, including an original approach called *cindynics*, which tries to formalize and structure the hidden drivers of the risk considered at the organization level.

We will then present three examples of the use of quantitative models of risk in assessing or selecting reduction measures.

LOSS CONTROL – A QUALITATIVE VIEW

The main objective of loss control measures is to reduce or contain the long-term economic weight of exposures by impacting on one or both of its two traditional quantitative dimensions, frequency and severity.

Action on *frequency* (or probability) tends to reduce the number of events by acting on the chain of causes that generate them. In other words, root hazards are reduced, or the resources involved put out of "harm's way". The generic name for such measures is *loss prevention*.

Action on *severity* (or impact) tends to limit the consequences(financial or others) of the event that has taken place or might take place; in other words the action is on the impact. The generic name for such measures is *loss reduction*.

As we may guess immediately, this clear distinction is sometimes blurred when actual mechanisms are implemented that tackle both frequency and severity.

Loss prevention (action on the causes)

Eliminating the exposure

If the prevention technique used is completely successful, then, in theory, the risk is reduced to *zero* and no further risk treatment will be called for concerning the specific exposure involved. From its own viewpoint, the organization has eliminated this exposure. However, there are two ways to achieve this, either the risk is "physically" eliminated altogether, or it is "totally" transferred to a third party.

Risk avoidance or suppression   While considering a project (avoidance) or during the review process for an existing activity (suppression), the management may conclude that the benefits involved are outweighed by the risks, the opportunity is not worth the threats involved. The situation is such that some "uncontrollable" events might lead to the destruction of the organization or such impairment that it could not rebound. Confronted with such scenarios, the executives have no other choice but to kill the project or eliminate the activity.

However, the extent of the "suppression" may be debated. Let us assume that a distillation process uses an alcoholic solvent with a risk of explosion and that a new process can be developed using water as the solvent. Some risk managers would call it "suppression", others "prevention". If the exposure is classified in the risk register as "explosion due to alcoholic fumes", it is evident that such an explosion will not be possible any more. One might call it a situation where the risk has been "suppressed". However, the author would like to limit the term avoidance/suppression to the situation where an opportunity, for the organization and/or for the society in general, is forgone due to the high threats at stake.

In the case of suppression/avoidance, society as a whole is not subjected to the risk, or not any more: hence, risk avoidance means eliminating societal risk as well as organizational risk.

Contractual risk transfer (for risk control)   This is a situation where an organization, considering its know-how, financial strength, and overall level of resources, finds an activity "too risky" to be engaged in but can find a partner, such as a subcontractor or supplier on the upstream side, or a customer or partner on the downstream side, to do the job. Therefore, from the point of view of the organization, the result is similar in this case to avoidance of narrowly defined exposure since the activity at risk is "physically" transferred to a third party. This new party is in charge of the risky operation that in most cases is a part of the manufacturing process. Thus the organization can draw the profits from the opportunity without being subjected directly to threats beyond its means. Let us note that there is always an element of "physical transfer" in such a case.

As an illustration, let us take the example of a small company specialized in precision work on metals, including surface treatment. The company management may decide that its last activity involving the use of long-term contaminants of the environment (heavy metals) and the compliance with always stricter federal regulation has become uneconomical in the long run. However, if all the parts to be processed have to be "surfaced" then the company must choose a course of action, either asking its customer to organize for the operation to be performed elsewhere, at the risk of losing the contract altogether, or finding a "reliable" subcontractor to do the job in a transparent manner for its customers.

Thus the supplier or, in the situation described above, the subcontractor now bears both the liability for the activity and its consequences. This is why it is also referred to as the "transferee", whereas the organization subcontracting is the "transferor". By the same token there is still a risk for society as a whole. Thus the organizational risk is shifted while the societal risk remains.

However, for the organization there is still a "residual" risk and that is the main distinction with avoidance/suppression. Furthermore it has created a new risk of dependency from the contractual partner. Let us examine the situation and assume that an element of the manufacturing process is transferred.

A few questions come to mind.

Since the organization is still marketing its products or services, does it remain exposed to product liability or not? Even though it is still responsible for the quality of the finished good, it does not control directly the quality of the outsourced operations but it may have recourse against the supplier or subcontractor in case a defect in the final product is identified to them.

Why is it "cheaper" to outsource, as the other party (or subcontractor) will expect to be rewarded for the risk it takes? If the internal cost of production plus "cost of risk" is more than the cost of outsourcing, it means that the partner in the contract is better at producing (cheaper labour costs?) or better at managing the risk ... there lies the crux of a third question.

Why would "society" condone such a move? Precisely, the only reason why society would encourage such practices lies in the third party's ability to handle the risk better. Thus this outsourcing as the contractual transfer of risk results in a net "loss reduction measure" for the societal risk. There is an additional profit associated with the reduction of the cost of risk; the economic system acknowledges the benefit for society by rewarding the transferor and transferee with a "bonus".

Let us stress again that whenever considering a contractual transfer for loss control, an organization should carefully ponder pre- and post-transfer conditions, so as to be sure that all consequences of the choice have been given due consideration. In other words, it must be fully aware it might create new exposures to be reckoned with. In the case of outsourcing, for instance, supplier and transportation risks are generated.

Furthermore, any risk manager's nightmare would be that the contractual transfer of risk be deemed invalid when confronted with a court decision thus leaving the organization with no resources to face a dangerous situation. If the courts are involved, the case is likely to be substantial enough to have made it to the justice system and that there would be no "risk financing mechanism" in place for this "transferred" exposure.

Derived from the societal concern mentioned above, a simple rule may apply to test the soundness of any contractual transfer for risk control: the transfer is an efficient risk control measure if and only if the societal risks involved are treated in the process, i.e. the risk borne or perceived by society is reduced. In other words, the transferor should be able to prove in a court of law, if called upon, that the transferee was chosen for its expertise in managing such an exposure. This is the test through which any outsourcing decision should be subjected: not only is it cheaper, but also is it a sound management decision from the viewpoint of all "stakeholders" (society as a whole) and not only from the point of view of the shareholders!

Let us be reminded here that there may be many considerations, other than risks, to lead to an outsourcing decision. However, in any contractual situation, the risk implications for the contracting parties should always be given appropriate consideration, as well as the implications for all other impacted stakeholders.

This form of contractual transfer is very different from the contractual transfer for risk financing that will be discussed further at length in the following chapter, as part of the risk financing mechanisms.

Reducing the probability of occurrence

This concept applies to all measures leading to a reduction in the frequency or the probability of adverse events, without eliminating them altogether. There is a residual probability that cannot be ignored.

It would not only be fastidious to attempt to compile an exhaustive list of all possible prevention measures but it would in fact be impossible. They are usually associated with the "frequency risks". In the "frequency risks quadrant", the more common applications are:

- Defensive driving education to reduce the number of accidents in which the vehicles of a fleet are involved.
- Medical check-up for health coverage.
- Ergonomically designed workstations.
- Safety measures to reduce workers' compensation claims.
- Control measures in supermarkets to reduce theft.
- Quality management to reduce product liability hazard.

However, systems safety not traditionally associated with risk management deals with "severity losses" and operates conceptually like prevention in reducing the probability of a major disruption below an "acceptable" level.

Loss reduction (action on the consequences)

There are two main types of loss reduction measures: "active" measures and "passive" measures. The difference between the two is that the former needs to be activated at the time of the event. Some authors use the terminology pre- and post-event. However, this might be misleading. All risk management measures should be planned and put in place before any loss occurs even if the actual trigger is at the time or after the event.

Pre-event or passive reduction

Segregation of loss exposures is the simple application of the old saying "Do not put all your eggs in the same basket". It is mostly used to reduce real estate and property losses or net revenue losses. It allows for the continuation of the activity when damage occurs to production or distribution facilities. There are two alternatives.

Separation or segregation without redundancy   Separation consists in splitting a large asset into several smaller ones. A site could be divided by firewalls, if indeed fire is the exposure to be treated. It could also be that several distant buildings are built on the same site rather than one unique large building. On the other hand, if machinery breakdown is the problem, several lines could be installed in the same building.

For other perils like social unrest, workers' walkouts or natural disaster, a different location, another country, another continent may be the answer. For economical risks, it may be another activity with counter-cycle effects.

The idea behind "separation" is that the full capacity is necessary for normal operations. Any damageable event will generate some disturbance in the normal level of activity, even if limited because of the multiple sources. These "smaller" entities may well increase initial investment costs and a loss in economies of scale (hence higher production costs).

In some cases, logistical constraints may justify a multiple sites approach, like storage for a chain of supermarkets when one platform alone would not be able to serve a whole country. In other words, other considerations may well lead to sound risk management decisions.

Duplication or segregation with redundancy   It is a generic term that refers to any situation where for the sake of the protection of goals and objectives, excess capacity must be purchased that is to be kept idle and put to use only should damages to the main capacity occur. It is therefore an additional investment with no other return than reducing uncertainty.

The most frequent and widely spread case is information systems back-up. The main site is doubled with a "shadow system" and it may go so far as multiplying by two all costs, investment, maintenance and personnel. However, it is rarely the case nowadays when specialized companies offer "back-up" contracts in which they guarantee "computer energy" with a limited downtime. In a way, these companies "mutualize" the risks of major customers to offer their service at a reasonable price.

For the same risk some use "facility management" but it is more closely related to a contractual transfer for loss control (see above).

The word duplication is somewhat narrow as it refers to a second site identical to the first and there are situations where an intermediate solution between separation and duplication may be the correct answer. This is the reason why the expression "segregation with (or without) redundancy" was coined.

Let us keep in mind that some prevention measures (pre-event measures by nature) have also a loss reduction impact. To name but two of these:

- Fleet vehicles where all statistical evidence points to a permanent ratio between frequency and severity ("frequency leads to severity"). Therefore, reducing frequency reduces severity automatically.
- Ergonomic considerations have the same effect on severity and frequency for labour accidents and work related health conditions (workers' compensation).

Post-event or active reduction

"Classical" loss reduction techniques   The definition stated above gives a good idea of the principles involved; mitigate the consequences of an event potentially damageable. Therefore, it is appropriate to illustrate with a few applications.

One of the best-known illustrations is a sprinkler used to limit damages caused by fire to property and real estate. Suffice to say here that it is based on the principle of drowning any starting fire through an automatic deluge of water. This safety device or any automatic fire extinguishing system, compulsory for many risky industries if they want to find an insurer, are widely reviewed in specialized publications like those offered by the CNPP (Centre National de Prévention et de Protection) in France and the Fire Safety Board in the USA. Any reader interested in further information may want to read this literature.

Another example is product recall. It aims at reducing any product liability claims that may be filed against the organization experiencing it. It can be heavily damaging to the reputation or brand image, one of the main assets of any company nowadays. The industrial branches most familiar with these processes are the automobile and food industries. So far the pharmaceutical industry has been relatively spared (at least in the news media!).

Product recall can be efficient and limited only when products tracing is ensured through the tracking of batches (part of a total quality management process), which is enforced in food and pharmaceutical industries among others.

In the workers' compensation area, rehabilitation and return to work plans impact primarily on severity but also to some degree on frequency.

Post-event redeployment planning   The organization survival is really at stake in the case of *low-likelihood and high-severity* exposures, i.e. mainly when its reputation is at risk of being destroyed or at least tainted. Therefore, this is when the "recovery planning" exercise is fully justified ethically, as a good citizen, and financially. This exercise will take into account, not only the shareholders' but also the employees' and more generally all stakeholders' present and future (sustainable development) interests.

Today, more than ever perhaps, any CEO's motto is "Keep the cost down". This applies also to the elements in the cost of risk. Everyone is in it in an effort to cut corners. This is why it is important to turn around the organization's risk culture by taking away what many executives still view as the ultimate safety net: the insurance covers and bring the premium budget to zero. The real starting point for a risk culture turnaround is then:

Sever all current insurance costs.

Start afresh from a "zero" cover and premium level.

Now, the recovery planning exercise can be efficient and based on the following hypothesis: "Assume that tonight a fire burns down our main facilities and everything it contains, but no employees are injured. When the employees report to work the next morning, what do we do?"

It is also the cornerstone any risk mapping exercise using the risk owner's approach, i.e. splitting the entire organization into several "risk centres" to develop a complete exposures diagnostic as well as mitigation methods. This should really be the prerequisite of any risk management decision, without any reference to insurance. The organization can then determine what to do and what funds will be required only to implement the post-event strategy. Thus the defined exercise is the key to strategic resilience.

If the study is conducted with a truly strategic approach in mind, the traditional denomination as survival planning is inadequate and seems only reactive. This new strategic proactive approach should thus be more appropriately named "strategic (post-event) redeployment plan".

The word "plan" may be misleading here. Indeed some aspects are more a framework or an ongoing thinking process to lead to a mindset where changes are sought to be uncovered early in order to build a very reactive organization able to adapt to changes and thus avoid crisis or abort them at an early stage, unless they can be seen as benefiting in the long term for all stakeholders.

During the course of this process, risk control measures, vital for the continuity of operations, will be elaborated at the same time that the exposures are identified and analyzed. Of course, whether they will be implemented or not will depend on their cost/benefit analysis presented to the finance department.

As a matter of fact, this approach may differ from the traditional step approach to risk management decision making as defined in most textbooks. It is just a reminder that no rigid approach to risk management is likely to provide the best benefits in the real world. Two essential elements need to be considered:

- First, the risk centre manager or risk owner's risk mapping approach simultaneously provides answers to two fundamental questions for the risk management professional that will eventually lead to a continuity plan at the level of each operational manager.
  - What risk am I exposed to? This is answered by developing a diagnostic of the exposures (risk map).
  - How can I secure the objectives?
- Second, the ultimate risk manager of any organization is its CEO or its board. Thus, should the continuity plans fail, the CEO and/or board is/are to review the existing strategy. It is their responsibility to make sure that all opportunities are exploited at best whereas risks are not only contained but even turned into opportunities.

The main steps in the "resilience" planning process are summarized in below:

- Starting from an objective appreciation of the organization, elaborate the scheme that will ensure continuous operations for all the departments, no matter what might happen to current facilities ("continuity planning").
- Identifying the critical ressources vital to the daily operations of each department, define concrete prevention measures to preserve them, evaluate costs (investment, maintenance and operational) and implement them.
- Search for temporary relocation for all departments and define procedures to monitor evolution (regular updating) and evaluate costs involved.
- Determine temporary equipment and communication vehicles required in case of an emergency, where to get them and the costs associated.
- Envision the situations in which "sufficient" continuity would not be achieved and/or "reputation impairment" would make it necessary to funnel the remaining resources to fuel new endeavours. Broadly speaking, shape possible futures for the organization.
- The above solutions must be approved by top management and then explained and sent in a crisis manual to all managers involved in the implementation. Precise instructions regarding the implementation of practical measures are essential; communication channels with the crisis management team must also be clearly identified and opened at all time.

The approach to loss control developed so far aims mostly at the immediate causes of the random event and their mostly unfavourable consequences. In other terms we have treated the case of the event development rather than the organizational causes that may be uncovered through root case analysis (or *hidden drivers*). In France, some specialists have tried to develop a model that would go beyond traditional systems safety to offer a framework in which the human element would not be the only physical component of a complex system. The cindynics attempt at encompassing also the social and psychological dimensions of any individual. You will find below a brief introduction to cindynics.

AN INTRODUCTION TO CINDYNICS

Some trace the first step in cindynics to the earthquake in Lisbon. Science starts where beliefs fade. The earthquake in Lisbon in 1755 was the source of one of the most famous polemic battles between Voltaire and Jean-Jacques Rousseau. The main result was the affirmation that mankind was to refuse fate. This is reflected in Bernstein[1] comment's "risk is not a fate but a choice".

In a way, the Lisbon episode may well be the first public manifestation of what is essential in managing risks: a clear refusal of passively accepting "fate", a definite will to actively forge the future through domesticating probabilities, thus reducing the field of the uncertain.

This new scientific approach to perils and hazards started in December 1987 when a conference was organized at the UNESCO Palace. The name *cindynics* was coined from the Greek word *kindunos*, meaning hazard. Many industrial sectors were in a state of shock after major catastrophes like Chernobyl, Bhopal, and *Challenger*. They offered an open field for experience and feedback looping. Since then, the cindynics continue to grow through teaching in many universities in worldwide. The focal point is a conference organized every other year. Many efforts have been concentrated on epistemology and attempts at developing objectives measures.

G.-Y. Kervern[2] has been, and still is, instrumental in establishing bridges between the many developments in cindynics that stem from researches on hazard, danger, risk, trauma, threats, and opportunities to name but a few of the many concepts used in the realm of studies of the future. The diversity of vocabulary is representative of the very transversal nature of the scientific approach needed to further our understanding of risk. Different business sectors, communities, local authorities, health specialists, including the World Health Organization, all conduct researches but fail to exchange enough. Who among the risk management practitioners in the industry have heard of the Haddon matrix, commonly used in healthcare circles? This is why a common conceptual framework could help in formalizing the bridges that most isolated individuals had attempted to build so far.

Basic concepts

The first concept is *situation*, which requires a formal definition. This in turn can be understood only in the light of what constitutes a peril and hazards study. According to the modern theory of description, a *hazardous* situation (*cindynic situation*) can be defined only if:

- The field of the "hazards study" is clearly identified by:
  - Limits in time (life span)
  - Limits in space (boundaries)
  - Limits the actors' networks involved.
- The perspective of the observer studying the system.

At this stage of the development of the science of hazards, the perspective can follow five main dimensions:

- First dimension – memory, history and statistics:
  (*A space of statistics*)
  It consists of all the information contained in the data banks of the large institutions (Electricity de France power plants, Air France flights incidents, forest fires monitored by the Sophia Antipolis centre of the Ecole des Mines de Paris, claims data gathered by insurers and reinsurers).
- Second dimension – representations and models drawn from the facts:
  (*A space of models*)
  It is the scientific body of knowledge that allows to compute possible effects using physical and chemical principles, material resistance, propagation, contagion, explosion and

geo-cindynic principles (inundation, volcanic eruptions, earthquake, landslide, tornadoes and hurricanes, for example).

- Third dimension – goals and objectives:

(*A space of goals*)

It requires a precise definition by all the actors and networks involved in the cindynic situation of their reasons for living, acting, and working.

In truth, this is an arduous and tiresome task to express clearly why we act as we act, and what motivates us. However, it is only too easy to identify an organization that "went overboard" only because it lacked a clearly defined target. For example, there are two common objectives for risk management "survival" and "continuity of customer (public) service". These two objectives lead to fundamentally different cindynic attitude. The organization, or its environment, will have to harmonize these two conflicting goals. It is what we call "social transaction", which is hopefully democratically solved.

- Fourth dimension – norms, laws, rules, standards, deontology, compulsory or voluntary controls, etc.:

(*A space of rules*)

It is all the normative sets that make life possible in a given society. For example, the need for a road code was felt as soon as there were enough automobiles to make it impossible to rely on the courtesy of each individual driver: the code is compulsory and makes driving on the road reasonably safe and predictable. The rules for behaving in society, for example how to use a knife or a fork when eating, are aimed at reducing the risk of injuring one's neighbour as well as a way to identify social origins.

On the other hand, there are situations in which the codification is not yet clarified. For example, skiers on the same track may be of widely different expertise thus endangering each other. In addition some use equipment not necessarily compatible with the safety of others (cross-country sky and mono-ski, etc.). How to conduct a serious analysis of accidents on skiing domains? Should codes be enforced drawn from experience? But can rules be defined if objectives are not clearly defined beforehand? Should we promote personal safety or freedom of experimentation?

- Fifth dimension – value systems:

(*Space of values*)

It is the set of fundamental objectives and values shared by a group of individuals or other collective actors involved in a cindynic situation.

As an illustration, when our parents declared that "the motherland is in danger", the word motherland, or "patria" (hence the word patriot), meant the shared heritage that, after scrutiny, can be best summarized in the fundamental values shared. The integrity of this set of values may lead the population to accept heavy sacrifices. When the media use the word apocalyptic or catastrophic, they often mean a situation in which our value system is at stake.

These five dimensions, or spaces, can be represented on a five-axis diagram and the resulting diagram is a representation of the "hyperspace of danger".

In combining these five dimensions, these five spaces, one can identify some traditional fields of research, both theoretical and applied:

- *Combining facts (statistics) and models* gives the feedback loop so crucial to most large corporations' risk managers.
- *Combining objectives, norms, and values* leads to practical ethics. Social workers have identified authority functions in this domain. These functions are funded on values that limit

the objectives and define norms that they enforce hereafter. If there is no source of authority to enforce the norms, daily minor breaches will soon lead to major breachs and soon the land will dissolve into a primitive jungle.

This new extended framework provides a broader picture that allows visualizing the limitations of the actions too often conducted with a narrow scope. Any hazard study can be efficient only if complete, i.e. extended to all the actors and networks involved in the situation. Then the analysis must cover all of the five dimensions identified above.

Dysfunctions

The first stage of a diagnostic to be established as described above consists of identifying the networks and their state in the five dimensions or spaces of the cindynic model. The next step will be to recognize the incoherencies or dissonances between two or several networks of actors involved in a given situation.

These dissonances must be analyzed from the point of view of each of the actors. It is therefore necessary to analyze dissonances in each dimension and between the dimensions.

In this framework, the risk control instrument we call prevention is aimed at reducing the level of hazard in any situation.

In a social environment, for example, some actors may feel that an "explosion is bound to occur". This is what will be called the cindynic potential. The potential is increasing with the dissonances existing between the various networks on the five spaces.

A prevention campaign will apply to the dissonances in an attempt to reduce them without trying to homogenize all five dimensions for all the actors. A less ambitious goal will be to try to install in each dimension between all the actors' network a "minimum consensus" for a common life. In other words, it is essential to find:

- *Figures, facts or data* accepted by the various actors as a statistical truth.
- Some *models* as a common body of knowledge.
- *Objectives* that can be shared by the various actors.
- *Norms*, rules or deontological principles that all may accept to abide by.
- *Values* to which all may adhere, like solidarity, no exclusion, transparency, and truthfulness.

The minimum foundation is to establish a list of points of agreements and points of disagreement. Agreeing on what divides is essential.

The definition of these minimum consensus is the result of:

- Lengthy negotiations between the various actors' network *and, most often*
- One particular network that acts as a catalyst or mediator. It is the coordinator of the prevention campaign for the entire situation.

The "defiance" between two networks, face to face, has been defined as a function of the dissonances between these two networks following the five dimensions. Establishing confidence, a trusting relationship, will require reducing the dissonances through negotiations, which will be the chore of the prevention campaign. This process can be illustrated by three examples.

Family systematic therapy   Dr Catherine Guitton[3] focuses her approach on dissonances between networks:

- The family requesting therapeutic help.
- The family reunited with the addition of two therapists.

When healing is reached on the patient pointed to by the family, the result was obtained thanks to a work on the dissonances rather than a direct process on the patients themselves.

Adolescents and violence   Dr M. Monroy's[4] research demonstrates that violence typically found in the 15–24 age groups is related to a tear along the five dimensions. This system can be divided into two subsystems between which a tremendous tension builds up:

- The traditional family with its set of facts, models, goals, norms, and values.
- An antagonistic unit conceived by the adolescent, opposed, often diametrically and violently, to the "family tradition".

These dissonances can lead the adolescent to a process of negotiation and aggression with violent phases in which he will play his trump card, his own life. From this may stem aggressions, accidents and even, sometimes, fatal solutions to this process of scission, specific to adolescence.

The case of the sects   It is in this process of scission that the success of some sect attracting an adolescent following may be found. Their ability to conceal from the adolescents their potential dangers comes from the fact that they sell them a ready-made "turnkey" hyperspace. The kit, involving all five dimensions, is provided when the adolescent is ripe. As a social dissident, the adolescent needs personal equipment in all five dimensions.

Violence in the sects stems from the fact that the kit thus provided is sacred. The sacredness prevents any questioning of the kit. Any escape is a threat to the sacredness of the kit. Therefore, it must be repressed through violence, including brainwashing and/or physical abuse or destruction, as befits any totalitarian regime that has become a master in large-scale violence.

In a recent book on the major psychological risk (see Bibliography) where the roots of the hazard level in the family are analyzed according to the cindynic framework, Dr M. Monroy tries to grasp all the situations involved by numbering all the actors involved in most of these situations.

Network I   Family
Network II   Friends and peers
Network III   Schooling and professional environment
Network IV   Other risk takers (bike riders, drug users, delinquents)
Network V   Other networks embodying political and civilian society
               (sources of norms, rules, and values)
Network VI   Social workers and therapists

This list of standard networks allows us spot to the dissonances between them that build the cindynic potential of the situation.

---

[3] Fournier, Anne, Guitton, Catherine, Kervern, Georges–Yves and Monroy, Michel 1997. Le risque psychologique, *Editions ESKA*, Paris.
[4] Monroy, Michel 2000. La Violence de L'excellence (Pressions et contraintes en enterprise), *Houmes & Perspectives*, Paris.

In the case of exposures confronting an organization, an analysis of the actors' networks according to the five dimensions facilitates the identification of the *deficits* specific to the situation. For example, the distances between what is and what should be provides an insight into what changes a prevention campaign should bring about. These deficits should be identified through a systemic approach of hazardous situations. It can be:

- Total absence of a dimension or even several (no data available).
- Inadequate content of a dimension (an objective such as "let us have fun").
- Degeneration, most often a disorder, of a dimension (Mafia model in Russia).
- Blockade in a plan combining two dimensions:
  - Blockade of feedback from experience (dimension's statistics and models).
  - Ethical blockade of authority functions insuring that rules are respected in the social game (dimension's norms and values).
- Disarticulated hyperspace in the five dimensions creating isolation, lack of cohesiveness between the dimensions (*fiefdoms splitting a corporation*).

These deficits always appear in reports by commissions, established to inquire into catastrophes. It is striking to realize how all these reports' conclusions appear to love similar explanations.

How do these situations change? Situations with their dissonances and deficits "explode" naturally unless they change slowly under the leadership of a prevention campaign manager.

In the first case, nonintentional actors of change are involved. The catastrophic events taking place bring about a violent and sudden revision of the content of the five dimensions among the networks involved in the "accident". Usually all five dimensions are modified, with revised facts, new models, new goals, implicit or explicit, new rules, and new values.

In the second case, which all organizations should prefer, the transformer chooses to act as such. He is the coordinator of the negotiation process that involves all the various actors in the situation. Deficits and dissonances are reduced through "negotiation" and "mediation". The cindynic potential is diminished so that it is lower than the trigger point (critical point) inherent to the situation.

General principles and axioms

Exchanges between different industrial sectors, cindynic conferences and the research on complexity by Professor Lemoigne (University of Aix en Provence, derived from the Nobel Prize winner Herbert A. Simon) have developed some general principles. The cindynic axioms explain the emergence of dissonances and deficits, Table 4.1.

The main utility of these principles is to reduce the time lost in fruitless unending discussions on:

- How accurate are the quantitative evaluations of catastrophes – quantitative measures result from conventions, scales, or unit of measures (axiom 2).
- Negative effects of proposed prevention measures – in any action positive and negative impacts are intertwined (axiom 7).

Perspectives

In a cindynic approach, hazard can be characterized by:

- Various *actors' networks* facing hazardous situations.
- The *way they approach* the whole situation.

Table 4.1 Cyndinic axioms

Cindynic axioms	
1 *Relativity*	The perception of danger varies according to each actor's situation. Therefore, there is no "objective" measure of danger. This principle is the basis for the concept of situation.
2 *Convention*	The measures of risk (traditionally measured by the vector Frequency–Severity) depend on convention between actors.
3 *Goals* Dependency	Goals are directly impacting the assessment of risks. The actors in the networks may have conflicting perceived objectives. It is essential to try to define and prioritize the goals of the various actors involved in the situation (*insufficient clarification of goals is a current pitfall in complex systems*).
4 *Ambiguity*	It states that there is always a lack of clarity in the five dimensions. It is a major task of prevention to reduce these ambiguities.
5 *Ambiguity* *Reduction*	It states that accidents and catastrophes are accompanied by brutal transformations in the five dimensions. The reduction of the ambiguity (or contradictions) of the content of the five dimensions will happen when they are excessive. This reduction can be involuntary and brutal, resulting in an accident or voluntary and progressive achieved through a prevention process. The theories by Lorenz on chaos and Prigogine on bifurcations offer an essential contribution at this stage. *It should be noted that this principle is in agreement with a broad definition of the field of risk management. It applies to any event generated or accompanied by a rupture in parameters and constraints essential to the management of the organization.*
6 *Crisis*	It states that a crisis results from a tear in the social cloth. This means a dysfunction in the networks of actors involved in a given situation. Crisis management consists in an emergency reconstitution of the networks. *It should be noted that this principle is in agreement with the definition of a crisis as included here above and the principle of crisis management stated.*
7 *Ago-Antagonistic* *Conflict*	It states that any therapy is inherently dangerous. Human actions, medications are accompanied with inherent dangers. There is always a curing aspect, reducing danger (cindynolitic), and an aggravating factor, creating new danger (cindynogenetic).

- The structuring of these approaches following the *five dimensions*. (Statistics, models, objectives, norms, and values)
- The identification of *dissonances* between the various actors networks.
- The *deficits* that impact the dimensions.

Dissonances and deficits follow a limited number of "cindynic principles" that can be broadly applied. They also offer fruitful insights into measures to control exposures that impact the roots of the situation rather than, as is too often the case, reduce only the superficial effects.

For more than a decade now, the approach has been applied with success to technical hazards, acts of God and more recently on psychological hazards in the family as in the city. It can surely be successfully extended to situations of violence (workplace, schools, neighbourhoods, etc.). In some cases, it will be necessary to revisit the seven principles to facilitate their use in some specific situations.

The objective is clear: situations that could generate violence should be detected as early as possible, they should then be analyzed thoroughly, and their criticality reduced and, if possible, eliminated.

Cindynics offer a scientific approach to understand, act and improve. Thus, they offer an entirely new perspective to the risk management professional; they dramatically enlarge the scope of his action in line with the trend towards holistic or strategic risk management while providing an enriched set of tools for a rational action at the roots of danger.

As discussed in the introduction, cyndinics offer a perspective to analyze and understand "hidden" organizational drivers that cannot be easily taken into account in qualitative or quantitative models of risk reduction.

Now we will study how quantitative modelling can contribute to risk reduction, offering a way to justify the loss control measures implemented, by quantifying their efficiency.

QUANTITATIVE EXAMPLE 1 – PANDEMIC INFLUENZA

For the first example, we will use the 1999 study of the Center for Disease Control and Prevention in Atlanta, regarding the economic impact of pandemic influenza in the United States (Meltzer et al.[5]). We will show how this study can be translated into a Bayesian network, and illustrate how the conclusions drawn from this study could be easily obtained from the model.

Introduction

Following a first direct infection of humans by the avian influenza virus in 1997, experts predicted that another influenza pandemic is highly likely, if not inevitable, although the time of its occurrence cannot be predicted. The World Health Organization put together guidelines to help countries estimate the potential consequences of such a pandemic and the potential effect of interventions.

A paper on influenza pandemics published in 1999 by Meltzer et al. has recently been the foundation of various studies and reports in different countries. For instance, the French "Institut de Veille Sanitaire" quotes the Meltzer paper in its strategy,[6] and the figures mentioned in the White House report on pandemic influenza[7] are close to those found by the Meltzer team. A similar report has been published in the Netherlands.[8]

The objectives of most of these studies were:

- To evaluate the range of illness cases, hospitalizations and deaths in the event of an influenza pandemic.
- To compare the different risk reduction strategies (in number of illness cases, hospitalizations and deaths avoided).

We propose to implement this model within our exposition, occurrence, impact framework, and show how a simple version of this model as a Bayesian network could help towards having a synthetic view of the problem and of the risk control strategies.

Our model will mainly be based on French data as described in the mentioned report[9].

---

[5] Meltzer et al. 1999. The economic impact of pandemic influenza in the United States: priorities for intervention, *Emerging Infections Diseases*, 5(5):659–671.

[6] Estimation de l'impact d'une pandémie grippale et analyse de stratégies, Institut de Veille Sanitaire, Département de Maladies infectieuses, June 2005.

[7] National Strategy for Pandemic Influenza, Homeland Security Council, November 2005.

[8] van Genugten, Marianne L.L., Heijven, Marie-Louise A. and Jager, Johannes C. 2003. Pandemic influenza and healthcare demand in the Netherlands: scenario analysis, *Emerging Infectious Diseases*, 9(5), May.

[9] We used this study and others as a basis for our analysis, in order to rely on realistic figures, although the conclusions drawn from the analysis below should be considered as illustrative only.

The influenza pandemic risk model

Exposure

The appropriate exposure measurement here is the population size. This could be questioned as each individual is not really independently exposed to the virus even if the presence of contaminated people in the neighbourhood increases the probability of becoming ill. However, considering a pandemic situation, we assume that the virus is omnipresent, and therefore that the probability of being contaminated is mainly dependent on the persons' characteristics.

Occurrence

The probability of occurrence is defined here as the probability of one person being contaminated. We must clarify here that we do not address – nor do the scientific papers mentioned above – the probability of the pandemic occurring. This probability is very difficult to assess. The possibility of a mutation of the avian influenza virus is an option that most experts consider "certain", although without being able to specify a time horizon. It is therefore not impossible that a new pandemic can happen with another virus – not connected with the present avian influenza virus. If we really needed to set a probability for the occurrence of the pandemic, we could simply say that "influenza pandemics have occurred for centuries, three times (1918, 1957, and 1968) in the twentieth century alone". The probability of a pandemic occurring in a given year could be then estimated at about 3 %.

All the studies mentioned above consider the occurrence of the pandemic as certain, and analyze the consequences of comparing different strategies.

Now again, the probability that an individual is contaminated is not particularly easy to estimate.

Most studies consider various scenarios, summarized into a variable called "gross attack rate". Gross attack rate is defined in the Meltzer study as the percentage of clinical influenza illness cases per population. It is assumed to vary from 15 to 35 %. Infected persons who continue to work are not considered to have a clinical case of influenza.

This 15 to 35 % interval has been used also in the French study, and will be selected for our model, although the Netherlands report considers an attack rate as high as 50 %.

The "gross attack rate" being set, the individual probability of contamination would depend mainly on age. This dependency has been estimated from the actual distribution of cases among age groups observed from the 1918, 1928–29, and 1957 epidemics and pandemics.

According to this estimation, the number of cases is distributed among age groups as shown in Table 4.2.

This yields the probability distribution for individual occurrence shown in Table 4.3.

Table 4.2 Estimate of age distribution of cases and population

Age group (yrs)	French population	Percentage of all cases
0–19	14.98 millions	40 %
20–64	34.93 millions	50 %
65+	9.72 millions	10 %

Table 4.3 Probability of individual contamination as a function of age group and gross attack rate

Age group \ Gross attack rate	15 %	25 %	35 %
0–19	24 %	40 %	56 %
20–64	13 %	21 %	30 %
65+	9 %	15 %	21 %

Impact

If contaminated, the possible consequences of the illness vary. The French study considers only three possible outcomes:

- No medical care needed
- Hospitalization
- Death

The original Meltzer study considered also "outpatient visit" as a possible outcome.

The consequences of the illness depend on the "risk group" of the patient. Individuals are categorized as high risk if they have a pre-existing medical condition that makes them more susceptible to influenza-related complications. High risk individuals are found in all age groups, but with different proportions.

The disease outcome – or the "impact" variable, according to our model – will in turn depend on age and risk group.

First, let us analyze the repartition of high risk individuals through age groups. The Institut de Veille Sanitaire report estimates this repartition as shown in Table 4.4.

Finally, the same report proposes the estimates shown in Table 4.5 for hospitalizations and death rates, depending on both the age group and risk group.

This table reads as follows: the most likely number of hospitalizations for 1000 people belonging to the 20–64 year old, high risk group is 125.

One important point here is that only *ill people* are mentioned in this table. This means that among 1000 people in the 20–64 year old group, and assuming a 25 % gross attack rate:

Table 4.4 Percentage of high risk population among age group

Age group(yrs)	% High risk individuals
0–19	14 %
20–64	5 %
65+	50 %

Table 4.5 Death and hospitalizatin rates per 1000 individuals
(lower, most likely, and upper estimates)

	Death rate (triangular distribution)	Hospitalization rate (triangular distribution)
Low risk		
0–19 yrs old	0.1–5.0–20	1–20–80
20–64 yrs old	0.2–7.5–20	2–30–80
65+ yrs old	3–15–20	10–50–80
High risk		
0–19 yrs old	1–10–30	5–100–300
20–64 yrs old	1–15–30	5–125–300
65+ yrs old	15–20–30	50–150–300

- On average 210 people would become ill (Table 4.3).
- Among these 210 people, around 10 would on average be considered high risk, and 200 would be considered low risk (Table 4.4).
- Among the 10 high risk ill people, one (12.5 % of 10) would need to be hospitalized (Table 4.5).
- Among the 200 low risk ill people, six (3 % of 200) would require hospitalization (Table 4.5).

The impact analysis could stop here, if we legitimately consider that deaths and hospitalization cannot be reduced to an economic cost, but should be analyzed as independent impact variables of the pandemic risk. However, following Meltzer, we can nevertheless estimate "the economic impact of pandemic influenza", and consider a cost variable. This variable is not used in the French Institut de Veille Sanitaire report, so we will use a simplified version of the Meltzer figures for illustration purposes only.

The main factor of estimated cost in the Meltzer paper is the "Average present value (PV), using a 3 % discount rate, of expected future lifetime earnings and housekeeping services, weighted by age and gender (30) and adjusted to 1995 dollars (by multiplying by a factor of 1.07)." We will not comment on this evaluation, as we use it here simply for illustration.

This yields the estimation shown in Table 4.6.

In our example, we will use simplified figures in euros, Table 4.7.

Table 4.6 Economic impact (directa and indirect costs) of
health outcomes due to an influenza pandemic in the United
States(in thousands of 1995 US$)

	0–19 yrs old	20–64 yrs old	65+ yrs old
Death	1020	1045	75
Hospitalization	3	7	8

Table 4.7 Simplified economic impact (direct and indirect costs) of health outcomes (€k)

	0–19 yrs old	20–64 yrs old	65+ yrs old
Death	1000	1000	100
Hospitalization	5	5	10

The Bayesian network

This example is quite straightforward to implement as a Bayesian network. The exposure variable being equal to the population, we will assume it to be constant – even if the population is regularly increasing, the analysis made should be considered as relative to the population size rather than absolute.

The structure of the Bayesian network, Figure 4.2, is directly derived from the above discussion.

The probability tables used in the network can also be imported from the data provided by the studies used.

In Figure 4.3, we have displayed the probability tables close to the node they refer to. In order to simplify the analysis, we have ignored the triangular distributions recommended for

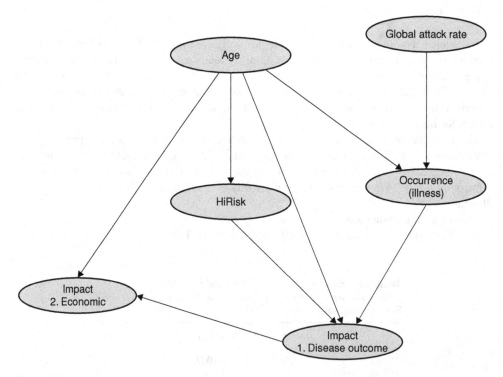

Figure 4.2 Structure of Bayesian network representing occurrence and impact for pandemic influenza

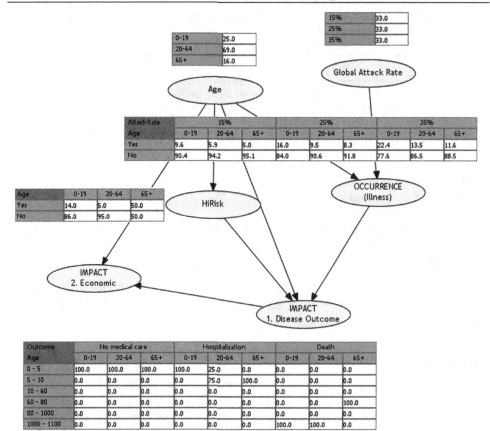

Outcome	No medical care			Hospitalization			Death		
Age	0-19	20-64	65+	0-19	20-64	65+	0-19	20-64	65+
0 - 5	100.0	100.0	100.0	100.0	25.0	0.0	0.0	0.0	0.0
5 - 10	0.0	0.0	0.0	0.0	75.0	100.0	0.0	0.0	0.0
10 - 60	0.0	0.0	0.0	0.0	0.0	0.0	0.0	0.0	0.0
60 - 80	0.0	0.0	0.0	0.0	0.0	0.0	0.0	0.0	100.0
80 - 1000	0.0	0.0	0.0	0.0	0.0	0.0	0.0	0.0	0.0
1000 - 1100	0.0	0.0	0.0	0.0	0.0	0.0	100.0	100.0	0.0

Illness	Yes						No					
HiRisk	Yes			No			Yes			No		
Age	0-19	20-64	65+	0-19	20-64	65+	0-19	20-64	65+	0-19	20-64	65+
No medical care	890.0	860.0	830.0	975.0	962.5	935.0	1000.0	1000.0	1000.0	1000.0	1000.0	1000.0
Hospitalization	100.0	125.0	150.0	20.0	30.0	50.0	0.0	0.0	0.0	0.0	0.0	0.0
Death	10.0	15.0	20.0	5.0	7.5	15.0	0.0	0.0	0.0	0.0	0.0	0.0

Figure 4.3   Structure and tables of Bayesian network representing occurrence and impact for pandemic influenza

death and hospitalization rates per 1000 individuals, and only used the most likely estimates (Table 4.5).

Risk control

Meltzer's original paper already mentioned above was focused on the use of influenza vaccines, while the analysis carried out by the French Institut de Veille Sanitaire also considered post-treatment strategies. Here we will study four simple strategies derived from the French report:

Table 4.8 Effectiveness of specific influenza vaccination (the figures reported here are the estimated number of cases, hospitalization and deaths that could be avoided thanks to the vaccination)

	0–19 yrs old	20–64 yrs old	65+ yrs old
Illness	40 %–60 %–80 %	40 %–55 %–75 %	40 %–45 %–60 %
Hospitalization	50 %–70 %–85 %	50 %–65 %–80 %	45 %–55 %–70 %
Death	60 %–80 %–90 %	60 %–75 %–85 %	60 %–70 %–80 %

- Administer influenza specific vaccine:
  - For the whole population,
  - For high risk population only.
- Administer antiviral drugs, such as neuramidase inhibitors (oseltamivir):
  - For the whole population,
  - For high risk population only.

Here we will study how to implement such strategies in a Bayesian network. But first, let us introduce the assumptions we used for the effectiveness of the different treatments we considered.

Pre-exposition treatment (vaccination)

The effectiveness of a specific influenza vaccination was estimated by looking at the use of such treatments in non-pandemic periods. These assumptions are summarized in Table 4.8.

This table shows that the vaccination has an impact both on the occurrence and on the consequences of the flu. For instance, on average 60 % of the cases could be avoided for young people, while 70 % of the hospitalizations and 80 % of the deaths could be avoided for the same category. For the sake of simplicity, we will assume that the vaccine only has an impact on occurrence, and we will use the median estimate. This is equivalent to using the simplified data in Table 4.9:

Post-exposition treatment (antiviral drug)

Similarly, the effectiveness of the post-exposition antiviral treatment was estimated from experience gathered during non-pandemic periods.

In our simple example, we only consider the post-exposition treatment, although prophylactic treatments could be considered as well, Table 4.10.

Table 4.9 Simplified version of the vaccination effectiveness table

	0–19 yrs old	20–64 yrs old	65+ yrs old
Illness	60 %	55 %	45 %
Hospitalization	60 %	55 %	45 %
Death	60 %	55 %	45 %

Table 4.10 Effectiveness of antiviral drugs (the figures reported here are the estimated numbers of hospitalizations and deaths that could be avoided thanks to the treatment)

	Antiviral effectiveness
Illness	—
Hospitalization	25 %–30 %
Death	30 %–35 %

Similarly, in Table 4.11, we will use simplified data, assuming that the treatment only reduces the probability of hospitalization.

Implementation within a Bayesian network

Implementing the risk control strategies within a Bayesian network is again quite simple.

As discussed in Chapter 1, a risk control strategy modifies the distribution of exposure, occurrence or impact, or of one of their drivers.

Here, the considered strategies will introduce new drivers in the model. "Vaccination" will become a new driver of "occurrence (illness)", and post-exposure treatment will become a new driver of "impact (disease outcome)". Indeed, these nodes are particular cases of more general "Prevention" or "Protection" nodes.

In the current model being analyzed, there are only a few drivers on which one can take action, Table 4.12.

Now we can see how the different intervention strategies impact the distribution of drivers, as shown in the Bayesian network in Figure 4.4:

- The "None" strategy is the reference one (no pre- or post-treatment).
- The "VAll" strategy corresponds to "Vaccinate the general population".
- The "VHiRisk" strategy corresponds to "Vaccinate the high risk population".
- The "PTAll" strategy corresponds to "Administer post-exposure treatment to the general population".
- The "PTHiRisk" strategy corresponds to "Administer post-exposure treatment to the high risk population".

Table 4.11 Simplified version of antiviral drugs effectiveness

	Antiviral effectiveness
Illness	—
Hospitalization	25 %
Death	25 %

Table 4.12   Exposure, occurrence, and impact drivers

	Drivers	Comment
Exposure	—	The total population is exposed to this risk – nothing can be done to control it. This node is not represented in the Bayesian network.
Occurrence	—	The probability of occurrence can be changed through prophylactic actions: vaccination, prophylactic administration of antiviral drugs.
	Age	The age distribution is exogenous data in this problem, and cannot be changed.
	Global attack rate	In this example, the global attack rate is considered exogenous data. One could consider restricting the circulation of people (partial closing of public transport, etc.) to reduce this attack rate. This option is not discussed in our reference papers.
Impact	—	Severity of disease outcome can be limited thanks to post-treatment cures.
	Age	See above.
	High Risk	High risk people belong to specific categories such as pregnant women, infants, immunity-depressed persons, etc. This is again exogenous data: the rates of such people in the overall population cannot be controlled.
	Occurrence	As in all risk models, occurrence is a driver of impact (there is no impact if the peril does not happen). See above on how to control this driver.

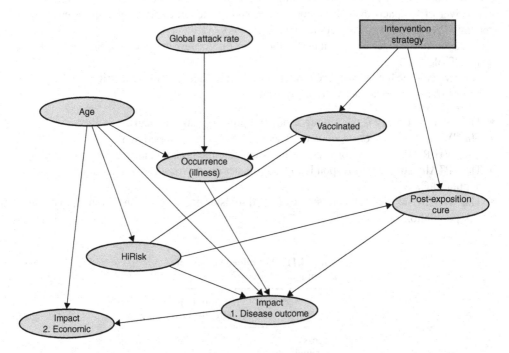

Figure 4.4   Structure of the Bayesian network representing the occurrence, the impact, and the risk control strategies for the pandemic influenza

Table 4.13 "Vaccinated" node probability table

HiRisk			Yes					No		
VacStrat	None	VHiRisk	VAll	PTHiRisk	PTAll	None	VHiRisk	VAll	PTHiRisk	PTAll
Yes	0.0	1.0	1.0	0.0	0.0	0.0	0.0	1.0	0.0	0.0
No	1.0	0.0	0.0	1.0	1.0	1.0	1.0	0.0	1.0	1.0

In order to represent the two possible alternatives of each strategy (treatment of the general population or of the high risk population only), we have to make sure that the "Vaccinated" and "Post-exposure cure" nodes also depend on the "HiRisk" node. This can be easily interpreted by looking at the "Vaccinated" node probability table, Table 4.13.

In this table, we see, for instance, that, being a high risk person, one would have a 100 % probability of being vaccinated if one of the VHRisk or VAll strategies was selected, while a nonhigh risk person would not be vaccinated (probability = 0 %) unless the VAll strategy was chosen.

Strategy comparison

Now we can examine the effectiveness of the different strategies. Let us first stick to the economic analysis, as inspired by Meltzer's original paper.

This analysis is very simply done using a Bayesian network: we just need to add a utility node. A utility node represents some quantity we would like to optimize, or at least to monitor. Here, let us assume we would like to monitor the average (expected) cost for one individual, as a function of the chosen strategy.

As explained in Chapter 1, the total risk cost is the sum of the loss control cost and of the actual risk cost.

The French Institut de Veille Sanitaire paper reports the treatment cost as follows:

- Vaccination: 12 euros.
- Post-exposure treatment: 2 euros.

Of course, these costs are not significant compared to the risk cost – since the average death probability with no strategy is about 0.2 %, the average risk cost would be around 2000 Euros for each individual. We will report them anyway in order to have a complete mode, Figure 4.5.

Figure 4.6 shows the results: all strategies are automatically compared according to the considered utility function.

Cumulated point of view

This analysis shows that, when selecting the "Vaccinate all" strategy, the total cost strategy is about €740 (€0.74k). This strategy reduces the risk cost by a factor of 2 compared to all other strategies. Altogether, and under these assumptions, the average economic cost of the pandemic influenza would reach €45 billion for a country like France, and twice as much if a strategy other than "Vaccinate all" is selected.

Obviously, this estimate relies heavily on the estimated cost of one death (around €1 million) and the assumed effectiveness of vaccination in limiting the probability of death.

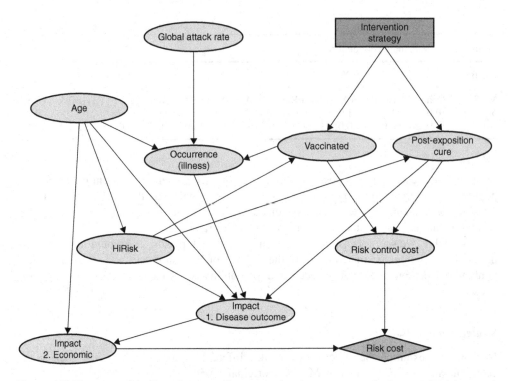

Figure 4.5 Structure of the Bayesian network representing the occurrence, the impact, the risk control strategies, and the risk cost for the pandemic influenza

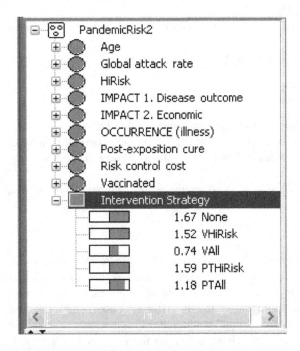

Figure 4.6 Average individual cost of different strategies

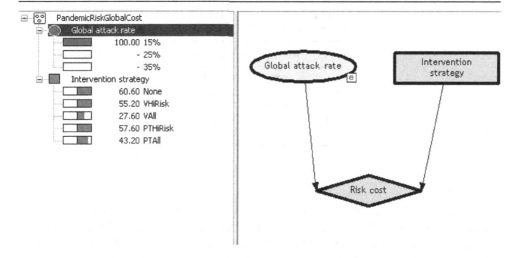

```
⊟ 🔲 PandemicRiskGlobalCost
   ⊟ ◯ Global attack rate
       ▬▬▬         100.00 15%
       ▭                - 25%
       ▭                - 35%
   ⊟ ▪ Intervention strategy
       ▭▬           60.60 None
       ▭▬           55.20 VHiRisk
       ▭▬           27.60 VAll
       ▭▬           57.60 PTHiRisk
       ▭▬           43.20 PTAll
```

Figure 4.7   Model of the cumulated cost – as a function of the attack rate and of the intervention strategy (billions of euros)

Other "utility" criteria could be considered, such as an efficiency criterion: the cost per avoided event (contamination or death), proposed in the above-mentioned studies. Using this criterion, the "Post-Treat High Risk population" strategy would be the most efficient. This type of criteria would only be used when severe limitations on resources must be taken into account. We believe, however, that this type of argument should be treated with caution.

One important point to understand here is that the presented Bayesian network does not take into account the "Exposure" dimension of risk; since the exposure is constant (all the population is exposed). This network actually represents the occurrence and the impact for a single "exposed unit", i.e. a person. If we consider the overall population, all the risk drivers would disappear as they would be averaged over the population. For instance, "Age" cannot appear in the overall risk model, since its distribution in a given country is constant. The age distribution of the country could be used as a driver of the overall risk model if one was, for instance, working for a worldwide organization considering the allocation of funds or medicines among different countries – but this is another story.

From the cumulated cost analysis point of view, only a very simple model is required: we simply need to represent the dependency between the chosen strategy and its cost. The "Global attack rate" should also be considered, since this variable is unknown, and the chosen distribution (33.3 % for each assumption) simply represents our ignorance.

This network can be built quite easily using the initial Bayesian network. We simply have to read the individual average cost for a given set of hypotheses (i.e. an hypothesis on "Global attack rate", and another one on "Intervention strategy") from the initial network, to multiply this cost by the exposure (60 million people) and to input this value in the new network, Figure 4.7.

This model will show that the "Vaccinate all" strategy is superior whatever the assumption on "Global attack rate" is, and also that the hierarchy of intervention strategies does not change when the "Global attack rate" changes.

Table 4.14 Variance analysis of the
cumulated risk cost (in billions of euros)

Strategy	Average	Standard deviation
None	102.0	3.1
VHiRisk	88.6	2.9
Vall	44.9	2.1
PTHiRisk	95.0	3.0
PTAll	69.7	2.6

Discussion

Another important point is that our analysis is performed only on an average basis. Both the individual and cumulated risks are averaged out. Even for a nonmathematician, it is easy to understand that averaging the individual cost to 740 euros is actually not meaningful. This average cost is simply a probability weighted sum of very different situations (no medical care needed, with zero-cost, and a one million euro death cost). On the other hand, one feels that the overall cost of 44 billion euros is a relatively solid figure. But is it so? What would be the "worst" case scenario? Or at least how can we differentiate between an optimistic and a pessimistic scenario?

This requires an analysis of variance. In general, an appropriate evaluation of the variance of the cumulated cost would require a Monte Carlo simulation. In this particular example, however, and since the exposure is very large (60 000 000 units are exposed), we may use the Central Limit Theorem (CLT) approximation.

Since the cost for each individual is a random variable, we have to sum $N = 60$ million independent variables with the same distribution.[6] The CLT approximation would yield a cumulated cost normally distributed with an average value of $N.c$ and a standard deviation of $\sqrt{N}.\sigma$ where c is the individual cost (€740) and σ the standard deviation of the individual cost (€265k for the "Vaccinate all" strategy).

This would finally yield the variance analysis shown in Table 4.14.

The standard deviation of the estimated cumulated cost is small compared to its average value (whatever the strategy being used). This shows – assuming a normal distribution – that it would be extremely unlikely that any other strategy would outperform the "Vaccinate all" strategy.

In this example, we see how a simple quantitative analysis could help select the best strategy. Although the results are quite straightforward in this example, and could have been derived from a simple calculation, the benefit of the model is to easily implement dependencies and hypotheses, and to perform what-if simulations.

We have also shown important features of loss control through quantitative modelling:

- The analysis starts with an individual (exposure, occurrence, impact).
- A loss control driver is any action that changes the distribution of one of the risk factors (exposure, occurrence, impact), or of one or its drivers.
- In order to analyze the response of the risk cost to a given driver, the individual model (exposure, occurrence, impact) should be summarized into a cumulated cost model, either through a simple calculation, or through a Monte Carlo simulation.
- The response to a risk driver can be considered using either average values or extreme values.

We will now return to the Basel II operational risk example, in order to illustrate the last two points in detail.

QUANTITATIVE EXAMPLE 2 – BASEL II OPERATIONAL RISK

We will reuse the "fat fingers" operational risk model already introduced in Chapter 3. With this simple example we will show how the use of inference in Bayesian networks can help identifying potential risk reduction drivers. We will also discuss the difference between drivers considered at the individual level and drivers of the cumulated cost.

The individual loss model

The individual loss model was presented in Chapter 3 and is displayed in Figure 4.8 for convenience.

Analysing the potential severe losses

Once the Bayesian network model has been built for this example, we can now evaluate the distribution of potential losses. For this, we just have to set the occurrence node to "True", and read the distribution of the impact (see Figure 4.9).

Then we can use the inference functionality of the Bayesian network in order to further analyze the conditions of a severe loss.

Identifying the loss control actions

This analysis calls for a potential loss control action: implement a double-check procedure for orders above €100k. Actually, two alternatives are considered: implementing a double-check procedure either above €100k or only above €250k.

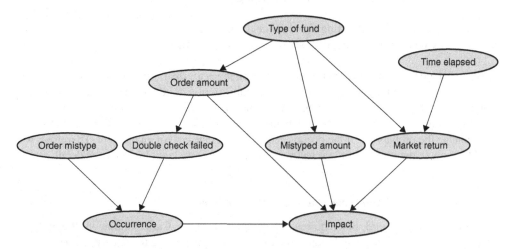

Figure 4.8   Fat fingers example (occurrence and impact model)

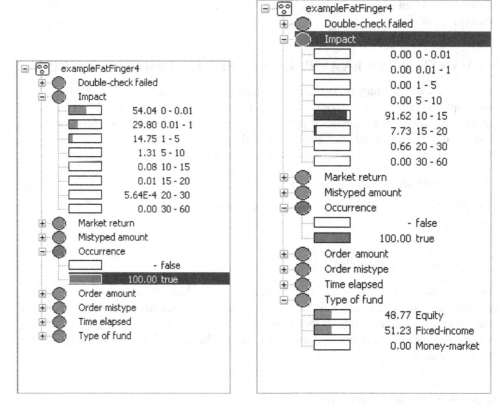

Figure 4.9   Analysing the conditions of a severe loss

This analysis can be done very simply using an influence diagram, Figure 4.10 and Figure 4.11. We just need to add two nodes to the existing network:

- One decision node, representing the order checking policy.
- One utility node, representing the average cost per incident.

As explained in Chapter 1, a loss control action changes the distribution of a risk driver. Here, the order checking policy would change the probability of a double-check failure (remember that, as a convention, we considered that the absence of double-check is equivalent to a failure).

Now this analysis is not sufficient. Changing the double-check policy would at the same time change the probability of the occurrence or the average cost of an incident. Therefore, we need to analyze the impact of the selection action on the cumulated loss in more detail.

Analysing the cumulated impact of loss control actions

As explained in Chapter 3, this requires implementing a Monte Carlo simulation. We will not describe the details of this simulation, which we implemented using the @Risk software from Palisade Corp. Chapter 5 contains several examples of the use of this tool.

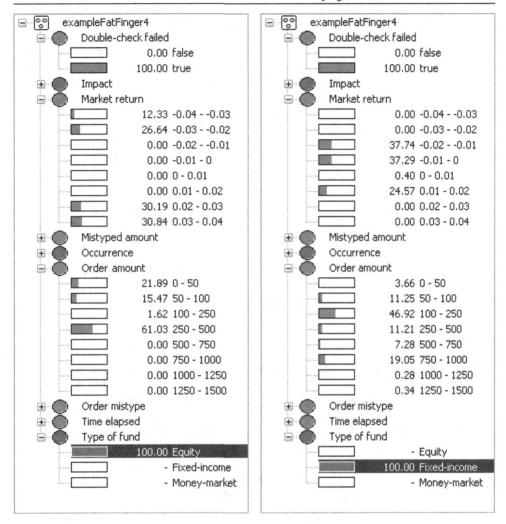

Figure 4.9   *(Continued.)*

Using this tool, we can get the distribution of the cumulated losses due to the "fat fingers" scenario, Figures 4.12–4.14.

We can see that this action concurrently shifts the distribution to the left, and narrows it, thus significantly reducing its variance. The impact of the risk control action can be summarized in Table 4.15.

Table 4.15   Summary of loss control action impacts

	Reduction on individual loss	Reduction on cumulated loss (mean)	Reduction on cumulated loss (99.9 % percentile)
Extended	9 %	49 %	43 %
Full	26 %	75 %	65 %

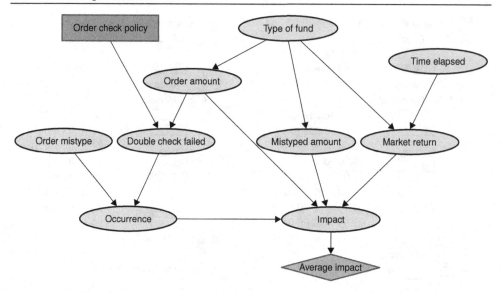

Figure 4.10   Augmenting the Bayesian network to evaluate the risk reduction measures

Discussion

This example gives a first point of view on how to use the exposure, occurrence, impact model as a basis for selecting a risk control action. Controllable drivers help identify potential risk control actions. Modifying exposure through action on a controllable driver can be considered as a risk avoidance approach (at least partially). Identifying controllable drivers of probability of occurrence is a prevention action. Finally, if the risk model contains controllable drivers of

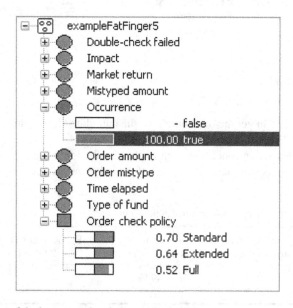

Figure 4.11   Impact of the loss control action on a single loss

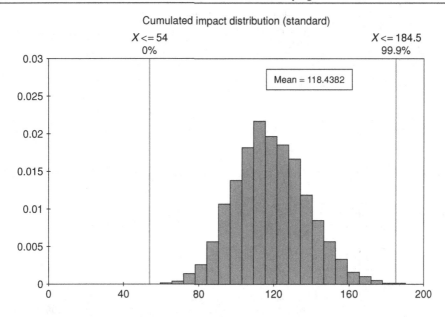

Figure 4.12   Distribution of cumulated costs with standard control policy

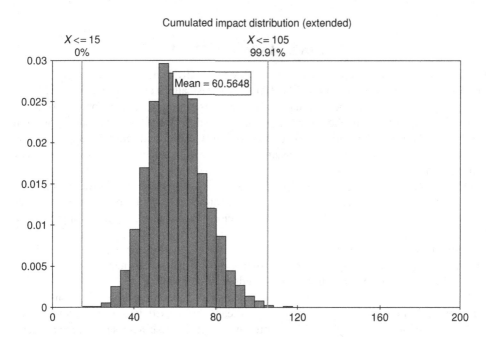

Figure 4.13   Distribution of cumulated costs with extended control policy

impact, they offer potential protection actions. From a quantitative point of view, the implementation of a risk control action on an existing model can be reduced to modifying a driver's distribution.

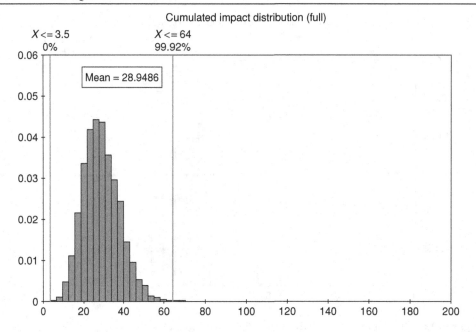

Figure 4.14   Distribution of cumulated costs with full control policy

QUANTITATIVE EXAMPLE 3 – ENTERPRISE-WIDE RISK MANAGEMENT

One of the key issues in risk management today is the ERM approach, which we prefer to develop as an enterprise-wide or integrated approach. Basically, it calls for all managers, indeed all staff, to be involved in the risk management exercise through the development of a "risk management culture" throughout the organization. In a deeply intertwined economy, it should even extend to the major partners, securing the supply chain, and require making sure that suppliers and subcontractors share the same views on risk management. This is the object of procurement risk management.

One of the daunting issues in integrating risk management in all the functions of the organization is to ensure that the quantification of risk is performed in a consistent fashion by all the actors. This is precisely where the Bayesian approach can help.

While the previous examples address specific risks in a bottom-up approach, we will now introduce an original example borrowed from a global risk assessment method developed within the risk management team of a major industrial company.

This example builds on Bayesian networks for risk modelling, as well as on an original definition of impact or severity. It has already been used in several applications in the above-mentioned company. We first present the global risk assessment method developed, and then describe an application to the risk assessment of a production plant, easily transferable to any case of a factory requiring a critical physical resource (water, fuel, gas, etc.).

Before describing further this example, we must give some preliminary warnings:

- This is a real-life example, far more complex than the simple examples we just presented. For this reason, it will not be possible to discuss it with the same level of detail.
- The model used here is *not* the exposure, occurrence, impact model presented throughout the book. However, we felt this was in line with the open-minded approach we recommend for risk reduction.

Context and objectives

A technical system like a plant, an infrastructure, an organization is impacted by various external natural events and possible human threats. The purpose of the global risk assessment presented here is to prioritize risks in order to manage them and achieve two main objectives:

- To bring a global understanding of the internal or external events which can have an impact on the availability of services or production provided by the system.
- To quantify as precisely as possible the risk of loss of availability, loss of production and eventually economic loss, of the system and the nonfulfilment of the legal or regulatory limits (like rejections levels, continuity of service, safety, etc.).

Risk analysis and complex systems

At this level, it is important to consider if the system we have to assess is a "complicated" or a "complex" system?

Complicated systems are typically designed, built, and operated by humans, like machines, software, technical systems, and procedures. Risk analysis of complicated systems relies on analytical modelling, with deterministic (causal) relations. Usually, fault tree style representations are used. Quantification is common; risk is defined as a product of likelihood and a consequence. As a process, risk analysis is more or less independent from the system, including a separation between analysis and decision.

A complex system is identified by the presence of particular criteria:

- The system is *holistic*: the whole is more than the sum of its parts, thus the usual analytic approaches may be not relevant.
- The system shows feedback and self-organization capabilities: including closed loops, the system has a capability to change according to the environment.
- The system is not deterministic: research of causal explanation is not sufficient to understand the system.
- The system is not reproducible: the comparison between experimentation and model is difficult or even impossible.
- The system is constructive: the observer is part of the system, the observation is not neutral regarding the system.

Usually, most systems which are not totally designed, built and operated by humans can be considered as complex: natural environments such as rivers, animals, plants. There are also complex systems dynamically designed, built,operated by humans such as organizations, technological systems, social systems, where the observer is part of the system. In the case of such complex systems, likelihood and consequences are difficult to quantify, thus decision must account for a large part of uncertainty. Risk is defined as uncertainty, and risk assessment has to accept a part of subjectivity.

An alternative definition of risk

When dealing with complex systems, it may not be appropriate to use the analytical approach of risks we introduced in Chapter 3. A specific conceptual work had to be undertaken to deal properly with complex systems, as far as the definition of risk is concerned. Here again, Bayesian networks can help to represent risks and produce risk maps and scenario analysis.

This alternative representation is based on a significant change in risk definition. Within this book, we generally define a risk as the triple (peril, object, consequence). The consequence of a loss is often financial. The risk manager is expected to put together the potential consequences of all risks being analyzed, and decide whether these consequences may significantly prevent the organization to reach its objectives. This analytical approach is often appropriate, but may be irrelevant when dealing with complex systems – in particular due to the built-in self-organization capabilities of the system.

When dealing with complex organizations, it may be interesting to adopt a holistic approach. Since "the risk manager's job is to ensure that, in any emergency situation, the organization has at its disposal adequate resources to allow it to attain its objectives under even the most strenuous circumstances" (Chapter 1), why not define a risk as *any event that may have a negative impact upon organization objectives*?

Given this definition of risk, the consequence (or severity) $S(X)$ of an event X is the probability that the organization does not achieve its objective O, *given* that the event has occurred.

$$S(X) = 1 - P(O|X)$$

Let $P(O)$ be the "unconditional" probability to achieve the objective O. An event having a major impact on $P(O)$ is therefore a major risk.

If $S(X) \leq 1 - P(O)$, this means that the probability of failure conditional to the occurrence of X is less than the unconditional one. Then, the event X is an opportunity. On the other hand, if $S(X) > 1 - P(O)$, then the event X is a hazard.

The *criticality* of a risk may be defined here as the product of the probability associated with a risk and its consequence:

$$C(X) = P(X).S(X) = P(X).(1 - P(O|X))$$

It is measured in terms of probability and consequences. Criticality is the probability that the risk X occurs and that the objective O fails. This definition enables us to take into account all the consequences of a given risk (for example, direct or indirect, financial, environmental, positive or negative, etc.).

Representation using Bayesian networks

Bayesian networks are well suited to implement this alternative representation of risk, and infer loss control recommendations. The "abstract" Bayesian network in Figure 4.15 shows how a global risk model can be implemented. Three types of links can be represented:

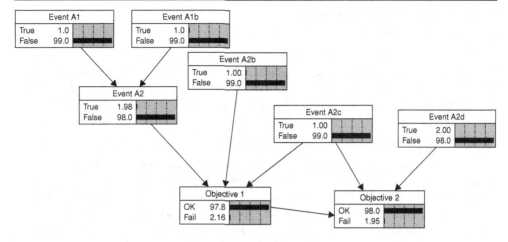

Figure 4.15 Simple Bayesian network structure incorporating events (risks and/or opportunities) and objectives. It can be defined as the "representation of a situation"

- Event → event. This represents the potential interaction between risks (domino effect). It is quite usual that the occurrence of an event will increase the likelihood of other events. If an accident with environmental consequences occurs at a chemical plant, the government may demand that similar installations should be closed for inspection. This decision may in turn have additional consequences.
- Event → objective. This represents the severity of the risk, i.e. the impact of the occurrence of the considered event on one particular objective.
- objective → objective. This type of link is used to express potential dependencies between different objectives.

In order to be able to actually implement such a model in practice requires the steps detailed below.

Selection of a time horizon

First, a time horizon must be defined. It corresponds to the overall duration the organization believes necessary to reach the objectives. The timescale of risk assessment generally ranges from six months to five years. Beyond five years, external uncertainties would become preponderant and a strategic prospective approach would become more adequate.

Identification of objectives

Then several independent (or partially independent) objectives can be considered at this horizon, all of them being specific cases of the general pre-event objectives defined in Chapter 1 (economic efficiency, environmental issues, ethics and good citizenship, functional objectives, etc.):

- Reach a predefined income or profit.
- Reach a certain level of client satisfaction.
- Obtain an environmental label.

- Increase reputation up to a given level.
- Develop business abroad.
- Etc.

For each identified objective, a binary variable is defined, being "true" if the objective is reached when the time horizon is reached, or "false" otherwise. A "target variable" or global objective, being generally a Boolean combination of intermediate objectives, may be further defined.

Identification of risks (events) and risk factors (context)

Once the time horizon, the intermediate objectives, and the target variable have been defined, all events that may change the probability of reaching the objectives must be identified (i.e. risks).

The identification of the significant events usually requires expert input – remember that we exclude here a strict analytical approach. An expert team should bring together experienced people within the organization or similar organizations, and risk managers. In order to be somehow exhaustive, the analysis of potential events should rely on a functional analysis of the organization in interaction with the external world (Figure 4.16):

- Environmental sphere: hydrosphere, geosphere, biosphere, atmosphere, climate.
- Resource sphere: human, technical, information, partners, financial.
- Financial sphere: shareholders, insurers, investors.
- Client sphere.
- Societal sphere: law, medias, nongovernment organizations.

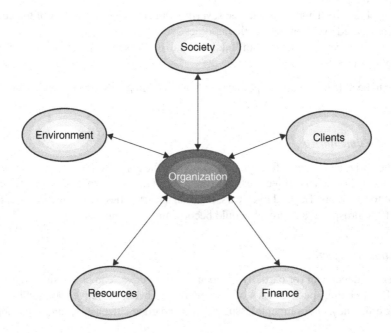

Figure 4.16 The organisation and its stakeholders. The various and often contradictory objectives and requirements of the stakeholders are the root causes of risks. This systemic diagram classifies the stakeholders groups on the basis of the flow exchanged with the organization (physical flows, resources, finances, power, etc.)

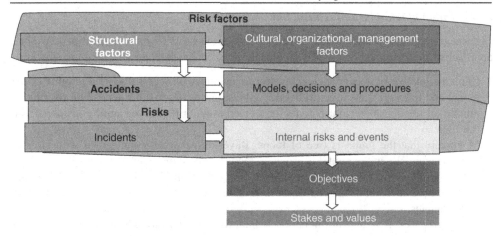

Figure 4.17   Structure of the Bayesian network used for global risk modelling. To avoid confusion and complexity, Bayesian networks used for complex system risk analysis have to be built according to a generic structure of risks and risk factors

Considering all potential aggressions against the organization or its relation with a specific "sphere" will help to identify a very large amount of risks. Of course, this method is not guaranteed to be exhaustive, but will be a precious guide to interview experts.

Several difficulties can be faced during this phase: profusion, self-censure of experts or, conversely, overamplification of the importance of their specialty, divergences. When working with a very large organization, the main trouble will usually be profusion. It is fundamental to keep in mind that only those events that may potentially impact the initially identified objectives should be considered.

Finally, the events identified must be defined clearly enough so that, once the time horizon is over, it would be possible to assess without ambiguity whether the event happened or not.

Structuring the network

The representation of a complex system integrating the internal risks as well as the external risks and the various risk factors quickly leads to a very complex network. To avoid confusion, we suggest building the Bayesian network according to a generic structure of risks and risk factors. The structure is derived from studies from E. Paté Cornell.[10] The network is built in a bottom-up sequence. At the bottom we have the objectives (or missions) and the values (or requirements) of the organization (or system) under analysis. The risks have an impact on objectives, and are being influenced by "risk factors". Different levels of intensity of internal and external risks are defined. An accident is, for example, the realization of a large-scale external risk, which influences at the same time different parts of the technical systems, its defence lines and its organizational context. The upper layer describes the impact of risk factors (existing variables like weather, organizational choices, social context, etc.).

The Bayesian network makes it possible to represent the interdependencies and correlations between the various risks and risks factors, Figure 4.17.

---

[10] Paté-Cornell, M. E. and Fischbeck, P. S. 1993. Probabilistic risk analysis and risk-based priority scale for the tiles of the space shuttle, *Reliability Engineering and System safety*, 40(3), 221–238.

Identification of relationships (causal links or influences)

In the next step, the dependency relationships between the variables must be identified. A sound approach to this identification process should take into account the following recommendations:

- Limit the number of dependencies. In order to guarantee an acceptable intelligibility of the model and to avoid very large probability tables, one needs to consider only a reasonable number of relationships (four parents for a given event or objective can be considered as a fair limit).
- Make sure that the graph is free of loops. Bayesian networks cannot deal with circular dependencies. When the model is growing, loops can be introduced involuntarily.
- Limit the number of levels. When an event influences an objective through a long path (more than four levels), this influence is usually insignificant compared to more direct dependencies.
- Avoid bypasses. If A has an impact on B both directly and through C, one may consider which dependency is the most significant, and either suppress the A → B link, or remove the C variable.

Quantification of the network

Some events in the networks will be considered as "root", i.e. won't have any cause in the graph. These variables correspond either to factors that cannot be controlled by the organization (climatic, political, or macroeconomic events, decisions of competitors or regulators, etc.), or decisions of the organization. The probability assessment of these variables is generally directly obtained from experts.

For intermediate variables, i.e. those variables which have at least one cause, the dependency is generally expressed through a logical or arithmetical relation (see Chapter 3). This expression is then "translated" into conditional probabilities.

When no such relation exists, the conditional probabilities have to be directly assessed by experts, and all the possible combinations of the parents of the considered node need to be evaluated. For instance, in Figure 4.18, this would require to consider at least 16 situations for R5 (if all causes R1 to R4 are binary variables). This is generally very tedious. In this case, only first-order relations will be considered (which means that the different parent variables are assumed not to interact).

Example of global enterprise risk representation

The network in Figure 4.19 represents a Bayesian network built for an application of the global risk assessment method. This model contains 39 variables and 57 links. For confidential

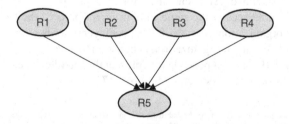

Figure 4.18   A simple node with no interaction between parent variables

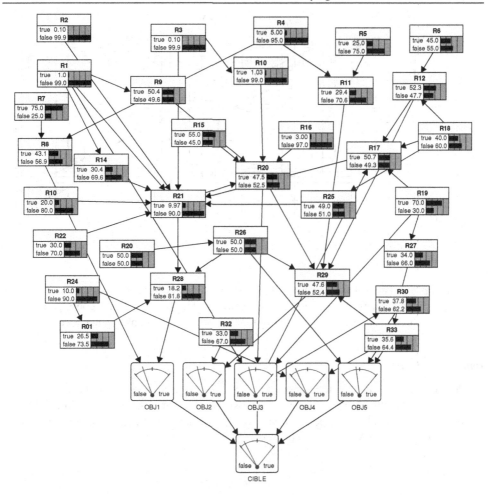

Figure 4.19   A typical network built for global risk assessment

reasons, variables and objectives names are not shown in this example. A more detailed example is discussed below ("Application to the risk management of an industrial plant").

Usage of the model for loss control

To illustrate clearly the possible usages of such a model, we will consider a small network (see Figure 4.19), that could be "extracted" for the global risk model.

Risk mapping

These definitions permit to directly build a risk matrix from a Bayesian network. In a risk matrix, or risk map (see Figure 4.20) the probabilities of occurrence of all the risks are on the x-axis, and the consequence of each one of them on the y-axis, evaluated in a particular situation or scenario.

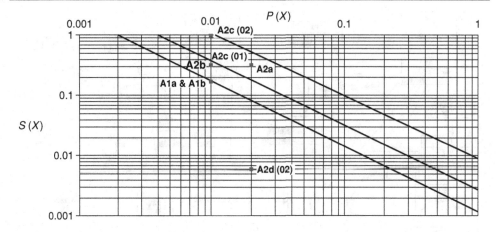

Figure 4.20   Example of risk matrix

In the top-right area of the graph are the most probable and serious risks. In the lower-left part appears the least probable and less severe risks. The lines of equal consequences are hyperboles which move away from the origin of the graph when consequence increases.

Importance factors

In addition to the risk matrix, the importance factor helps the comparison of the causes of loss of the mission and the efforts to manage the most probable contributors (see Figure 4.22).

To perform this analysis, a specific objective O_i is assumed to be failed. Importance factor $IF(X)$ of a given event X is the probability of occurrence of an event *knowing* that the objective O_i is failed:

$$IF(X) = P(X|\text{not}O_i)$$

In order to determine the influence of each event, the analyst needs to "force" the objectives in the "fail" situation for each of them. The Bayesian network will then recalculate the conditional probabilities $P(X_j|\text{not}O_i)$ for each variable X_j as displayed in Figure 4.21.

Scenario analysis

Scenario analysis makes it possible to study the evolution of the likelihood of mission failure according to various scenarios considered. More than the absolute value of the calculated probabilities, it is necessary to consider their evolution according to several scenarios. Stress testing and sensitivity analysis are performed in the same way, Figure 4.23.

In this particular framework, a scenario is defined as a *combination of events* at a deterministic level. Each scenario S has an impact, defined as the probability of missing the objective, given that the scenario has occurred:

$$I(S) = P(\text{not}O_i|S)$$

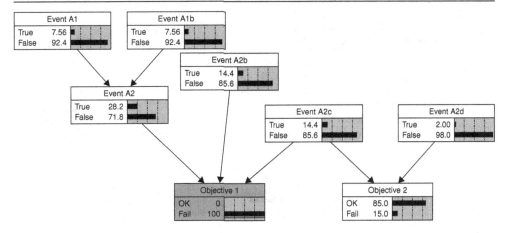

Figure 4.21   Importance factor analysis

Application to the risk management of an industrial plant

Description of the system

The system is an industrial plant located along a river. The plant needs water to cool its machinery. For example, it may be a chemical plant, a power production plant, etc. In this case the cooling system is called "heat sink". The heat sink of a plant has a great impact on the performance and the safety of the plant. In this application the case considered four plants located along a same river.

The heat sink is the combination of five technical subsystems: a water pumping or inlet (WI), a waterway (WW), filters of the pumping station (FPS), two heat exchange subsystems (HES1, HES2). The technical system constraints are such that the failure of one element is sufficient to cause the failure of the whole system.

The technical system has two main objectives: ensure the cooling of the machinery, and thus ensure the continuity of production, and also provide sufficient cooling to ensure that the temperature of the water rejected by the machinery does not exceed legal requirements. Missing any of these objectives would result in a loss of production.

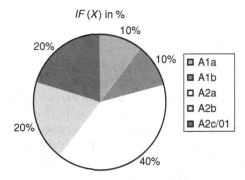

Figure 4.22   Example of importance factors

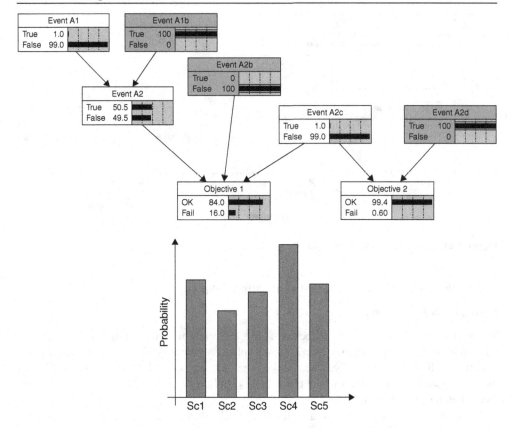

Figure 4.23   Principle of scenario analysis

The subsystems are impacted by various external natural events, as represented in the Figure 4.24 (river status, natural accidents, etc.). These events are influenced by risk or risk factors (season, month, climate conditions, river management, etc.).

In addition human events should be considered (use of river by other stakeholders, technological accident or malevolent acts, etc.). These events are also influenced by risk or risk factors.

Assessment of the external risks

Natural risks   The weather, the season and the hydraulic regime are the most important natural risk factors. We observe in our case relatively high variations of the flow (high in periods of raw water and weak in periods of low water level) and various external natural risks (silting up of the headrace canal, stranding of the raw water system in the river, obstruction of the drainage ducts, freezing of the river, fast detachment of packages of sediments in the headrace canal, development of shells in feed lines). These risks may be aggravated in the long term by climate changes. This part of the model required the collection of expertise on the following subjects: characteristics of the river (temperature, flows, low water levels, floods, etc.), specificities of the design of each heat sink system, the physical events like silting, stranding, obstruction,

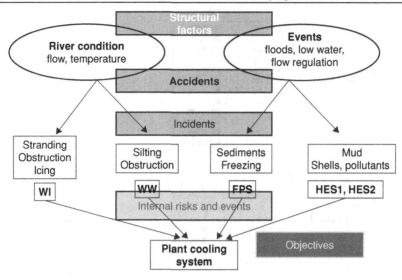

Figure 4.24   Impact of natural risks on the technical system

river freezing, filling, development of shells; and requirements on rejection (chemical, thermal, biological, and radioactive). Extreme flows were described with probabilistic distributions used for extreme values: Gumbel distribution and Weibull distribution. The risks are correlated: low water levels appear in summer preferentially, when the temperatures are high; floods appear especially in autumn, when the river temperature decreases; etc. – Figure 4.25.

Human risks   Now we focus on malevolent acts, and the so-called "human threat". We define here a human threat, or human hazard, as a potential and intentional action to harm people, environmental or technical systems, including information systems, to create hazardous events and situations, or to disrupt social organization. This definition includes terrorism, political violence, sabotage, rioting, looting, blackmail, etc. We propose elements to represent the threat in the form of a Bayesian network.

In the context of threat analysis, the basic questions of risk analysis (What can go wrong? How likely? What are the consequences?) come down to four questions:

- What does the author of the malevolent action expect?
- What can he make fail?
- What are his chances of succeeding?
- What would be the consequences if he succeeds?

From a literature survey, we make the assumption that the threat profile results from the combination of a motivation, an organization, a target selection and available attack modes.

- Motivations: they may be political, sectarian, criminal, or psychotic.
- Type of organization: may be networked, hierarchical, unorganized, etc.
- Target: selected among industrial plants, infrastructures, symbolic places, high populated areas, and key people.

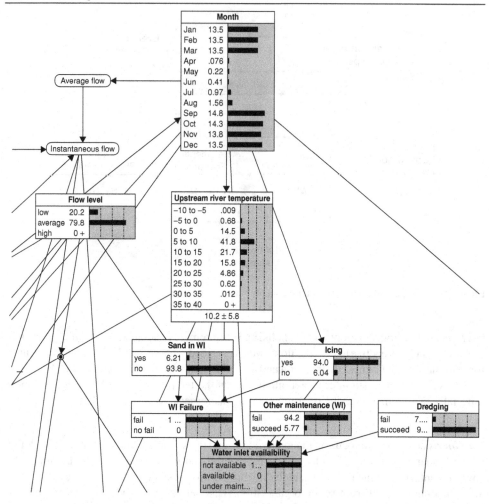

Figure 4.25 Subpart of the Bayesian network used. This subpart is used to represent the consequence of various natural events on the availability of a specific subsystem (the water inlet, WI). In this figure, the WI has been set on the "not available" position. This simple analysis shows that icing is responsible for 94 % of WI failures, sand only 6%, and the autumn and winter months are especially critical

- Attack modes: they may vary from conventional light (small arms, small explosive charges) to conventional heavy (heavy weapons, explosive trucks), or unconventional (chemical, radiological, biological, IEM). Also to be considered are attacks through lethal use of systems by hijacking or attack through infrastructures (networks).

In addition, malevolent acts have a collateral effect on the environment, infrastructures, and social and economical systems not calculated by the attackers themselves. In this case, a probable threat may be a collateral effect due to an attack on a third party target. For example, upstream pollution may be the consequence of sabotage targeting an oil plant. There are also economical and societal impacts. Even if they do not materialize, continuous threats have in the long term disrupting effects, by distracting resources, retaining people to work in certain locations supposed to be targets, making work procedures used in the industries more complex, etc.

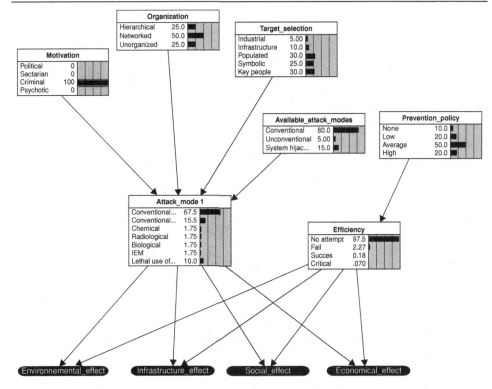

Figure 4.26 The network representing human threats. The consequences of human threats are then associated with the system through a vulnerability analysis

A threat profile is thus the combination of four variables (profile, organization, target, attack mode). Using this structure, we can build a part of the Bayesian network that describes more particularly the human threat potential profiles, Figure 4.26.

Integration of external risks in the global risk assessment

Vulnerability analysis The question is now to "connect" this network to the system network. We have to understand what happens if a major threat materializes upstream of the heat sink, targeting either a critical resource or the system directly. What are the consequences, in terms of safety, availability and environmental rejection? In this study, the link between risk assessment and threat analysis is established through a vulnerability analysis matrix.

This matrix enables to establish a connection between the threat assessment network and the pre-existing internal risk assessment network. For each given threat profile, the lines represent the threat effects, and the columns the elements of the systems that are vulnerable. The cell numbers express the likelihood that the threat considered may harm the element of the system should it really occur as well as the likelihood of recovery. Prevention, protection, maintenance, and repair elements of the technical system are part of this analysis. The achievement of this step of the study led to a network for the industrial plant, Figure 4.27.

Indeed, the company operates four plants, located along the same river, separated by distances of about 10–100 km. At the final step, we are able merge the global network, connecting also the external threats, Figure 4.28.

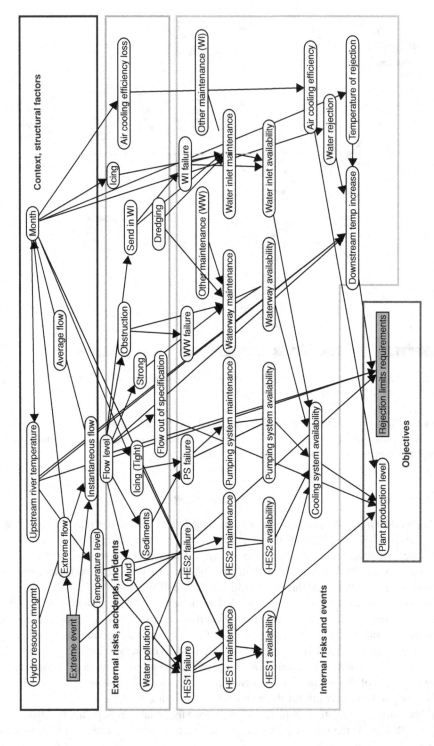

Figure 4.27   The network used to represent external natural risks and their consequences on the system

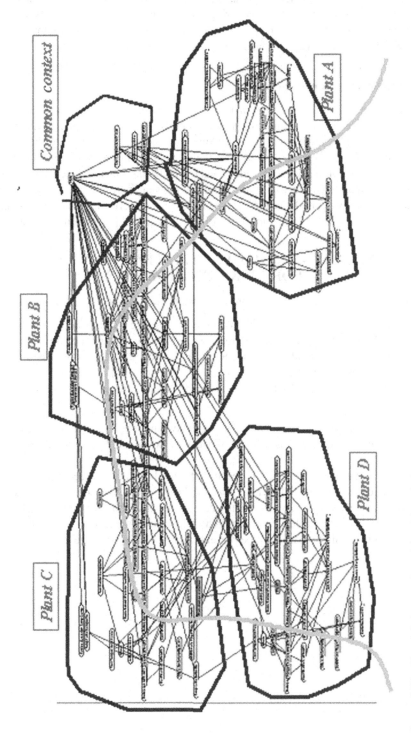

Figure 4.28   The global network used for risk analysis

A "network of networks" represents external natural risks and their consequences on the four plants located along a same river. This network permits to analyse the influence of upstream plants on downstream plants through possible pollutions, and the scenarios of common failure modes in some climatic and hydrological conditions.

Usage of the model for risk management

The impact of an external risk or of a combination of risks on a given plant is directly calculated from the Bayesian network according to the formulas presented in this chapter. A risk matrix prioritizing the external events can be drawn. Another risk matrix prioritizing the internal events (subsystems failures) can also be, with or without maintenance (risk management), an option. The weak points of the system are identified by the IF diagrams. A specific IF diagram can be drawn to compare the influence of the months of the year, permitting to analyze vulnerability windows of the systems. Thus, the Bayesian network supports the risk management by providing relative comparison of the impact of various strategies of prevention and protection.

SUMMARY – USING QUANTITATIVE MODELS FOR RISK CONTROL

Quantitative models can be used for risk control in two different ways:

- First of all, by using the model: drivers of exposure, occurrence and impact can be identified and their distribution modified in order to reduce one of these constituents of risk.
- Second, by extending the model: dependencies can be added in the model (for instance, through the implementation of additional controls). When using a Bayesian network model, decision and utility nodes can be added to the model in order to implement a decision support tool.

The evaluation of risk control actions "utility" is not always enough, since it is generally related to average risk control (expected cost of risk). Control of extreme risks may require different actions.

As mentioned in the introduction, going beyond the model is always recommended when dealing with risk reduction: not all drivers of risk have been taken into account. Organizational drivers, for instance, are very rarely taken into account, because most models will reflect the organization as it is (whether it has been acquired from experts or databases, the knowledge used in the model is implicitly based on the present organization – structure, controls, etc.).

Risk Financing: The Right Cost of Risks

INTRODUCTION

Risk financing is part of the overall medium- and long-term financing of any organization. Therefore, its main goal is derived from the goals of the finance department, i.e. maximizing return while avoiding bankruptcy, in other terms obtaining the maximum return on investments for the level of risk acceptable to the directors and stockholders. In economic terms, that means riding on the efficient frontier.

To reach this goal the organization can use a set of tools aimed at the impact of the losses it may incur spreading through time and space and more generally take care of the cash flows at risk. However, deciding whether it can retain or must transfer the financial impact of its risks cannot be based merely on a qualitative assessment of risks. A quantitative evaluation of risks is necessary to support the selection of the appropriate risk financing instruments, to negotiate a deal with an insurer or understand the cost of a complex financing process.

In this chapter, we deal with the benefits of building a model which quantifies the global cost of risks, thus providing the risk manager with a tool that allows him to test several financing scenarios.

The chapter deals with the benefits of quantification to enhance the process of selection of a risk financing solution. Financing is the third leg of risk management based on the initial diagnostic and after all the reasonable efforts at reducing the risks have been selected. Risk financing, even more than risk diagnostic or reduction, requires an accurate knowledge of your risks. "How much will you transfer?", "How much will you retain?" are questions about quantities the answers to which require obviously fairly precise figures.

Insurance premiums are set on the basis of quantitative models developed by the actuaries of insurance and reinsurance companies. Thus, insurance companies have an accurate evaluation of the cost of your risks. The problem is to ensure a balanced approach at the negotiation table. It is not conceivable to have a strong position when negotiating your insurance premiums equipped with only a qualitative knowledge of your risks. You may try, but it will be difficult for you to convince an insurer.

A complex financing programme is usually expensive to set up, and sometimes to maintain, therefore the organization must make sure that the risks to be transferred are worth the effort. As part of their governance duties, the board of directors will expect from the finance director a convincing justification of the proposed programme in terms of both results and efforts as part of their governance duties.

Any decision concerning the evaluation or selection of a financing tool must be based on a quantified knowledge of your risks. Defining the appropriate layers of risk to be retained or transferred involves a clear understanding of the distribution of potential losses. Deciding whether you are able to retain a €10m loss requires at least that you know the probability of occurrence of such a loss.

Before developing any risk financing programmes, the first decision concerns what risks must be financed. This issue should be addressed during the diagnostic step. Diagnostic has been extensively developed in Chapter 3. This step provides a model for each loss exposure and sometimes a global risk model. This model quantifies (1) the probability of occurrence of a given peril, (2) the distribution of losses should the peril occur, and (3) the distribution of the cumulated losses over a given period.

Developing and implementing a risk financing solution involves at least being able to measure beforehand the cost of retention and the cost of transfer. We set out to demonstrate it in this chapter; this is possible only by combining the risk model and a mathematical formalization of the financing tool cost.

RISK FINANCING INSTRUMENTS

Until the early 1990s, risk financing was practically identified with purchasing insurance covers in traditional national oligopolistic markets. As a matter of fact, the large number of actors did not result in a very active competition. It was very limited in reality as the tariff was set in committees, organized by the national insurers' associations, with the blessing of public regulators. After all, the requlators' main mission is to ensure the long-term financial soundness of the sector, and tariffs were set at a level that guaranteed the result! The insurers' solvency was guaranteed, while the insured costs and the insurance premiums were not related to such consequences with regard to profits, as to endanger any economic sector. Globalization and the mergers that accompanied it have completely changed the insurance world's landscape.

The basic missions of risk financing are still derived from the financial objectives, from the return and the solvency. Therefore, risk financing must secure, in most instances even before any loss has occurred, the "exceptional" fund sources, which will provide the cash flows in order to compensate for the outflows generated by the losses, while containing the cost of risk.

However, in a stable economic world, insurance mechanisms were considered a very good solution, where fixed assets represented the bulk of the firm's value: the provided compensation facilitated the replacement. In an economy of "scarcity", customers had to wait for the supply chain to restart. The new global landscape is totally different, with skyrocketing liability exposures and firms' value based less on fixed assets and more on the expected future profit flow and on the reputation among stakeholders.

Now is the time for aggressive financial strategies, when the market value of the firm is 20 to 100 times its book value, which has clearly become irrelevant. This revolution of financial markets implies a profound revision of risk financing habits. This is what generated the birth of what is known nowadays as strategic risk financing.

The world of "risk financing" is much more sophisticated and many new instruments have appeared, and are developed everyday at the whim of some ingenious consultants', brokers' or insurers' marketing plans. All are anxious to create niches to replenish dwindling margin on traditional markets. The most common of these instruments are discussed further later. Therefore suffice to say at this stage that, if they include an insurance mechanism, they are based on sharing the risk between insurer and insured (profit sharing, retrospective rating where the insured repays most of the claims) or some mechanism of provision building with the insurer to achieve a mutualization through time (finite). Other instruments use the financial markets and aim at reconstituting long-term funding (options, SPV – special project vehicle).

However, the fundamental objective is always the same, to reduce profit volatility, which the financial markets penalize heavily. The main mission of large companies' executives is to keep financial analysts and institutional investors "happy". A sanction or a falling in price/dividend ratio could end their jobs or swallow their stock option plans' value. For small and medium size businesses, at least in Europe, the banker is the man who must be convinced, in order to get the funds needed for development: he is even at more adverse risk than investors.

Whatever the expanding offers of ever more complex instruments, the choices are dictated by two very basic questions:

- What is the volatility of outcome?
  Is it transferred to a third party, in part or totally? In other words, from the organization's point of view, do they know the cost of risk a priori (budgeted with certainty before the year and before any loss) or a posteriori (after the end of the year, only when all claims are known and accounted for)?
- What is the long-term cost of the instrument?
  Within the insurance industry, it is covered by the "load" and by the transaction's cost in the financial markets. It is sometimes more difficult to define and evaluate risk retention mechanisms.

The value of any asset, any activity, can be divided into two components: the "fundamental" (the present value of the expected cash flow generated by the asset over its economic life) and the "value of risk".

Then, the fundamental "strategic" question for any CEO or board of directors is: "What risks should be retained to build an efficient frontier risk portfolio, and which are more economically transferred?" There is never only one "right" answer, but there is always a better answer in a given situation. This is the reason why the risk financing mix must be regularly reviewed to reflect the organization's appetite for risk, as well as the market's appetite for that same risk.

Therefore, there is no risk financing plan relying only on retention or only on transfer. Any plan is a hybrid; each organization can find its optimal balance through a mix of different instruments. This is the time where their risk appetite is levelled or where the "anguish factor" (for the risk averse) just balances out the marginal transfer cost.

For SMEs (small and medium size businesses), buying insurance covers remains the most sensible alternative, at least for all risks that are insurable at a reasonable price. The new tools, more sophisticated but complex to implement, are based on simple financial principles and can be embedded in traditional insurance programmes to provide the advantages without the burden (retro tariffs based on results, interest on reserves, "large" deductibles, annual stop-loss, which will be explained further later).

For any risk financing mechanisms, there are five elements to be examined:

1. Planning (how is the instrument designed and implemented).
2. Where will the funds come from (when called upon to compensate a loss)?
3. What are the accounting consequences before and after the loss.
4. What are the fiscal implications, before and after the loss?
5. *Who bears the uncertainty of the outcomes (volatility)?*

The risk financing "continuum" consists of all the risk transfer and risk financing products which are available in banking and reinsurance. For all likelihood risk classes a most cost-effective solution exists, Figure 5.1.

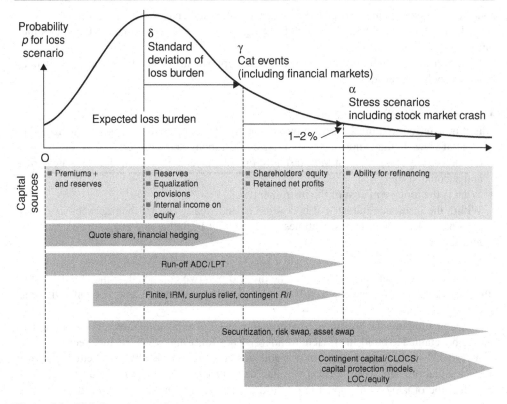

Figure 5.1   Risk financing continuum

Retention techniques

The first approach to retention mentioned earlier is the cash flow question: "Where do the funds needed for loss compensation come from?" When it is an internal source, it is called retention.

We have already revised this rudimentary vision with a more sophisticated point of view that instead questions who bears the uncertainty of the outcome: retention means the uncertainty is entirely borne by the organization.

However, for any given retention mechanism, there remains the issue of careful planning, which is necessary to ensure funds are available on time, in order to compensate for a single unexpected large event or a series of abnormally frequent smaller losses, putting a severe strain on the ongoing costs of the organization. In other words, it is necessary to:

- Verify the retention tools will inject funds to the current cash flows, when needed (*not too early, not too late*).
- Carefully monitor accounting procedures used for these retention tools (*with special attention to fiscal consequences*).

Current treatment

It is the least complex form of retention. However, it needs planning and cannot be haphazard. Therefore, it can be used safely only when historical data on losses are available as a basis for future losses forecasts. These forecasts must provide future cost evaluation with a "reasonable degree" of certainty. Then, the following applies:

- A budget line is introduced in the budget (planning).
- Losses will be paid as they occur, taken out of current cash flows (the actual budget line must be divided in monthly cash needs – in this case this would be one of the risk manager's duty).
- Losses are accounted for as current costs.
- Losses are tax deductible once these are actually paid for (or a "certain" cost).
- *The risk (uncertainty) rests totally with the organization.*

The limitation of such an instrument is clear: losses must be forecast with a degree of certainty compatible with budgeting practices. It can only be safely used in the case of low-severity, high-frequency risks (a motor vehicle fleet of more than 100 or 150 is an example, health insurance for employees in a large organization is another example).

Reserves

When a given exposure does not lend itself to the current treatment, it is possible to investigate the feasibility of "reserving". Annual additions to the "fund" will allow dipping into it when compensation for a loss is due.

Planning for a reserve is actually a purely accounting mechanism whereby the annual addition is considered as a current cost for managerial accounting purposes, but not fiscally deductible. It will appear at the bottom of the debt column in the balance sheet, just above the capital and the general reserves as it still belongs to the shareholders.

When a loss occurs, the amount is deducted from the reserve and the cost of the loss is offset, at least as long as the reserve is large enough at the time of the loss to be reported to the shareholders. However, for tax-related purposes, the loss is considered as a deductible expense when, and only when, the amount is final and the payment is due.

So far, the whole process described is purely accounting and fiscal, no actual flows of cash are involved and clearly all uncertainty is borne by the organization; the "reserving" approach has, however, mutualized the cost through time, therefore yearly fluctuations of profits have been somewhat mitigated.

There remains a crucial question – as for any "risk financing mechanism" – where does *cash* actually come from? There are three possibilities:

- Current cash will be tapped if no other source has been set up (would normal cash levels meet the expenses?). This is often called an "unfunded reserve".
- Borrowing provided a specific line of credit has been secured ahead of time for this specific use to match the "reserve level". This is often called "borrowing for losses". *Note*: If borrowing is not associated with a reserving mechanism, the impact on the results may actually increase the fluctuations, adding an additional "risk" to the underlying risk to be treated.
- Set aside financial short-term assets (near cash) equivalent to the reserve, which could be turned into cash at short notice to meet the requirements generated by the losses. This is often called a "funded reserve".

Captives (insurance or reinsurance)

This is the most complex form of retention and it requires specific expertise and substantial initial investment.

What is a captive?   In the field of risk financing, a "captive" refers to an insurance (or reinsurance) company which is a subsidiary of a large industrial or financial conglomerate.

Its specificity is to underwrite solely (or mostly) covers for its mother company and its subsidiaries (or sister companies).

As it is in most common cases, the captive is a reinsurer. The different subsidiaries of the group buy their cover from a direct insurer admitted in to the country. The mother company has a contract with the direct insurer who cedes the bulk of the reinsurance of these covers to the captive company under pre-agreed terms ceding commission, type of reinsurance, attachment points, etc.).

In most cases, the direct insurer retains none or a very small part of the risks and this type of agreement is often referred to as a "fronting agreement", hence the words "front" or "fronting company" used to refer to the direct insurer issuing the insurance contracts.

Thanks to this mechanism, the bulk of the insurance premium cash flows, paid by the subsidiary of the group, remain in the group and improve the cash position of the whole group (via the captive and its reserving capabilities). In some cases, the premium flows directly to the captive, minus the "fronting commission" paid to the direct insurer delivering the policies.

It is frequent that the cover limits greatly exceed the underwriting or premium capacities of the captive, or simply the retention level at which the group executives feel comfortable. In such a case, the captive will buy reinsurance on the international reinsurance markets.

The existence of a group captive insurer does not imply that all insurance covers are insured or reinsured through it. It may have as well been established to handle only some classes of risks and may also refuse to reinsure covers for some subsidiary deemed too risky, especially if the traditional markets offer adequate covers at reasonable prices.

What are the advantages of a captive?   The objectives of creating a captive may vary from one group to the other. However, if the emphasis differs widely, some of the common reasons are the following:

- To secure claims information data in a largely decentralized group:
  One of the most frustrating exercises for the risk management professional is to obtain reliable historical data on claims from the subsidiaries. This goal is not often mentioned in the literature concerning captives whereas it is often one of the most valuable advantages of the captive. The direct insurer documents and manages the claims but keeps the captive, the final payers, regularly informed of the statistical data for all subsidiaries and that information can be fed into the RMIS (Risk Management Information System). This is one of the reasons why lower excess may prove useful to insure more accurate information flows.
- To obtain a better reward for prevention and reduction efforts deployed in the group thanks to premium conditions which are more responsive to better loss experiences recorded inside the group:
  The reinsurance agreement held with the captive forces the direct insurer to isolate the claims history of the group from the other contracts within the books, thus creating an internal mutualization that disconnects the group experience from the overall market claims ratio. Therefore, the risk manager will be shielded from automatic premium increases applied by the insurers to an entire market segment to balance their results. The impact on the tariffs is all the more important if captive retention level is significant.

However, the organization is not totally cut off from market fluctuations. It must fulfil its legal obligations and purchase all the compulsory covers (quite a large number in France as a matter of fact). It heavily relies also on the reinsurance markets to place its captive reinsurance programme. At any time, the amount required in retrocession and the state of the market will influence the overall cost of risk.

- To gain a direct access to reinsurance markets:

For decades, the reinsurer was the "bad guy", the hidden master of the destiny for the insured deciding on the fluctuations in insurance premiums that the underwriter had no choice but to pass on to the "consumer".

The captive gives the risk manager direct access to the reinsurance market allowing him to understand the mode of operation of the market, its expectations, and anticipate the cycles.

The reinsurers, ever larger with the globalization merger movements, have fully integrated the captive phenomenon and its irreversibility. Most of them have set up specific departments to handle the captive reinsurance business and even provide risk management.

Furthermore, this direct connection induces better knowledge of each group risk management policy and its long-term effect on claims history. Furthermore, the dialogue that has been established provides the reinsurance underwriter with first hand knowledge of the quality of the risk management policies conducted in large industrial groups.

- To facilitate the standardization of covers among the subsidiary:

As mentioned earlier, the captive is a forum through which all information pertinent for risk management purposes in all the group subsidiaries flows. It is therefore ideally located to insure homogeneity of policies and covers worldwide.

In some cases, the captive is the leader of all international master policies; for others only a reinsurer for a global programme with a unique leader, whenever possible.

- To keep large cash flows within the group:

The captive, being an insurance/reinsurance company, is allowed to set up appropriate reserves, provided it is indeed requested. Therefore, premium cash flows are kept within the group and invested to provide investment income that would otherwise go to the outside insurer. The result for the cash flows is illustrated in Figure 5.2.

- To create capacity to cover risks that the traditional market would not insure:

Some risks cannot be insured through traditional markets, or only partially, or at prohibitive premium conditions. These events, although probabilistic in nature, are not insurable

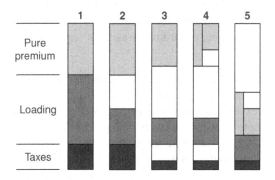

Figure 5.2   Theoretical cash flows preserved through the use of a captive insurer

for some of the reasons listed below, and often advanced by underwriters to refuse a risk:

- Mutualization is not possible – insufficient numbers of insurance prospects or insufficient premium turnover to build a viable offer.
- No outlet on the reinsurer market to place excess cover.
- Technical difficulty in appraising the risk (nature, new technology, new markets, etc.).
  In the insurance industry, the phrase used for the availability of a cover is "creating underwriting capacity".
- Listed below are a few of the risks, potentially catastrophic for the insured, which, in case of an occurrence without outside sources of funds, could hinder the survival of the organization:
  ◇ Pollution and damage to the environnement,
  ◇ Product recalls,
  ◇ Image or reputation deterioration (and costs exposed to restore),
  ◇ Product liability (for some industries not favoured by the insurers),
  ◇ Some "acts of God",
  ◇ Political and economical (other than those insurable),
  ◇ And more generally any peril potentially significant for the insured and for which there is no established traditional market.

As mentioned before, with the captive, as with any reinsurer partner on the market, the risk manager has direct access to the reinsurance capacity. He can also establish reserves to face the long-term losses arising from otherwise uninsurable exposures. He can attempt a mutualization through time if it is not open through space. In some cases, he can even use financial reinsurance to "post-finance" some losses, thereby averaging the impact on cash flows and profits for several years to come.

Conditions for a successful captive   When an organization chooses to use a captive for risk financing purposes, it must be fully aware that it is entering a new world: the world of professional insurance underwriting, even reinsurance in most instances. Managing insurance or a reinsurance company requires a number of specific competencies which cannot be improvised!

Furthermore, if the captive has to have any significant impact on the risk financing programmes, it must be able to retain a substantial share of the risk. Sizeable capacities will require adequate financing and the initial investment will be heavy. The question is always the same, are the funds used to finance the captive put to the best possible use for the group, or will they be missed for other more rewarding investment opportunities.

Pointers for success:

- Prepare a thorough diagnostic of exposures (especially those to be retained).
- Get a board commitment on a rough estimate for capital expenditures involved.
- Identify clearly those exposures that the organization will not retain under any circumstances.
- Define maximum retention levels by classes of exposures and perils.
- Always make sure that the reinsurance programme for the captive puts a ceiling on annual losses to be internally financed (stop-loss) and a cap on large individual losses (single excess of loss).
- Obtain or gather history of claim losses over several years.

- When fronting is necessary or elected, select carefully the fronting company for financial soundness, underwriting competencies and claims management efficiency.
- If necessary, brokers specialized in reinsurance can bring technical and market assistance.
- Hire efficient management (if necessary, through the services of captive management facilities).
- Carefully select the captive domicile.
- Periodically review investment, underwriting, and reinsurance policies.

This list is in no way exhaustive. However, it stresses the work involved in the proper use of a captive insurance company. It is not a decision to be taken on the spur of the moment because of a difficult cycle in the insurance industry and looking only at short-term gains. It is a long-term commitment of funds and efforts that can be a success only if a thorough feasibility study has been conducted, often with the assistance of a neutral outside service provider.

Transfer techniques

Contractual transfer (for risk financing – to a noninsurer)

Contractual risk transfer has already been mentioned as a loss control measure; however, the transfer here is only aimed at the financial impact of the exposure. The third party will not bear the legal responsibility of the exposure, but only all or part of its financial consequences should a loss occur falling within the scope of the contract. Therefore, this type of contract is by nature hazardous. They are by nature similar to an insurance contract; however, the transferee is not a professional insurer. The party transferring the exposure is called the transferor; the party accepting the financial consequences of the exposure is called the transferee.

The fact that the contract is not insurance has four main consequences:

1. There are no insurance taxes on the transaction.
2. The transferee does not have to be an accepted insurer.
3. The insurance law does not bind the parties (nor does the transferor have the protection of the same law) and the contract may be drafted as they wish.
4. The transferred exposure does not have to be insurable (see below conditions for insurability).

However, as in the case of an insurance contract, the transfer applies only under the terms and conditions of the contract. Furthermore, the protection is efficient only if, at the time of the claim, the transferor is willing and able (solvent) to comply with his obligation.

In any event, it is essential for a risk management professional to clearly distinguish between the two forms of risk transfer mechanism. Although the distinction is not always as clear-cut, the ultimate question from the transferor point of view is the following: "Should the transferee be unable or unwilling to pay, could I be directly involved in the claim?" If the answer is:

- *Yes*: it is a risk transfer mechanism for risk financing.
- *No*: it is a risk transfer mechanism for risk control.

Purchase of insurance cover

This is the most common contractual risk transfer mechanism for risk financing; compensating for claims remains the insurance core function in the economic cycle.

It is worth remembering here a few common sense rules to be applied to anyone purchasing insurance covers:

- Cover only those risks for which there is a real exposure.
- Read carefully the definition of the insured perils.
- Describe carefully and accurately the risk to be insured (answer with precision and honesty all questions asked by the underwriter).
- Read carefully all exclusions (it can provide useful information as to the risks really incurred).
- Regularly open to competition – open or clause bids (but always keep in mind long-term relationship, especially with long tail covers like product liability or professional indemnity).
- Contract only with insurance company of good standing (solvency ratio, financial rating, etc.).
- Evaluate the balance losses/premium on your contracts for the insurer.
- Always use a professional competent insurance intermediary.

One common rule is that, over the long term, insurance covers are always more expensive than retention. The services provided by both the intermediary and the insurer must be paid and the stockholders get a return on their investment, the capital on which the insurance company capacity is built. However, retention limits are often low for any given organization and the purchase of insurance is a necessity.

A solid knowledge of the insurance products and services and of the market mechanisms is an essential component of any risk manager core competencies. The scope of this chapter is risk financing therefore the presentation on insurance is limited (if need be, the reader can further his/her understanding of the insurances from specialized books).

So far, we have referred only to an insurance contract with premium conditions fixed before the period of cover is started and where no revision clause based on experience exists. If such a clause exists, the insured will bear part of the uncertainties and they are considered as hybrid techniques.

Hybrid techniques

As mentioned earlier, hybrid means in fact that the uncertainty of the outcome of a risk is shared between the organization and one or several third parties.

Pools and closed mutual

Originally, the captive insurance companies were formed by US companies as a direct insurer handling only their business and they are known as "closed single parent" captives. The American fiscal authorities (IRS) refused to consider the premium paid to such subsidiaries as tax deductible expenses unless the captive wrote a substantial book of business for third parties. This position prompted different approaches to the "captive" issue.

Some used their captives to offer covers to economic partners and even total strangers "opening" their books of business. But then it becomes an additional line of business, may lose its orginal purpose of risk financing, and requires additional investment in both capital and competences (underwriting and claims settlement).

The trend in Europe has been to form captive reinsurer companies with the use of a fronting insurance company as mentioned above. Depending on the attachment point of the reinsurance programme, the scheme is more or less a hybrid.

However, if the closed single parent captive or pure captive is a form of retention, in spite of its reinsurance programme, there are variations from the pure model to models including some risk sharing with other entities, which can be considered as hybrid. They are centred on four main schemes.

Rent a captive   When the premium volume of an organization is not large enough to justify the creation of a fully owned subsidiary, it is possible to rent a captive, in other terms to set up a specific account in a company owned by an outside interest, broker insurer or reinsurer, who has set up the company to house such programmes. It offers reasonable capacity for a lower cost and ensures that the organization benefits from its loss control efforts. However, part of the cash flow's advantage may be lost.

Shared captives   In contrast with the one parent model, in these schemes several parents join forces to establish a shared captive. If the parents are from the same industry, the captive is known as group captive, or if they choose to insure only a specific type of risk, it is then called an association captive. But there is always an important proviso: the parents must share a common view on loss control efforts, quality management, and claims management and accept some degree of risk sharing with competitors or partners. Most such captives have been established in the USA. However, in France, some open mutuals like the SHAM for hospitals, MAF for architects, and SMABTP/Auxiliaire for the construction world, or SMACL for local authorities were created in the same frame of mind. The form of the company may be a stock with shares owned by all the owners or a mutual.

Pools and risk sharing groups   These are arrangements in which organizations faced with the same risks and a tough or nonexistent insurance market decide to "pool" or put together their risk in order to make a global premium volume likely to attract an underwriter. These agreements may take widely different legal form and share a level of retention in some cases to increase their appeal to the market. This has been the case in the 1970s and 1980s in the USA for professional indemnity in the medical industry and the legislator even enacted some specific laws to allow such grouping. In France, "pools" tend to be operated only by insurers who pool to offer covers that no single insurer would (Nuclear Liability Pool, Environmental Pool, etc.).

The degree of "transfer" versus "retention" in each case is variable. Most of these agreements have by-laws that rule the retention levels for each adherent and the risk retention level of the "pool" or "mutual" and therefore the "hybrid" content for each organization taking part in the agreement.

In all such agreements, however, it is essential for any prospect member to be very weary of the conditions under which they can pull out of the agreement, individually by leaving the pool or captive, or collectively by folding down the captive.

Protected Cells Companies (PCC)   One of the problems with any type of shared risk financing mechanism is the risk that an adverse claims development in some of the partners may jeopardize the financial soundness of the whole programme. Clearly, the choice is made when the amount of risks involved would not justify the formation of a single parent company. Therefore, sharing a mechanism with others is a necessity while each organization wishes protection from a general failure. This is achieved through an additional mechanism that enjoys growing popularity and is known under the name of protected cell, insofar as it is "protected" from contamination from the performances of the other organizations sharing the same mechanism.

These cells are like small companies, isolated in terms of assets and liabilities up to a point. The concept is simple but the fiscal and legal implications must be dealt with in detail to ensure the long-term sustainability of the schemes, especially if challenged in court by unsatisfied creditors (lenders or service providers).

Claims history-based premiums

All the conditions and precautions relative to creating a captive or joining a pool may well discourage even some large businesses that may still wish to benefit from their loss control efforts. For such candidates, there exists an option that should be considered: insurance contract with premium adjusted to reflect the claims history experienced during the life of the contract.

As soon as an organization has a dependable loss experience history over several years, it can choose a higher level of deductible, even an annual stop-loss that it will be able to finance internally. Henceforth, it can negotiate with its insurers a cover that will be in effect a surplus line, even if all claims, hence those below the stop-loss limit, are handled by the insurer. The cover can then stabilize the premium around the long-term annual average with a small variation for exceptional losses.

Only the premium for exceptional losses belongs to the insurer. The provisional "premium" should be reviewed every three to five years to respond to the trend in losses experienced over the period. The insured then takes part in the profit or losses as reflected in the annual accounts for the programme. The period chosen allows for some offsetting of the yearly variation to stabilize the cost of risk element for the insured.

With this approach, it is clear that we are close to a retention mechanism managed by a third party and whereby the insurer is compensated for services in the bottom layer and receives a risk premium only for the excess line. However, the bottom line, like an SIR (self-insured retention) can be subject to different treatments. In the ultimate case, the insurer only receives a fee for his handling of the SIR and takes no risk in it. In other programmes, even the risk for this first line may be shared between insured and insurer in varying degrees.

The definition above is more a conceptual framework than an actual programme. It can be used to explain a number of different risk financing products offered on the market, from full retro plans to limited profit sharing plans. However, it is really put to use only in cases of relatively high frequency exposures. The list would never be up to date as brokers and consultants are always eager to create new forms to be included in sophisticated plans among other "financing alternatives".

Choice of retention levels

At this stage, the professional reader confronted with a real life situation must be asking one crucial question: "What is the right level of retention for my organization?" The answer is simple, indeed simplistic, it can be disappointing but there is no way around it:

The ideal retention level is the level with which the board is "comfortable".

This is a reminder that the final choice in risk financing is in the hands of top management; it is their safety that is at stake, theirs and their organization's.

There are, however, a few guidelines:

- Whatever is the "ideal" level chosen, it will apply only to the "conscious" retention, i.e. the retention linked with "identified" exposures. It is advisable to have some leeway, a margin for those exposures that have not been identified. Losses will happen some day and they will have to be financed out of current cash flows (or the postponement of an investment project like some Japanese firms did for development in Europe, frozen to help rebuild the key facilities destroyed by the Kobe earthquake in 1995).
- Nonvoluntary, or compulsory, retention must be considered first (those for which there is no known or available transfer mechanism).
- Then an appropriate level of retention must take into account all the basic financial balances and the objectives of the firm:
  – Cash flow,
  – Liquid assets, acid test, quick ratio, etc.,
  – Stockholders (or stock market) reaction of a lessening growth pattern,
  – Stockholders (or stock market) reaction to a decrease in the profit per share (the dividend per share).

In the real world, it is rare that a firm will adopt a retention level in excess of 5 to 10 % of its annual profit. This is not an accepted norm; rather a founding based on factual evidence.

One last reminder, risk financing is always based on the final assumption that, should the survival of the firm be at stake, then financing the losses will take precedence over any other consideration. All funds available will be channelled to close the breach in the hull.

As mentioned earlier, this is the reason why in the wake of the Kobe earthquake several Japanese firms, with no pre-financing plans for earthquake in an area deemed safer than others in Japan, froze all investments abroad, and especially in Europe, to fund the rebuilding of vital interests in Japan. In the same fashion, Union Carbide had to reduce is worldwide activities and shrink to a much smaller operation to preserve its existence. The sale of subsidiaries was the likely consequence of the process of indemnification of the victims of Bhopal but did preserve the "core business".

Financial reinsurance and finite risks

The first generation of alternative risk financing mechanisms was used by both insurers and insured. It is mostly articulated around two concepts both taking into account the time value of money: one being mostly a post-financing technique (financial reinsurance) and one a pre-financing technique (finite risk). Using capital markets to address potential risk financing needs has become known as risk securitization.

As far as financial reinsurance and finite insurance/reinsurance products are concerned, their impact on the reinsurance programmes for captives and pools alone justifies the understanding of their mechanisms by any risk management professional.

Gathered under the same topic, the two concepts are clearly distinguished in specialized circles. "Finite risk" applies to a specific amount of cover of future losses over a policy period, typically several years. "Financial reinsurance" applies to the purchase by an insurer or a reinsurer of past losses, already incurred but not already paid for. Readers interested in large corporations involved in the global economy will need to get much more familiar with these approaches that are often needed to build enough capacity to cover professional indemnity or environmental liabilities that can far exceed the world's traditional insurance markets' capacities.

Readers interested only in small and medium size organizations may skip the presentation of these products, which require a sizeable stake!

The specifics of financial reinsurance are stressed in the tinted box that follows. The major specificity, however, lies in the present value approach to losses and the post-financing mechanism. A key factor in placing financial reinsurance is therefore the forecasting of future cash outflows linked with incurred losses. Both amounts and timing are essential in this process, as interest is the major risk transferred in the transaction.

The "aggregate limit" is stated in monetary terms for the reported claims portfolio transferred and the premium paid upfront by the transferee is reduced to take into account the interest earned on the funds while the reinsurer pays the losses over the period.

It should be noted that this mechanism provides to the insurer (or the captive) an improvement on his balance sheet. A portfolio of losses is written out of his liabilities for the amount of the full reserve while, on the asset side, only the present value of the set reserves is paid. Therefore, he gains an immediate improvement of his current results and safety ratio.

During the 1990s, financial reinsurance has become ever present in the markets and its products have diversified and become more sophisticated. However, the key question remains the extent to which the reinsurer shares in the actual development risk for reported losses, starting with no share at all in the original version stated above. French readers will find a detailed presentation of the financial reinsurance in the quarterly *Revue Risques* from which this presentation is largely inspired. American readers can refer to the different publications, including those by the Insurance Institute of America.

The most common product, which risk managers in large organizations could find useful, is detailed here. It could be used especially to outsource post-financing for exposures not insurable in the traditional insurance markets.

Integration of interest on investment: interest earned on the investment of the premium is an essential part of the contract and recognized as such. Traditional reinsurance does not ignore this aspect and in many branches negotiations between insurers and reinsurers take into account interest earned on long tail claims (automobile liability for bodily injuries, product liability, workers compensation, etc.) However, they do not appear explicitly in the terms of the contract.

Contractual limit for insurer liability: the object of the contract is to cover claims already reported at their estimated outstanding cost (reserve) and, occasionally, it may be extended to IBNR (Incurred But Not Reported) that appear in the insurer (or the captive reinsurer) books. But the reinsurer liability is strictly limited to the transferred claims and to the reserve deemed correct at the time of transfer. All financial reinsurance contracts therefore contain an "aggregate limit", i.e. the maximum that the reinsurer will pay to or on behalf of the insurer over the period.

Profit and loss sharing: financial reinsurance contracts also include a mechanism that allows the insurer to get back part of the premium should the claims close for less than the reserves set up. The insurer is responsible for any excess and the sharing of this excess may constitute an underwriting risk for the reinsurer. In some cases, the aggregate limit is set at a level that includes a line of cover in excess of current reserve to allow for long-term claims development. This is more like a line of "excess of loss" traditional reinsurance added to the first layer of pure financial reinsurance. See below "Prospective aggregate cover".

Long-term commitment: Financial reinsurance is by essence a long-term approach and supposes a long-term commitment for both parties. It can be an additional tool to protect insurance lines that traditional reinsurance would exclude from cover. The principle is a full payment for incurred losses allowing only for the risk of timing of the outflows to be transferred. The reinsurer is more a financial institution than a traditional reinsurer is. Fully analyzing the exposures involved and expecting a portfolio effect to "mutualize" the risks.

Prospective aggregate cover

This product offers a future protection from current exposures, i.e. for claims not yet occurred or not yet reported.

Thus, the insurer (or the captive reinsurer) pays a premium in exchange for the protection of the reinsurer that will pay for a stated proportion of the claims up to the "aggregate limit".

If no claims occur, or if the frequency and severity are less than expected, the reinsurer will return to the ceding company part or the entire technical surplus thus made.

When compared to traditional reinsurance that arrangement is like a quote-part contract with a limited cover over the period and the inclusion of the interest earned on the premium in the profit sharing agreement attached to the contract.

Capital markets products for risk financing[1]

Traditionally, the only role played by the capital markets in the insurance industry and in related risk financing matters was that of a purveyor of funds. The capital thus raised was used to underwrite risks. The question addressed here is how and when capital markets can be used as an alternative to traditional insurance or reinsurance markets.

Capital market products for risk financing currently used can be grouped into three categories, Figure 5.3:

- *Insurance-linked securities* are financial investments, most of the time in the form of bonds that have insurable risks embedded in them. The investor receives a higher return for the security as it includes a premium as a retribution for the embedded risk. Losses to the investor linked with the embedded risk benefits another organization, which uses the proceeds to offset its insurable risks.
- *Insurance derivatives* are financial contracts valued on the base of the level of insurable losses that occur during a specific time period. An insurance derivative increases in value as specified insurable losses increase and, therefore, the purchaser of the derivative can use this gain to offset its insurable losses. The seller of an insurance derivative accepts insurable risks and receives a commensurate return for doing so.
- *Contingent capital arrangement* is an agreement entered into before losses occur and that enables an organization to raise cash by selling stock or issuing debt at prearranged terms following a loss that exceeds a certain threshold. The loss can arise from insurable risks such as property damage resulting from an earthquake or a liability loss resulting from pollution. The organization agreeing to provide the contingent capital receives a commitment fee.

[1] Published by the French Insurers Association – see issue number 9.

Securitization

Securitization means to create a marketable investment security based on the expected cash flows from a financial transaction. A financial institution can use securitization to transfer income-producing assets off its balance sheet in exchange for cash. For example, a card issuer might securitize its credit card receivables, or a bank might securitize its mortgage receivables.

As an example of a mortgage securitization assume that a bank that extends loans to individuals who purchase homes would like to transfer its mortgage receivables (an asset) off its balance sheet. The bank could sell receivables for cash to an intermediary, usually called an SPV (Special Purpose Vehicle). In turn, the SPV will issue securities to investors to finance the purchase of the assets.

More generally, an organization sells income-producing assets to an SPV in exchange for cash. The income-producing assets are taken off the organization's balance sheet and reside in the SPV as collateral to securities sold to investors. The investors purchase the securities for cash and receive a return commensurate with the risk inherent in the income-producing assets that back the securities.

Insurance companies, including insurance or reinsurance captives, can participate in a number of ways linked to all classes of assets owned by such companies. However, what is referred to as "insurance securitization" is a unique from of securitization.

The concept of an insurance-linked security can best be explained through an example. An investor purchases a bond from an SPV that provides a higher interest rate than the "risk-free" interest (US Treasury bonds), thus including a risk premium. The bond would be relatively free of credit risk as it is collateralized by liquid investments held by the SPV.

In return for the "risk premium" he receives, the investor's return is linked with a risk like the occurrence of a hurricane during the term of the bond. The return to the investor will be reduced if a hurricane strikes causing damages in excess of a stated level. When the threshold is exceeded, the return falls in direct proportion with the total loss incurred. The "loss" reference can be a given portfolio of an insurance company, an industry index, or the losses of a given organization (captive).

In fact there may be different classes of bond (tranches), usually three. Of course, these incur variable degrees of risk and the risk premium is proportional to the risk assumed. In increasing level of risk they are:

- Bonds with a guaranteed minimum return.
- Bonds with a protected principal.
- Bonds with no guarantee (even for the principal).

Through this mechanism, the investor buying the bond is really underwriting an insurable risk that could be insured through a traditional insurance contract. It is a marketable security through a financial market. In other terms, the process of insurance securitization has "securitized" the risk of hurricane loss by linking the returns provided by the investors in a marketable security.

In the case of insurance securitization, the SPV takes a specific role that does not apply in other settings:

- The SPV transforms an insurable risk into an investment risk and vice versa.
- The SPV receives cash from both the investors and the organization transferring the insurable risk. It holds cash as collateral for its obligation to repay interest and principal on the insurance-linked securities and its obligation to pay any losses that occur.

- Depending on the jurisdiction involved, the SPV might qualify as an authorized insurer (or reinsurer), which enables the organization transferring its risk of loss to treat the transaction as insurance (or reinsurance) for tax and accounting purposes. The main advantages of treating the transaction as insurance (or reinsurance) are that the losses do not have to be taken into account on the income statement or the balance sheet as they occur and that the "premium" paid to the SPV are tax deductible at the time of payment.

Insurance derivatives

A derivative is a financial contract that derives its value from the value of another asset, such as a commodity. A derivative can also derive its value from the yields on another asset or the level of an index, such as the Standard & Poor's stock index.

An insurance derivative is a financial contract that derives its value from the level of insurable losses that occur during a specific time period. The value of an insurance derivative can be based on the level of insurable losses experienced by a single organization or on the level of an insurance industry index of insured losses.

The two major categories of insurance derivatives are swap and options. These are routinely used by organizations to offset, or hedge, their financial risks like interest rates and foreign currency exposures.

Swaps   A swap is an agreement between two organizations to exchange their cash flows based on the movements in the value of another asset, yields on an asset, or an index of values or yields. Thus, the swap derives its value from an underlying asset. The cash flows are exchanged back and forth between the organizations on a continuous basis throughout the term of the swap.

An organization can use a swap to transfer its insurable risk, in which case the swap is an insurance derivative. Insurance companies (or captive) can spread their risks through a swap arrangement. For example, one insurance company could exchange a portion of the cash flows (premiums and losses) arising from a hurricane exposure in the southwestern United States with a portion of the cash flows arising in another insurance company for tornado risks in the midwestern United States. Clearly such a swap mimics a reinsurance contract. It could also be construed to mimic an insurance contract.

A major advantage of swaps is that they cost less than insurance-linked securities. Their main disadvantage is that they are not collateralized therefore the issuer faces the risk that the other party (the counterpart) will not meet its obligation.

Insurance options   An insurance option derives its value from insurable losses, either an organization's actual insurable losses or an index of losses covered by a group of insurance companies. The value of an insurance option increases as the value of the underlying insurable losses increases. Therefore, an organization can use a gain from an insurance option to offset its losses from insurable risk.

An over-the-counter option is placed privately and is customized to meet an organization's specific needs. Exchange-traded options are traded on an organized exchange, such as the Chicago Board of Trade.

A call option gives the holder the right, but not the obligation, to buy an asset; a put option gives the holder the right, but not the obligation, to sell an asset. The price at which the asset can be either purchased or sold is called the strike price.

Insurance options, as do swaps, have the same cash flow characteristics as insurance policies. For a call option, imagine that the underlying asset is individual insurable losses and that the strike value (similar in concept, but involving a value other than price) is set equal to the deductible or self-insured retention level under an insurance policy.

In this case, the call option is an insurance option that serves the same function as an insurance policy with a large deductible. The buyer of the call option pays a premium and receives cash when the value of the insurable losses exceeds the strike value, during the period of the option. The seller of the option is in the opposite position because she receives a premium and must pay cash if the value of insurable loss exceeds the strike value.

As a result of their differences in placement and administration these two types of option serve different purposes. Whereas the OTC option will be designed to finance a given reinsurance or retrocession line for an insurer or a reinsurer, it requires extensive advice from fiscal and legal counsels so that it fulfils its expected need. For the bearer it is a closed operation not easily transferable and for the emitter it will require in due course to prove the extent of the loss, more or less like for a traditional reinsurance contract. Exchange traded options are bought and sold on an organized market with approved forms that simplify the emission and placement phases but they cater to a general class of business (like hurricanes, or other natural disaster) and may not compensate exactly the loss suffered. This goes two ways: some may be overcompensated, others undercompensated as it is an objective trigger (a level of a hurricane, the force of a wind, the lack or excess of snow in a given zone at a given period, etc.). The advantage is that the "insured" will not have to prove or measure the extent of her losses as the proceeds do not indemnify but provide the compensation stipulated in the contract.

Contingent capital arrangements

Contingent capital arrangements are agreements entered into before losses occur and that enable an organization to raise cash by selling stock or issuing debt at prearranged terms following a loss that exceeds a certain threshold. Therefore, in this type of transaction the organization does not transfer its risk of loss to investors. Instead, after the loss has occurred, it receives an injection of funds in the form of long-term debt or equity to pay for the losses.

The terms of the funds injection are pre-agreed to; therefore the organization is usually able to receive more favourable terms than it would receive if it were to raise the funds after a large loss, assuming its weakened financial position would permit such a raise in the first place!

Investors in a contingent capital arrangement become creditors of, or equity investors in, the organization following a loss. A contingent capital arrangement is set up as an option, so the organization that purchases such an arrangement is not obligated to exercise the option even if the loss exceeds the threshold specified in the agreement.

In the case of equity, it may be compared with an insurance transaction. The indemnity received from the insurer in the event that a covered loss occurs is a "free" injection of equity to restore previous stockholders to their financial position, at the cost of a reduction in current earnings (the insurance premium): it is a pre-loss financing mechanism. The insurer bears the risk of uncertainty associated with the exposure; thus it is a transfer-financing tool.

The equity contingent capital arrangement is much cheaper than insurance. The cost of the option is substantially smaller than the insurance premium; however, the injection of equity capital is accompanied by a dilution of future earnings thus reducing the future earnings of current stockholders: it is a post-loss financing mechanism. As the current stockholders bear the risk of uncertainty involved with the exposure thus financed it is clearly a risk retention tool.

The contingent capital arrangement can take either of three forms.

Standby credit facility   A standby credit facility is an arrangement whereby a bank or another financial institution agrees to provide a loan to an organization in the event of a loss. The credit is prearranged so that terms, such as the interest rate and principal repayment schedule, are known in advance of a loss. In exchange for this credit commitment, the organization taking out a line of credit pays a commitment fee.

This type of arrangement was referred to earlier in the presentation of retention risk financing instrument as "borrowing for losses" in connection with setting reserves.

Contingent surplus note   Surplus notes are specific to the statutory accounting rules applied to insurance companies in the USA (and where accounting rules similar to the US's apply). They are sold to investors and counted as policyholder surpluses rather than as a liability on an insurer's balance sheet. The main benefit of the surplus note is that it increases an insurer's assets without increasing its liability, whereas regular debt increases both similarly. Thus, surplus note allows the insurer to increase its capacity to write business.

Contingent surplus notes are prearranged so that the insurer has the option to obtain funds by issuing surplus notes at a pre-agreed rate of interest. Thus, the insurer can bolster its surplus following a loss.

In the USA, they are made available to an insurer through a trust known as a contingent surplus note (CSN) trust. The trust receives funds from investors and places them in liquid investments, such as US Treasury securities.

The investors receive a higher interest rate than similar maturity securities. The cost to the insurer is this differential in rate or risk premium granted the investors. If it exercises its right to issue surplus notes, the insurer must repay interest and principal to the CSN trust over time so that funds are available to provide interest and principal repayments on the trust notes to the investors.

Catastrophe equity put option   Catastrophe equity puts are another way for an insurer (or a captive) or a non-insurance organization to raise capital in the event of a catastrophic loss.

As mentioned above, a put is a right to sell an asset at a predetermined price. In the case of a catastrophe equity put option it is the right to sell stocks at a predetermined price in the event of a catastrophic loss.

The major advantage of this arrangement is that they make equity funds available at a pre-agreed-to price when an organization needs them the most, and would be least likely to obtain it were it not pre-arranged, i.e. immediately following a catastrophic loss.

If an organization suffers a loss of capital due to a catastrophe, its stock price is likely to fall, lowering its price earnings ratio and rendering equity financing more expensive: the dilution of future earnings for current stockholders, as exposed above, would be much greater.

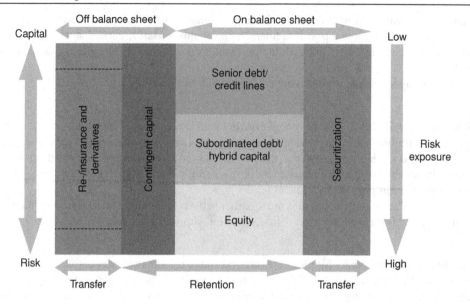

Figure 5.3   The "insurative" model

Furthermore, the pre-agreed price sends a signal to the market and may well stop the fall of the stock price.

A subsidiary question linked to the dilution is to know into which hands the new equity will fall. The sell must be carefully tailored to avoid too much new equity giving headway to a hostile takeover bid.

Companies worry endlessly about the optimal mix of debt and equity. They are missing the point. [. . .] By including both the cost of paid-up capital and off-balance-sheet capital, managers and investors would be more accurate in their estimates of company's true cost of capital, and therefore of a company's real value.

Risk financing and risk quantifying

As mentioned above, the risk financing plan is part of the organization's financial strategy and as such must strive to reach two conflicting objectives: high return and low probability of insolvency. Therefore, risk financing is the phase of risk management where it is essential to have a global approach to risks, threats and opportunities, throughout the organization.

The economic efficiency of each of the instruments must be measured against those two targets and quantifying the probability and the impact of the exposure after the proper control have been implemented (see Chapter 4) is a key to assessing the value and/or cash flow at risk to assess the need for pre-financing and the possibility of post-financing. Any form of pre-financing, be it retention or transfer, means that some of the "financial energy" that could be used to invest in productive projects has to be diverted and put aside to serve if and when the risk materialize.

Quantifying the risks to be financed is therefore the key to the resilience of the organization and its sustainable growth to ensure long-term return to stockholders.

Table 5.1   Outcome of the satellite launcher risks model

Failure probability	1.5 %
Loss given failure	€100m with 75 % probability
	Between €0 and €100m with 25 % probability

USING QUANTITATIVE MODELS

Example 1: Satellite launcher

Mr Drajab is risk manager in a commercial space company. OrbitalService is specialized in telecommunications satellite launching. The company has 30 planned missions during the next five years. As a risk manager, Mr Drajab is in charge of evaluating the financing solutions to hedge the potential risks incurred during this period.

A given mission is usually exposed to two types of risks:

- Total failure of the mission (due, for instance, to the launcher explosion): all the satellites embarked are destroyed or unusable.
- Partial failure of the mission: for a technical reason, a satellite is put into a lower orbit than was initially planned.

We assume that these risks have already been modelled. The outcomes of the model are summarized in Table 5.1.

This table reads as follows:

- The overall probability of a mission failure is estimated at 1.5 %.
- Once a problem occurs, the probability for things to go seriously wrong is high and estimated at 75 %. In this case, the launcher and all the satellites on board are destroyed. The cost of such an accident is very high and estimated at €100m.
- In some "favourable" situations, even when a problem occurs, the mission can be partially recuperated, and the satellite can be put on a lower orbit. The probability of this eventuality is estimated at 25 %. If this happens, the satellites are expected to deliver a reduced service, or even not to be usable at all. Therefore, the impact is assumed to be uniformly distributed between €0 and €100m.

Mr Drajab would like to set up a financing programme for the next five years.

The insurance market is not very liquid for these kinds of specific and high-severity risks. At least, insurance premiums are expensive enough to justify Mr Drajab considering other options for risk financing.

The first option Mr Drajab considers is retention, and more specifically the use of a captive insurance company, that OrbitalService may specifically create to fulfil its insurance needs.

Would OrbitalService be able to retain some risks? Instead of transferring every launch risk to an external insurance company, the option of retaining some of the potential failures could be appealing. This approach would result in a combination of financing tools: part of the risks would be retained within a captive insurance company, and additional potential losses would be hedged by an external insurance company. The principle of this combination is described in Figure 5.4.

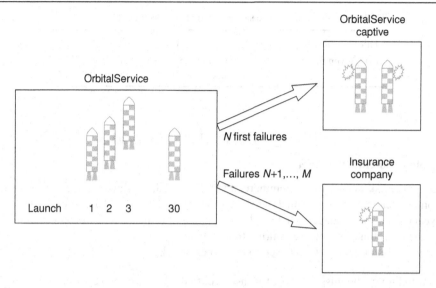

Figure 5.4   A combination of financing tools for OrbitalService major risks

In order to precisely tune this combination of financing tools, i.e. to decide where to set the limit between retention and transfer, Mr Drajab decides to evaluate the cost of the programme under several assumptions on the number of retained failures.

First, Mr Drajab performs a very simple probabilistic analysis to decide that considering the possibility of more than five failures is not realistic. Actually, assuming that the overall probability of one mission failure is 1.5 % – as stated by the model above – the probability of having exactly k failures is:

$$P\ (k \text{ failures}) = C_{30}^k\ p^k\ (1 - p)^{30-k}$$

This yields the probability distribution for the number of failures over 30 launches, as shown in Table 5.2.

Being exposed to more than five failures is therefore extremely unlikely (0.0005 %)! Should this happen, it would probably mean the model is not correct or else *launches are not independently exposed to the risk of failure.*

Table 5.2   Probability distribution of the random variable "Number of failures"

Failures	Probability	Cumulated probability
0	63.55 %	63.55 %
1	29.03 %	92.58 %
2	6.41 %	98.99 %
3	0.91 %	99.90 %
4	0.09 %	99.99 %
5	0.01 %	99.9995 %

He gets approval from the board regarding this point: they confirm that if OrbitalService would face more than five failures within the next five years, the consequences for the company would be far more critical than the mere losses due to failures. An in-depth analysis of accident causes would probably force OrbitalService to interrupt launching programmes.

Now, Mr Drajab needs to define the set-up and operating conditions of the potential captive. After going through this with the board, and after an analysis of the external companies' premiums, he decides to start his analysis with the following parameters:

- The initial capital of the captive cannot exceed €100m.
- The premium for covering one specific mission is €7m (in other words, the captive would be paid €7m for each covered mission).

Furthermore, Mr Drajab assumes that, whenever the captive's trading account is positive, it will be invested in the money markets. On the other hand, when it is negative, the captive has to refinance through loans.

We assume here, out of simplicity, that the captive can always refinance on money markets. In the case where a limit is set on the amount that can be borrowed, it can easily be taken into account and will be discussed later on.

Interest rates are assumed to be constant:

- The return of invested liquidity is 3 %.
- The cost of borrowing on the money market is 4 %.

Starting from these assumptions, Mr Drajab now needs to answer the following questions:

- How many failures can the captive hedge?
- What is the required initial capital in order *to be almost sure* that the captive would not be ruined (it can refinance its debt)?
- What are the risks transferred to the insurance company?

From a qualitative standpoint, it is clear that the number of hedged failures is related to the initial required capital: the higher the initial capital, the larger the number of hedged failures without being ruined. Mr Drajab therefore has to *optimize* the initial capital to make sure that the probability of being ruined is small enough. He has to do so within the imposed limits: the initial capital is constrained to be at the most €100m. Within these limits, increasing the number of hedged failures will thus increase the probability of being ruined.

It is time for Mr Drajab to formalize this financing problem and to quantify the identified relationships.

The captive is assumed to be ruined if its trading account is negative at the end of the 30 launches. The trading account is calculated as follows. At the beginning, the trading account is equal to the initial capital. The captive receives a €7m insurance prime per launch. If an incident occurs, the loss is deduced from the trading account. When the trading account is positive it is invested in the money markets. When it is negative, the captive has to borrow money.

Consider, for instance, that the number of failures the captive would hedge is set to two. If a mission fails, the financing option will depend on how many failures have already happened:

- If this is the first or second failure, then the captive would bear it.
- If this is the third, fourth, or fifth failure, then the external insurance company would bear it.

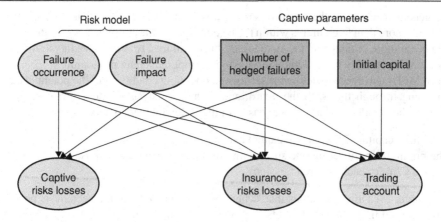

Figure 5.5   An influence diagram representing OrbitalService risk financing options

- Otherwise, the loss would not be hedged at all (remember this extremely unlikely situation has been ignored in our analysis).

The total losses either transferred to the external insurance company or retained by the captive are calculated as the sum of losses incurred over the 30 launches.

The quantification process will have three different outcomes:

- The total losses retained by the captive. This is clearly a random variable since it depends on the number of failures and on each individual failure loss impact.
- The total losses transferred to the insurance company. This is also a random variable for the same reasons previously explained.
- The trading account at the end of the 30 launches. Again, this is a random variable, depending both on the number of failures and on the cost of each failure.

These outcomes also depend on the number of failures hedged by the captive and its initial capital. *These two variables are the levers of the decision-making process.* Mr Drajab has to evaluate several alternatives for these two variables.

These relationships between random variables and decision variables can be represented on an influence diagram, as shown in Figure 5.5.

The calculation process described above is detailed in Table 5.3 and can also be implemented through an Excel spreadsheet.

In Chapter 3, we familiarized ourselves with this type of stochastic processes implementation. First, we have to create a "one-run" worksheet.

Now, in order to estimate the distributions of the target random variables, it is necessary to repeat the stochastic calculation above several times. In other words, it is necessary to implement a Monte Carlo simulation.

As for the examples presented in Chapter 3, this could very well be done using Excel. This would require implementing each simulation run on a single row (i.e. to "flatten" Table 5.3 onto a single row). Therefore, with 30 launches, each of them being defined by seven variables, a single row of the new Excel worksheet would be 210 cells wide.

Table 5.3 OrbitalService Excel formulas

Launch	Failure	Loss	No. of failures	Retained?	Retained loss	Transferred loss	Trading account
1	F1	L1	NF1	FR1	LR1	LT1	TA1
2	F2	L2	NF2	FR2	LR2	LT2	TA2
...	...	...	...	...	...	...	
30	F30	L30	NF30	FR30	LR30	LT30	TA30
TOTAL					**SUM(LRi)**	**SUM(LTi)**	**TA30**

F_i — IF RAND() < 1.5 % THEN $F_i = 1$ ELSE $F_i = 0$

L_i — IF $F_i = 0$ THEN $L_i = 0$ ELSE

(IF RAND() < 0.25 THEN $L_i = 100$ ELSE $L_i = $ RAND() * 100)

NF_i — NF1 = F1

$NF_i = NF_{i-1} + F_i$

FR_i — IF $NF_i < $ (# Hedged failures) THEN $FR_i = 1$ ELSE $FR_i = 0$

LR_i — $LR_i = FR_i * L_i$

LT_i — LTi = Li − LRi

TA_i — TA1 = InitialCapital + Premium − LR1

IF $TA_{i-1} > 0$ THEN $TA_i = TA_{i-1}*(1 + $ CreditRate$) + $ Premium $- LR_i$

ELSE $TA_i = TA_{i-1}*(1 + $ Interest rate for debt$) + $ Premium $- LR_i$

Finally, repeating this simulation 10 000 times would involve 2 100 000 cells. Although it is feasible to implement the Monte Carlo simulation this way, this would be very memory and time consuming.

A way to get through this problem is by creating a specific programme to implement the Monte Carlo simulation. This could be done, for instance, by using VBA (Visual Basic for Applications) within Excel. However, it is certainly easier, if possible, to use specific Monte Carlo simulation software. Several tools do exist for this purpose. For this specific application, we did use Excel add-in software – @Risk developed by Palisade Corp.

This software requires the user to:

- Specify how one scenario is sampled.
- Identify the "input" random variable cells.
- Identify the "output" random variable cells.

The user simply needs to describe the calculation process, exactly as in the case of creating the one-run worksheet above, and then needs to specify the probability distribution of each input random variable.

Returning to the OrbitalService spreadsheet, we will now implement @Risk formulas. As the simple one-run simulation worksheet, the @Risk spreadsheet implements the calculation process of loss, retained loss, transferred loss, and trading account for each of the 30 missions.

In the first column, each cell contains the mission index. Each of the cells in the second column contains a binary indicator of accident occurrence. This indicator is equal to 1 if and

	A	B	C	D	E	F	G	H	I	J
1		Launch scenario					OrbitalService Captive			
2										
3	Launch	Failure	Loss		No failures	Retained ?	Retained Loss	Trading Account		Transferred Loss
4	1	0	0		0	1	0	57		0
5	2	0	0		0	1	0	64		0
6	3	0	0		0	1	0	72		0
7	4	0	0		0	1	0	79		0
8	5	0	0		0	1	0	87		0
9	6	0	0		0	1	0	94		0
10	7	0	0		0	1	0	102		0
11	8	0	0		0	1	0	109		0
12	9	0	0		0	1	0	117		0
13	10	0	0		0	1	0	125		0
14	11	0	0		0	1	0	132		0
15	12	0	0		0	1	0	140		0
16	13	0	0		0	1	0	148		0
17	14	0	0		0	1	0	156		0
18	15	0	0		0	1	0	164		0
19	16	0	0		0	1	0	172		0
20	17	0	0		0	1	0	180		0
21	18	0	0		0	1	0	188		0
22	19	0	0		0	1	0	196		0
23	20	1	83		1	1	83.15619101	121		0
24	21	0	0		1	1	0	129		0
25	22	0	0		1	1	0	137		0
26	23	0	0		1	1	0	144		0
27	24	0	0		1	1	0	152		0
28	25	0	0		1	1	0	160		0
29	26	0	0		1	1	0	168		0
30	27	0	0		1	1	0	176		0
31	28	0	0		1	1	0	184		0
32	29	0	0		1	1	0	192		0
33	30	0	0		1	1	0	201		0
34	Total		83.15619101				83.15619101	201		0
35	OUTPUTS		83.15619101				83.15619101	201		0
36										
37	Prime per launch	7								
38	Interest rate (credit)	3%	0.60%							

Figure 5.6 OrbitalService Excel spreadsheet

Table 5.4   Example of @ Risk macro

Distribution	@Risk macro
Uniform	=RiskUniform(MIN,MAX)
Normal	=RiskNormal(MEAN,STD)
Lognormal	=RiskLognorm2(MEAN,STD)

only if an accident happens during the considered mission. As shown below on the influence diagram, each cell is an *input* random variable of the process.

Each cell in the third column contains the loss for the considered mission, if an accident should occur. This cell is distributed according to Table 5.1. Here again, each cell is an input random variable of the process. All other columns derive from these two columns and from the two decision variables: the initial capital and the number of hedged failures.

Creating an input random variable with @Risk simply involves entering a specific formula (see Table 5.4). For instance, creating the first column random variables – accident occurrence – is done simply by entering "=RiskBinomial(1,1.5%)" in the considered cell. For simple distribution, it is also possible to simply use built-in Excel macros: with the same purpose, the formula "=IF (RAND()<1.5%;1;0)" will do the job.

Now, defining an output random variable simply requires telling @Risk that a particular cell is being observed. This cell may be any cell: it may contain a formula involving any other cells or it may be an input random variable. This is simply done by adding to the cell expression RiskOutput(Name).

For example, the G35 cell contains the formula "=RiskOutput("RetainedLoss") + G34". This means that we want to observe the random variable defined in cell G34 and name it "RetainedLoss", Figure 5.7.

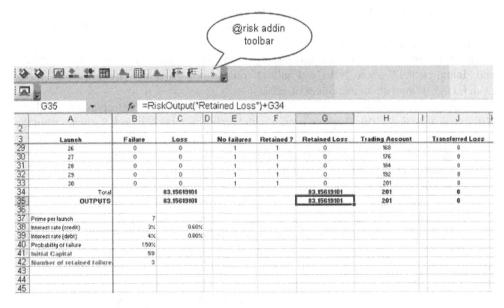

Figure 5.7   Risk addin toolbar

Table 5.5   Various simulations implemented

# Hedged failures	Initial capital	MC simulation runs	Trade account distribution
1	0	1 million	
1	€20m	1 million	
...			
1	€100m	1 million	
...			
4	0	1 million	
4	€20m	1 million	
...			
4	€100m	1 million	

Likewise, the H35 cell contains the formula "=RiskOutput("TradingAccount") + H34", and the J35 cell contains the formula "=RiskOutput("TransferredLoss") + J34".

Using such a spreadsheet, it becomes easy to calculate the distribution of risk losses retained by the captive, the distribution of risk losses transferred to the insurance company, and finally the distribution of captive trading account.

These distributions can be computed for several configurations of initial capital and of number of hedged failures.

Remember Mr Drajab is trying to adjust the initial capital to various risk retention levels. In other words, Mr Drajab will have to find an optimal initial capital to ensure the trading account of the captive will never end up being negative.

Here "never" is not the appropriate word. Assuming the captive trading account would actually *never* be negative, imposes the initial capital to be set up to the maximum loss possible, i.e. €100m for 1 loss hedged, €200m for 2 losses, and so on. Mr Drajab decides 0.1 % is a good probability limit: he will try to find the optimal capital in such a way that the captive has 99.9 % probability of not being ruined.

To reach this objective, Mr Drajab launches the simulations shown in Table 5.5 in order to fill the last column (probability of ruin).

This means that he generates 1 000 000 samples for each combination of "#Hedged failures" and "Initial capital", where "#Hedged failures" range from 1 to 4 and "Initial capital" varies from €0 to €100m with an increment of €20m.

The results are summarized in the influence diagram in Figure 5.8 representing all the different distributions. This diagram is built with Hugin Bayesian Network Software from the generated data and should be considered as a "Dynamic Report". Mr Drajab can use this tool in order to directly visualize and share the results of his potential decisions.

This presentation is more convenient than the mere @Risk report.

We first examine the TradingAccount variable.

In theory, this variable could be as low as −€3139m and as high as €348m.

The minimal value is reached when every launch is a failure and initial capital is €0m. The maximal value is reached when no failure occurs and initial capital is €100m. A maximal value is highly unlikely. Therefore the TradingAccount potential values have been distributed on seven equal sized intervals ranging from 0 to 350 million euros and an additional interval for negative values.

Let us assume Mr Drajab decides to create a captive with the following configuration: hedge one failure at the most and start with no initial capital. In this case, which is the one represented

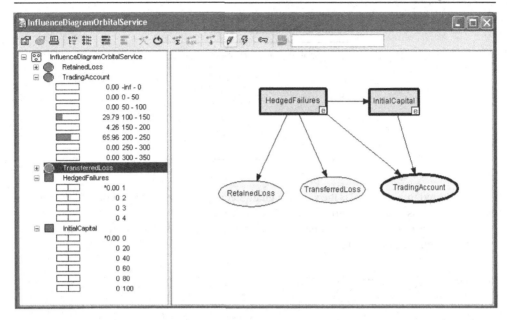

Figure 5.8 Summary influence diagram for OrbitalServices risk financing. Square nodes represent decision variables, oval nodes represent random variables. An asterisk (∗) is displayed close to the selected decision (in the picture above, the number of hedged failures is 1, and the initial capital is 0)

in the screen capture in Figure 5.8, the probability distribution of the trading account would be as shown in Table 5.6.

This means that the probability for the captive to be ruined – if the trading account at the end of the period is negative – is close to 0. Even a captive with a minimal capital can retain at least one failure!

What would be the optimal capital to be able to retain two failures? Selecting "2" for the decision node "HedgedFailures", and successively trying 0, 20, up to 100 for the initial capital in millions of euros, yields the data in Table 5.7.

Table 5.6 Probability distribution of the captive final trading account if hedging one failing with no initial capital

Interval (€m)	Probability
<0	0 %
0–50	0 %
50–100	0 %
100–150	29.79 %
150–200	4.26 %
200–250	65.96 %
250–300	0 %
300–350	0 %

Table 5.7 Probability of ruin when hedging at the most two failures

Initial capital (€m)	Probability of ruin
0	0.79 %
20	~0 %
40	~0 %
60	~0 %
80	~0 %
100	~0 %

The required initial capital is the smallest guaranteeing that the trading account of the captive would have a less than 0.1 % probability of being negative.

As shown in Figure 5.9, the probability that the captive is ruined if it hedges two failures without any initial capital is 0.79 %.

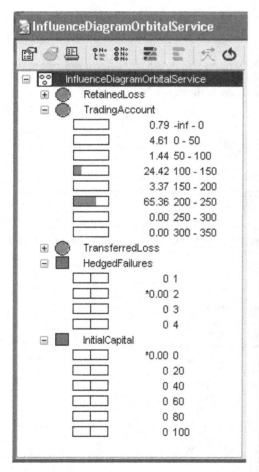 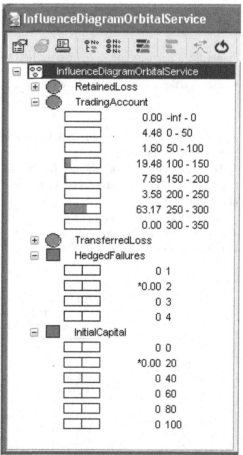

Figure 5.9 Summary influence diagram for OrbitalServices risk financing

Table 5.8 Initial capital required to be able to hedge one to four failures

Number of hedged failures	Required initial capital (€m)
1	0
2	20
3	>100
4	>100

This probability is higher than the confidence probability of 0.1 % specified by Mr drajab. Thus the initial capital must be increased in order to be able to hedge two failures.

By increasing the initial capital of €20m, it is possible to bring the probability to be ruined down to almost 0 %. Consequently, according to our analysis, the initial capital required to hedge two failures is about €20m.

Actually, the exact minimal capital would certainly be lower, but our model "resolution" (decomposition in 20 million euro intervals) does not allow us to be more accurate.

Now Mr Drajab simply needs to apply the same process to each number of failures he would consider to hedge (from 3 to 5), and find out the minimal required initial capital. The obtained results are summarized in Table 5.8.

In order to be able to hedge three or four mission failures with a probability of ruin below 0.1 % would require an initial capital higher than €100m, which is not acceptable according to the initial constraints.

Based on this analysis, it appears that:

1. It is rational to create a captive to retain at least one failure. Even with a minimal capital, it is close to certain that the final trading account of the captive will be highly positive.
2. Considering that OrbitalService is not willing to invest more than 100 million euros in the captive, it is not possible to hedge more than two failures with a satisfactory confidence.
3. The decision on whether to hedge one or two potential failures through the captive belongs to the OrbitalService board. This could be analyzed through usual return on investment criteria. By comparing Figure 5.8 and Figure 5.9, it is easy to see that these €20m invested would most likely generate an additional profit of €50m after five years. This could be further analyzed using financial criteria.

We will assume the OrbitalService board of directors has finally decided to invest 20 million euros in the captive and, hence, to retain two failures at the most.

Providing this situation, which part of the risks is being transferred to the insurance company? What are the expected losses the insurance company will have to hedge?

Once again, Mr drajab can use his dynamic report to check how the transferred losses are distributed. Distribution is directly read from the influence diagram and is described in the table in Figure 5.10.

Based on this table we are able to get a first estimate for the expected value of the transferred losses by averaging value of each interval weighted with its probability:

$$0.5 * 99\% + 25.5 * 0.11\% + \ldots + 550 * 0\% \approx €1.65m$$

Again, due to our model "resolution", this estimation is probably inaccurate. A more precise estimation could be found by averaging all transferred losses generated by the Monte Carlo

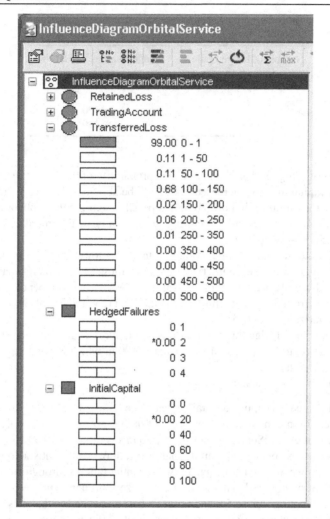

Figure 5.10   Distribution of transferred losses

simulation process given a number of hedged failures equal to 2 and an initial capital equal to €20 m. This method would yield a €0.95m estimation.

The external insurance company will have to hedge about €1m on average. But the probability for transferred losses to be greater than €100m is 0.77 % (this figure can be obtained from the table in Figure 5.10: 0.68 % + 0.02 % + 0.06 % + 0.01 %).

Furthermore the sample-based estimated standard deviation on transferred losses is about €10m (this is again empirically calculated from the table in Figure 5.10). These two figures are the main drivers for insurance prime calculus, and could help to negotiate with the insurance companies or insurance brokers.

Of course the insurance premium may take into account other factors, which we did not consider in our simple analysis. For instance, we assumed for our model that it is always possible for the captive to borrow money with a 4 % interest rate. This assumption may

Table 5.9   WWB property

Building type	Number	Exposure at risk
Local branch	2000	Infrastructure
Business centre	10	Infrastructure and information systems
HQ tower	1	Infrastructure and information systems

become unrealistic if the captive debt gets too high. In this case, interest rates would be higher than 4 % and the probability of ruin would increase. To estimate a realistic insurance prime would certainly require taking this risk into account.

This example illustrated how quantification of risks could help a risk manager to select a financing option and to get the base line figures to negotiate with insurance companies.

Quantification requires both a risk model and a formalization of the financing process. Monte Carlo simulation has been processed to generate potential losses, retained losses, transferred losses, or captive trading account and a Bayesian network (influence diagram) was built to summarize Monte Carlo simulation results.

Two software tools were used in this example to help the risk manager to deal with this problem.

Example 2: Defining a property insurance programme

We now present a simple example in order to illustrate how risk quantification can help a risk manager to select the appropriate features of an insurance programme for property.

Mrs Lareo is risk manager in an international banking group, WWB, and has to define an insurance programme for the bank's property. She focuses on the following types of events: fire, flood damage, explosion, and natural catastrophes. The considered property contains 2000 local branches, 10 business centres and one 100 storey tower where the headquarters are located (see Table 5.9). The geographical situation of the buildings is worldwide.

Mrs Lareo has outlined the framework of an insurance programme. Some quantitative features have to be fixed together with insurers or insurance brokers. But before dealing with them, Mrs Lareo would like to be aware of the right cost of transferred risks under several assumptions.

To meet these objectives, she has to model both the loss exposure she would like to insure and the insurance programme itself. Let us perform this analysis with her.

Exposure at risk consists of building infrastructures (walls, cabling for communication and energy, water, lifts, etc.) and in some cases of IT equipment (mainframes, servers, workstations, office computers, etc.). The IT equipment will be taken into account only for business centres but not for local branches, as the cost of equipment in branches is not significant. The HQ tower contains thousands of personal computers and houses some mainframes.

Those perils that are being studied are fire, flood damage, explosion and natural catastrophes. Among natural catastrophes Mrs Lareo is especially worried about earthquakes and hurricanes. Indeed two business centres are situated in Florida which is unfortunately regularly hit by hurricanes, and three business centres are situated in Japan where earthquake risks are high. The HQ tower stands in San Francisco Bay threatened by large magnitude earthquakes. Local branches are widespread all over the world, 20 % of them stand in a seismic area and 5 %

Table 5.10   perils on property

	Fire	Flood damage	Earthquake	Hurricane
Local branch (2000)	2000	2000	20 % 15% in California, 5 % in Japan	5 %
Business centre (10)	10	10	3	2
HQ tower (1)	1	1	1	0

stand in an area exposed to hurricanes. All buildings may be affected by fire or flood damage. A serious fire in the tower is particularly feared.

The Table 5.10 summarizes whether an event could happen on a given type of building and how many buildings may be affected in each case.

The probability that a building is affected by an event depends both on the type of building and the type of event. For example, in business centres and in the HQ tower, the electrical and network cabling is specifically designed to reduce the probability of a fire.

On the other hand, since the only method to avoid earthquakes is to stand in nonseismic areas, the probability of an earthquake does not depend on building type but rather on the seismic risk level of the area. Any local branch situated in the San Francisco area has the same probability of being damaged by an earthquake as does the tower. Whereas earthquake probability can be retrieved from statistics, fire probability should be evaluated using WWB security engineers' expertise. The same remark holds for hurricane probability. Climate and meteorology experts could provide statistics or forecasts to quantify the probability for a given area to be hit by a hurricane. Expertise is either external or internal to quantify the probability of a given peril (see Table 5.11 and Figure 5.11).

For fire and flood damage in local branches, probabilities will be estimated by empirical frequencies since these types of hazard occur rather frequently on the overall housing stock. Fire probability for business centres and the tower will be provided by engineers since the WWB has never experienced such events.

Probabilities for each event on each building are summarized in Table 5.12.

Flood damage is less likely in business centres (1 %) than in a local branch since local branches (5 %) are often situated on the ground floor of an inhabited building. Two types of earthquake have been considered here: medium magnitude earthquake (level 3–5 on Richter scale) and serious earthquake (higher than level 6 on Richter scale). The threshold level has

Table 5.11   Expertise source to quantify probability of event

	Expertise
Fire	Internal (engineer, hazards database) External (firemen, insurance company)
Flood damage	Internal (engineer, hazards database) External (firemen, insurance company)
Earthquake	External (geologists)
Hurricane	External (meteorologists)

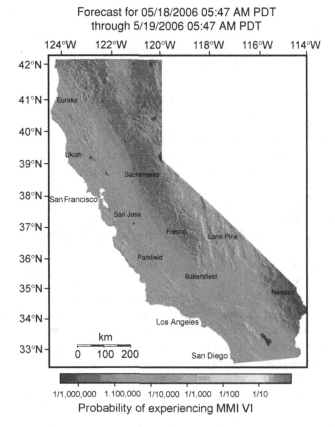

Figure 5.11 Example of external expertise source (US Geological Survey Earthquake Hazards Program: http://earthquake.usgs.gov/)

been selected to match the anti-seismic protection level. Both the tower and the business centres are protected against earthquakes of magnitude 3 to 5.

Impacts must be quantified for every building type and event type. Impact can be calculated as the product of the total building value (including information systems in the tower and business centres) by a damage factor. This damage factor is comprised of between 0 % and 100 % and depends both on the severity of the event and on specific protection measures. Damage factors cannot be known with certainty: they will be described as random variables.

Table 5.12 Event probabilities

	Fire	Flood damage	Earthquake	Hurricane
Local branch	2 %	5 %	1/50 for medium magnitude, 1/250 for serious earthquake	1/50
Business centre	1 %	1 %	—	—
Tower	1 %	1 %	—	—

Table 5.13 Building values

Building	Value
HQ tower	€1b
Business centre	€150–250m
Local branch	€150–250k

Total building values are summarized in Table 5.13.

The HQ tower value is estimated at €1b. Business centre estimated values are uniformly distributed between €150 and 250m. Local branch value is uniformly distributed between €150 and 250k.

Damage factors were obtained from internal and external experts and are given in Table 5.14. This table reads as follows.

There is an 80 % probability that a fire in a local branch will destroy less than 10 % of its value. This means that the loss due to a fire on a local branch would be less than €20k (10 % of an average value of €200k) in 80 % of cases. Similarly, this loss may be greater than €100k with 20 % of probability.

The tower is protected against earthquake with anti-seismic equipment. As a consequence, medium earthquakes will not affect it. For business centres, the situation is somewhat different. Anti-seismic equipment of those buildings being a little less efficient, we will consider that business centres may be damaged by a medium magnitude earthquake. The damage factor for medium earthquakes is at most 1 % which corresponds to a €2m loss for a €200m business centre.

Finally, the impact of a hurricane on a business centre is considered to be at most 0.01 % of its value.

All these data being gathered, Mrs Lareo is now able to design a risk model together with the WWB R&D department. Several submodels should be built. All perils may be considered to be independent. As a consequence, let us study the risk models for each peril.

All buildings are independent against the fire event or the flood damage event. For these two types of event, we can thus design one (exposure, occurrence, impact) model for each building type where the exposure is the number of buildings. We could also merge all these building-type-based models into a global model, by introducing the type of building as a causal factor for both occurrence and impact, Figure 5.12.

For earthquakes or hurricanes, we cannot assume any longer that buildings are independent given the peril. Indeed, when an earthquake hits a specific area, all buildings in this area may be affected. For these perils, the appropriate exposure is the number of geographical areas.

For the earthquake model, two areas will be considered: Japan and California. The probability for an earthquake is 1/50 for medium severity earthquakes and 1/250 for serious earthquakes (see Table 5.12). When an earthquake hits one of these areas, it affects all buildings in the area. In Japan, 100 local branches will be affected. In California 300 local branches, three business centres, and the HQ tower will be damaged.

The same type of model will suit for hurricanes. Only one region (Florida) is exposed to this risk for WWB. The probability for a severe hurricane to occur during one year is estimated at 1/50. If this happens, 10 local branches and two business centres will be damaged.

Mrs Lareo is now able to quantify WWB risks.

Table 5.14 Impact of various perils on different buildings

	Damage factor
Fire	
Local branch	[0 %,10 %] with 80 % probability
	[10 %,20 %] with 10 % probability
	[20 %,50 %] with 5 % probability
	[50 %,100 %] with 5 % probability
Business centre	[0 %,1 %] with 90 % probability
	[1 %,10 %] with 9 % probability
	[10 %,50 %] with 0.9 % probability
	[50 %,100 %] with 0.1 % probability
Tower	[0 %,1 %] with 99 % probability
	[1 %,2 %] with 0.9 % probability
	[2 %,100 %] with 0.1 % probability
Flood damage	
Local branch	[0 %,10 %] with 90 % probability
	[10 %,20 %] with 10 % probability
Business centre	[0 %,1 %] with 99 % probability
	[1 %,2 %] with 1 % probability
Tower	[0 %,0.01 %] with 100 % probability
Earthquake	
Local branch	Medium magnitude earthquake:
	[0 %,50 %] with 50 % probability
	[50 %,100 %] with 50 % probability
	Serious earthquake:
	[0 %,50 %] with 10 % probability
	[50 %,100 %] with 90 % probability
Business centre	Medium magnitude earthquake:
	[0 %,1 %] with 100 % probability
	Serious earthquake:
	[0 %,1 %] with 90 % probability
	[1 %,10 %] with 9 % probability
	[10 %,50 %] with 0.9 % probability
	[50 %,100 %] with 0.1 % probability
Tower	Medium magnitude earthquake:
	0 %
	Serious earthquake:
	0 % with 95 % probability
	[0 %,1 %] with 4 % probability
	[1 %,10 %] with 0.9 % probability
	[10 %,100 %] with 0.1 % probability
Hurricane	
Local branch	[0 %,10 %] with 80 % probability
	[10 %,50 %] with 20 % probability
Business centre	[0 %,0.01 %]
Tower	—

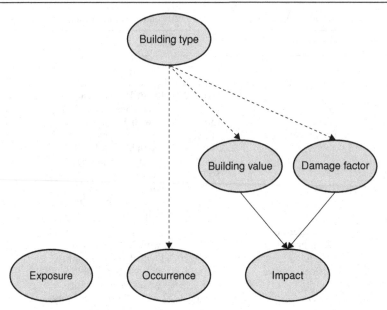

Figure 5.12   Detailed risk model for fire or flood damage event. The "Building type" node would be used for the global model where exposition includes tower, business centres and local branches

A financing programme for WWB had been designed some years ago. Mrs Lareo would like to update this programme and renegotiate insurance primes with her insurance broker, Erik Happyshark.

The financing tool which currently hedges WWB property against the perils mentioned above relies on the following principles. Two independent programmes have been designed, one for the local branches and business centres and the other for the tower. These programmes are illustrated in Figure 5.13.

For local branches, all losses under €0.100m are retained. Losses in excess of €0.100m and until €0.250m are retained by a WWB captive insurance company. Losses greater than €0.250 m are transferred to an insurance company.

For business centres, the same rules apply but losses are transferred as long as they are under €250m which is the maximal value for a business centre. An annual stop-loss of €750m is to be applied.

For the HQ tower, losses under €200m are retained in the captive whereas losses in excess of €250m and under €1b are transferred.

Let us consider some examples to understand how this financing tool works.

If a local branch is affected by a fire which impact is €0.050m, these €0.050k will be paid by WWB since they are under the excess limit (€0.100m). On the other hand, if damage due to fire is €0.175m, €0.100m will be retained by WWB and €0.075m will be transferred to the captive.

If one business centre is damaged by an earthquake which destroys 90 % of its €250m value, the €225m loss is financed as follows: €0.100m are retained, €0.150m are transferred to the captive, €224.750m are transferred to the insurance company.

If four business centres sustain the same losses, since a stop-loss of €750m is defined, only €75.750m will be transferred to the insurance company for the fourth centre. As a consequence

Table 5.15 How WWB financing programme works. An example

Loss	Retained under €0.1m	Captive	Insurance	Insurance capacity	Retained above stop-loss
				€750m	
€225m	€0.1m	€0.15m	€224.75m	€525.25m	0
€225m	€0.1m	€0.15m	€224.75m	€300.50m	0
€225m	€0.1m	€0.15m	€224.75m	€75.25m	0
€225m	€0.1m	€0.15m	€75.75m	0	€149m

€149m will be retained by WWB on top of the €0.400m. Table 5.15 details the computation process. Insurance capacity is the difference between the stop-loss (€750m) and the cumulative amount transferred to the insurance company.

Mrs Lareo has two main concerns. On the one hand, she thinks that a €100k excess for a local branch is too high. She would like to evaluate the impact of reducing this excess to

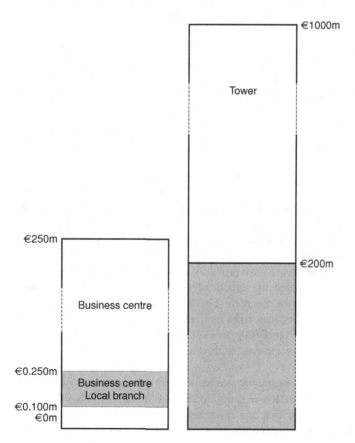

Figure 5.13 Two financing programmes for WWB property. A light grey rectangle means that risks are retained by WWB. A medium grey rectangle means that risks are transferred to a WWB captive insurance company. A white rectangle means that risks are transferred to an external insurance company

€10k. On the other hand, she would like to test the sensitivity of the transferred and retained risks to the HQ tower programme excess. This excess is currently €200m. What would be the transferred risks distribution if this excess was €100 or €150m?

To simplify the following analysis, stop-loss is ignored.

Both the risk models and the financing tool can be implemented within an Excel spreadsheet. The computation process for calculating annual global losses, losses retained, losses transferred to the captive insurer, and losses transferred to the insurance company is described in Table 5.16. This process must be applied for each peril.

From Mrs Lareo's point of view, this process has two inputs (excess for the first and second programmes) and four outputs (annual global losses, retained losses, captive losses, and insurance losses). A deep analysis has been conducted on both risk model and financing tools. This analysis helped Mrs Lareo to define a global input/output process whose purpose is to measure the impact of specific financing features on the cost of risks (retained and transferred).

Figure 5.14 shows an example of an Excel worksheet which implements the above process.

This calculation sheet allows Mrs Lareo to compute one year of losses. Since she wants to obtain the distribution of annual losses, she has to simulate many years of losses. Here again we use the Palisade Corp. software @Risk. First, we have to define the process outputs, using the RiskOutput() macro. This macro specifies which variable we want to sample in the worksheet (see Figure 5.15).

Then we are able to sample the process as many times as needed for given excess values.

As for the previous example, all results may be synthesized within an influence diagram. But here Mrs Lareo is mainly interested in two results: the expected annual loss and the standard deviation on annual loss. Instead of the standard deviation, the 95 % percentile will be considered as a measure of the uncertainty on annual loss.

For each couple of values for excess in the first and second programmes, the expected loss and 95 % percentile are presented in Table 5.17 (10 000 simulations have been run for each couple).

Let us discuss these figures. The first point is that neither expected values nor 95 % percentiles are sensitive to the excess of the second financing programme. This is due to the fact that a peril does not seriously damage the HQ tower (fire, flood damage) or it is rare (earthquakes). As a consequence HQ tower losses are much less than the excess of 100 million euros and therefore changing this excess has no impact on annual loss distribution. If perils threatening the HQ tower had either a greater probability to occur or a greater impact, then the excess on HQ tower programme would have probably great influence on annual loss distribution.

The second point is that the excess of the first programme has no influence on losses transferred to the insurance company. This is normal since changing this parameter has only impact on the balance between risks retained by WWB and risks transferred to the captive. Decreasing the excess from €100k to €15k (reduction factor is about 7) would reduce the retained losses by a factor approximately equal to 2 and increase the captive losses by a factor around 3.5.

A positive effect of reducing the excess of the first programme to 15 thousand euros is that the uncertainty on retained losses is divided by 3. Whereas the losses could fluctuate in a wide interval when excess is €100k and can reach about €9000k, these fluctuations are controlled and retained losses are more predictable.

From this analysis, Mrs Lareo could conclude that it is useless to decrease the excess for the HQ tower programme and that it may be interesting, in order to reduce Treasury fluctuations due retained losses, to decrease the excess of the first programme (local branches and business

Table 5.16 WWB Excel formulas

Building	Area	Value	Occurrence	Damage factor	Impact	Retained	Captive	Insurance
N1	A1	V1	O1	DF1	S1	R1	C1	I1
N2	A2	V2	O2	DF2	S2	R2	C2	I2
...	...	...	...	...	...	...		
TOTAL					=SUM(Si)	=SUM(Ri)	=SUM(Ci)	=SUM(Ii)

	INPUTS			OUTPUTS
Program #1 Excess	IN1		Retained	OUT1
Program #2 Excess	IN2		Captive	OUT2
			Insurance	OUT3
			Total	OUT4

Ni   Number of the building
Local branches are numbered from 1 to 2000
Business centres are numbered from 1 to 10
Tower is numbered 1

Ai   Geographical area of the building
Can take the values: California, Florida, Japan, other

Vi   Value of the building
- Local branch: uniform distribution[5] {150–250}
- Business centre: uniform distribution {150 000–250 000}
- Tower: Constant 1 000 000

Oi   Occurrence of the considered peril
- Fire: binomial distribution[6]
  - Local branch: 2 %
  - Business centre: 1 %
  - Tower: 1 %
- Flood damage: binomial distribution
  - Local branch: 5 %
  - Business centre: 1 %
  - Tower: 1 %
- Earthquake: all buildings in the same area (California or Japan) share the same value for the occurrence. In such an area, this occurrence follows a binomial distribution which depends on the severity of the earthquake.
  - Medium magnitude earthquake: 2 %
  - High magnitude earthquake: 0.4 %
- Hurricane: all buildings in the same area (Florida) share the same value for the occurrence. In such an area, this occurrence follows a binomial distribution with probability 2 %.

DFi   Damage factor follows a histogram-based distribution[7] detailed in the Table 5.14.

Si   If $Oi = 0$ then $Si = 0$
Else $Si = DFi * Vi$

Ri   For local branches and business centres covered by the first programme:
If $Si < IN1$ then $Ri = Si$
Else $Ri = IN1$
For the tower covered by the second programme:
If $Si < IN2$ then $Ri = Si$
Else $Ri = IN2$

Table 5.16 (*Continued*)

Ci	For local branches and business centres covered by the first programme:
	If Si < IN1 then Ci = 0
	Else Ci = MIN(Si-IN1, 250)
	For the tower covered by the second programme no captive is involved:
	Ci = 0
Ii	Ii = Si − Ri − Ci
IN1	Excess of the first programme. Can take two values: 15 and 100
IN2	Excess of the second programme. Can take three values: 100 000, 150 000, 200 000
OUT1	Annual retained loss for all perils
OUT2	Annual captive loss for all perils
OUT3	Annual insurance loss for all perils
OUT4	Annual total loss for all perils

centres) to 15 thousand euros. She also has some basic figures to calculate the impact of such a decision on the captive risk prime. She now feels ready to start the negotiation with Mr Happyshark.

This example illustrated how accurate knowledge and quantification of risks can help the risk manager to evaluate a financing programme and to identify the improvement drivers. To compute the right cost of the risks, Mrs Lareo will also need to take insurance and captive premiums into account. But this first quantitative analysis gave her some keys to understand how she could improve her current financing programme.

A tentative general representation of financing methods

Introduction

The examples presented above illustrate how quantification could help the risk manager to select or specify a set of financing solutions, to be aware of which risks are retained, and which risks are transferred, as well as to evaluate the global cost of risk.

We would now like to propose some guidelines to assemble several financing methods and to combine them within the general modelling framework which has been described in Chapter 3.

Table 5.17 Annual losses distribution parameters (expected value – 95 % percentile) for retained losses, losses transferred to the captive insurer, and losses transferred to the insurance company

Excess1	Excess2	Retained	Captive	Insurance	Total
€15k	€100 000k	1622–2787	2489–3320	414–1745	4525–12 424
€15k	€150 000k	1599–2736	2370–3183	375–1731	4345–11 778
€15k	€200 000k	1610–2726	2452–3342	399–1751	4461–12 319
€100k	€100 000k	3373–8127	714–995	401–1787	4488–12 288
€100k	€150 000k	3382–9144	714–1048	437–1715	4533–12 436
€100K	€200 000k	3384–8899	713–1019	457–1798	4555–12 434

	Building	Area	Value	Occurrence	RAND1	RAND2	Damage Factor	FIRE Impact	Retained	Captive	Insurance
1											
2											
1997	1995	Other	239	0	0.92	0.00	20.82%	0.00	0.00	0.00	0.00
1998	1996	Other	177	0	0.42	0.36	3.61%	0.00	0.00	0.00	0.00
1999	1997	Other	247	0	0.73	0.34	3.44%	0.00	0.00	0.00	0.00
2000	1998	Other	235	0	0.55	0.55	5.46%	0.00	0.00	0.00	0.00
2001	1999	Other	222	0	0.80	0.88	8.81%	0.00	0.00	0.00	0.00
2002	2000	Other	228	0	0.75	0.07	0.70%	0.00	0.00	0.00	0.00
2003 Business center	1	California	157489	0	0.28	0.96	0.96%	0.00	0.00	0.00	0.00
2004	2	California	158358	0	0.54	0.96	0.96%	0.00	0.00	0.00	0.00
2005	3	California	210109	0	0.69	0.81	0.81%	0.00	0.00	0.00	0.00
2006	4	Florida	242916	0	0.67	0.85	0.85%	0.00	0.00	0.00	0.00
2007	5	Florida	203585	0	0.26	0.31	0.31%	0.00	0.00	0.00	0.00
2008	6	Other	190812	0	0.96	0.57	6.12%	0.00	0.00	0.00	0.00
2009	7	Other	165110	0	0.81	0.10	0.10%	0.00	0.00	0.00	0.00
2010	8	Other	228351	0	0.63	0.72	0.72%	0.00	0.00	0.00	0.00
2011	9	Other	202137	0	0.13	0.08	0.08%	0.00	0.00	0.00	0.00
2012	10	Other	210212	0	0.80	0.34	0.34%	0.00	0.00	0.00	0.00
2013 Tower	1	California	1000000	0	0.57	0.48	0.48%	0.00	0.00	0.00	0.00
2014											
2015 TOTAL								887.44	418.20	469.24	0.00
2016											
2017											
2018 **Inputs**			**Outputs**								
2019 **Financing tool features**			**Annual losses**								
2020											
2021 **Program #1**			Retained	1434.32							
2022 Excess	15		Captive insurer	1812.32							
2023 Captive insurer max	250		Insurance company	0.00							
2024 Insurer max	250000		Total	3246.64							
2025											
2026											
2027 **Program #2**											
2028 Excess	150000										
2029 Insurer max	1000000										

Figure 5.14 WWB simulation process for risks and financing tools

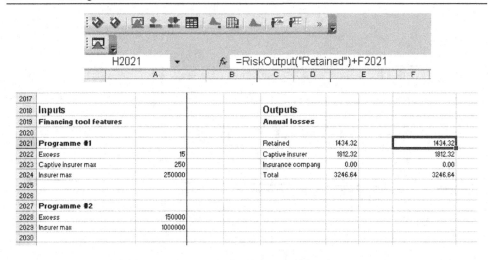

Figure 5.15 MonteCarlo sampling of annual losses with @Risk software. In this example we use the formula =RiskOutput("Retained") +F2021 to specify that the variable to be sampled will be named "Retained" and is to be retrieved from F2021 cell

Ultimately, the targeted objective is to calculate the cost of risk financing given the constraints of the organization. Since risk financing always combines retention and transfer, the cost of risk is the summation of the retention cost and the transfer cost.

The retention cost mainly includes those losses that are being retained and the financial profits that could be generated by investing funds dedicated to loss coverage.

The transfer cost includes insurance premiums or any specific due cost when not transferring to an insurer (structural fees for a captive, for example).

The cost of risk cannot be known with certainty. It is random since it depends both on financing method specification and potential losses. By applying a financing method to potential losses, an organization is able to estimate the distribution of potential losses that are transferred or retained as well as the distribution of potential costs.

Modelling potential losses has already been extensively discussed in Chapters 2 and 3. Modelling the process introduced above involves that the financing method is simply formalized.

A financing tool can be characterized by cost features (premiums, etc.) and hedging features.

Cost features can be very difficult to handle in a general model. For example, cost features for retro-tariff insurance can be very different from cost features for a cat bond. Furthermore, cost features are not useful to quantify transferred risks or retained risks, these are only involved in the calculation of the cost of risk.

On the other hand, the hedging features of the financing method condition both transferred and retained risk distributions. Dependencies between financing tools, risk losses, retained risk losses, transferred risk losses, and cost of risk can be summarized in the abstract influence diagram in Figure 5.16.

Risk financing building blocks

We will now explain how to build such a diagram by introducing a simple model for financing methods. This model, even if representative of a wide range of methods, may be oversimplistic

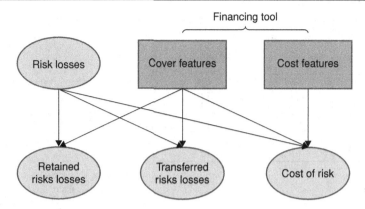

Figure 5.16   General influence diagram for risk financing

in special cases of risk financing. Its main purpose is to demonstrate that Monte Carlo simulation and Bayesian networks (influence diagrams) are the suitable tools to quantify risk financing solutions.

Whatever the complexity of a risk financing solution, we can consider it as a combination of basic covers. Let us first give a description of these building blocks for risk financing, and then show how they can be combined in order to build more classical financing tools.

The set of features of one particular building block are listed below:

- Definition of the covered peril.
- Cover definition.
- Start-loss (STL): cover in excess of. First euro to be covered per occurrence.
- Stop-loss (SPL): amount covered. The last euro covered is the summation of Start-loss and stop-loss.
- Excess (EXL): excess each and any occurrence.
- Fraction of loss (FOL): percentage of the amount covered.
- Start cumulative loss (STC): aggregate cover. First euro to be covered cumulatively.
- Stop cumulative loss (SPC): aggregate cover. The last cumulative euro to be covered is the summation of start cumulative loss and stop cumulative loss.
- Start number of occurrences (STO): first occurrence to be covered.
- Stop number of occurrences (SPO): maximum number of claims covered. The last occurrence to be covered is the summation of start number of occurrences and stop number of occurrences.

Cover definition identifies which object is covered. *Start-loss*, *Stop-loss*, *Excess* and *Fraction of loss* define the "slice" of loss impact which is covered. The *Start cumulative loss* and *Stop cumulative loss* specify limits on the cumulative loss. The *Start number of occurrences* and the *Stop number of occurrences* define a "slice" of loss frequency.

A euro is covered if it falls into the slice defined by the parameters. This elementary cover is defined by applying a conjunction operator (AND) to the defined parameters.

Figure 5.17 shows an instance of this elementary risk financing unit.

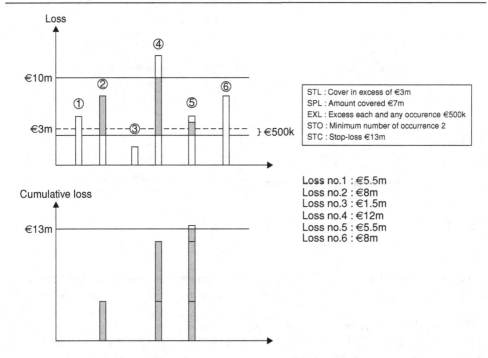

Figure 5.17 Elementary financing tool. Grey rectangles represent covered losses whereas white rectangles represent uncovered losses

This tool covers organization losses in excess of €3 and covers at most €7. An excess is applied to each occurrence whose amount is €500 000. Moreover, the first occurrence is not covered and a cumulative stop-loss of 13 million euros is applied.

The *first loss* is not covered.

The *second loss*, whose amount is €8m , is covered in excess of €3m. Therefore, only €5m are covered. Cumulative covered losses after the second occurrence sum up to €5m.

The *third loss* is less than €3m and is therefore not covered.

The *fourth loss* amounts €12m. The slice between €3m and €10m of this loss is covered. The rest is retained by the organization. Cumulative covered losses after the fourth occurrence sum up to €12m.

The *fifth loss* is €5.5m. Normally the slice in excess of €3m (€2.5m) should be covered, but the stop-loss of €13m is reached as soon as €1m has been covered for this loss. Then, only €1m is actually covered for that loss.

For each of the occurrences nos2, nos4, and nos5, an excess of €500 000 must be paid by the organization.

An elementary cover may be represented in a three-dimensional space which dimensions are the number of loss occurrences, the loss impact, and the cumulative loss, Figure 5.18. In such a space, the cover is represented by the volume delimited by a rectangle parallelepiped.

Those euros that are inside the dark grey volume are partly covered whereas euros that are outside must be retained by the organization or dealt with another tool.

Mathematically speaking the elementary cover can be specified as follows. For any selected euro in a given loss, let L denote the amount of euros under the selected euro, let C denote

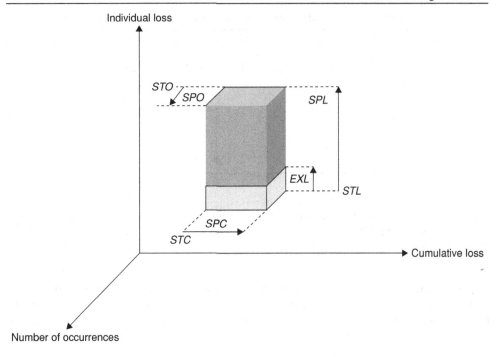

Figure 5.18   3D representation of an elementary cover

the cumulated covered euros before the selected euro, and finally let O denote the number of losses occurrences, starting from the beginning of the cover period. Then the considered euro is covered if and only if the three conditions below hold simultaneously:

$$STL + EXL \leq L \leq STL + SPL$$
$$STC \leq C \leq STC + SPC$$
$$STO \leq O \leq STO + SPO$$

In this case, the specified fraction of the considered euro (FOL) is covered. Otherwise this particular euro is not covered.

In this visual representation, building an efficient financing tool can be interpreted as positioning some elementary blocks in an appropriate way.

Usual financing tools revisited

Let us discuss how classical financing tools may be described using these building blocks.

- Retention (self-insurance and informal retention)
- First line insurance
- Excess insurance
- Retro-tariff insurance
- Captive insurer
- ART (cat bonds)

Table 5.18   Informal retention cover features

Parameter	Value	Comment
STL	Infinity	Every loss is retained. Nothing is transferred
SPL	—	
EXL	—	
FOL	—	
STC	—	
SPC	—	
STO	—	
SPO	—	

Informal retention   Informal retention is the "minimal" method to finance risks. Losses are paid when they occur. This kind of programme can be described by the instance of the model shown in Table 5.18.

Self-insurance   Self-insurance is very similar to informal retention. The main difference stems from the fact that self-insurance is a formal process set by the organization to handle losses. Therefore, there is a difference for the cost features but not the cover features.

First line insurance   First line insurance covers an organization between the first euro and a maximum amount. An excess can be applied on each occurrence. Table 5.19 describes an example of a product liability insurance, which covers losses for a maximum amount of €1m with a stop-loss of €10m, with an excess per occurrence of €100 000.

Excess insurance   Excess insurance covers an organization for losses that could occur, in excess of a given amount. Generally speaking, they are used on top of a first line insurance. Table 5.20 represents an excess insurance built on top of the previous one to cover liability losses for an amount of €5m in excess of €1m. No excess per occurrence is defined and a stop-loss of €50m is set.

Table 5.19   First line insurance cover features

Parameter	Value	Comment
STL	0	The first ero is covered
SPL	€1m	Losses between €0 and €1m are covered
EXL	€100k	€100 000 are retained for each event
FOL	100 %	
STC	—	
SPC	€10m	If cumulative loss exceeds €10m, losses are not covered any more
STO	—	
SPO	—	

Table 5.20   Excess insurance cover features

Parameter	Value	Comment
STL	€1m	Losses under €1m are retained
SPL	€5m	Losses between €1m and €6m (1 + 5) are covered
EXL	0€	
FOL	100 %	
STC	—	
SPC	€50m	If cumulative loss exceeds €50m, losses are not covered any more
STO	—	
SPO	—	

Retro-tariff insurance   Retro-tariff insurance aims to cover both individual losses and cumulative losses in excess. The organization retains losses that are under a limit per event and as long as its cumulative retained losses remains under a cumulative limit.

The organization has to pay a fixed prime for transferred losses (above the limit per event) and a loss adjusted prime for losses under the limit. This is why losses under the limit can be considered as retained.

Retro-tariff insurance cannot be represented with a single block since its space representation is not a rectangle any more but the union of two rectangles: a euro is covered if it lies between a minimal and a maximal individual loss *or* if it lies above a minimal cumulative loss.

In Tables 5.21 and 5.22, we present a retro-tariff insurance with a limit per event of €100 000, an amount covered of €1m, and a limit on cumulative losses of €5m. The insurance is obtained by combining through ensemble reunion an excess insurance block and a specific block which starts covering losses when a cumulative loss of €5m is reached, Figure 5.19.

Captive insurer   From the organization's point of view, a captive insurer can be modelled as any of the insurance tools.

Therefore we will change our perspective and study a financial tool used by captive insurers or classical insurers in order to cover their own losses: reinsurance. We will focus on quota-share reinsurance.

Table 5.21   Retro-tariff insurance – block 1

Parameter	Value	Comment
STL	€100k	Losses under €100 000 are retained
SPL	€1m	Losses between €100 000 and €1.1m(€100k + €1m) are covered
EXL	€0	
FOL	100 %	
STC	—	
SPC	—	
STO	—	
SPO	—	

Table 5.22 Retro-tariff insurance – block 2

Parameter	Value	Comment
STL	—	
SPL	—	
EXL	—	
FOL	100 %	
STC	€5m	As soon as cumulative loss exceeds €5m, losses are covered
SPC	—	
STO	—	
SPO	—	

Up to now, we considered that either a euro was covered or it was retained. With quota-share reinsurance, this rule does not hold any longer: a euro may be only partly covered.

When an insurer transfers his own risks to a reinsurer within the framework of a quota-share programme, the fraction of transferred losses is equal to the fraction of the premium paid to the reinsurer.

For example, if the reinsurer received 75 % of the risk prime paid by the insurer client, he will also have to pay 75 % of the losses: on a €1 loss, the insurer will retain 25 cents and transfer 75 cents to the reinsurer.

Table 5.23 represents a reinsurance quota-share programme which covers the insurer for 75 % of losses that could incur from the excess insurance tool described above. The cover definition includes all losses that are transferred by the organization to the insurer. Losses are being considered from the insurer's point of view.

Alternative risk transfer   Alternative risk transfer (ART) tools might be as complex as desired according to the organization objectives. A multi-stage process based on captive, reinsurance,

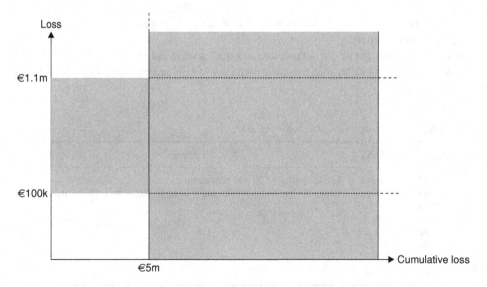

Figure 5.19 Retro-tariff insurance as a combination of two building blocks. The grey area is covered

Table 5.23 Quota share reinsurance

Parameter	Value	Comment
STL	€0m	From the insurer's point of view, a loss is covered as soon as it occurs
SPL	—	Limit is not defined here. But we know from the cover definition that losses should not exceed €6m
EXL	€0	
FOL	75 %	75 % of the loss is covered
STC	—	
SPC	—	
STO	—	
SPO	—	

and financial products might be necessary to meet coverage requirements. Besides the classical insurance tools, ART relies on financial markets to transfer some special risks (cat nat, market-based risks, etc.). Most of the used financial tools are cat bonds and insurance derivatives. Whatever the underlying technical difficulties may be to implement these tools, they transfer the risks from the organization to the financial market instead of an insurer. Cat bonds, swaps, and insurance options can be modelled as standard insurance.

Combining a risk model and a financing model

The model discussed above for an elementary financing block can be used to represent a large set of classical financing solutions. Representing more complex financing solutions involves combining several elementary blocks in order to cover the possible losses in the most appropriate way.

A financing solution may be considered as a set of elementary blocks which aims at covering the potential losses without forgetting some "holes". As a consequence, blocks will generally depend on each other. For example, if we want to build a two-layered insurance with an excess insurance on top of a first line insurance, the excess of the excess insurance should be equal to the amount covered by the first line insurance, Figure 5.20.

To decide whether a euro is covered by any of the elementary blocks involved in the financing tool being studied, we have to scan each of the elementary blocks in a given order and stop whenever the considered euro satisfies the cover conditions.

A financing tool can be thus considered as an ordered set of elementary covers. If we return to the above example, we have two elementary covers numbered 1 for the first line and 2 for the excess line.

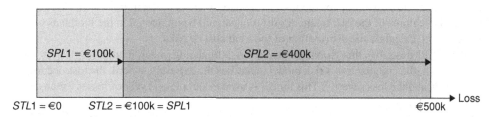

Figure 5.20 Amount covered by the first line is the excess of the excess insurance

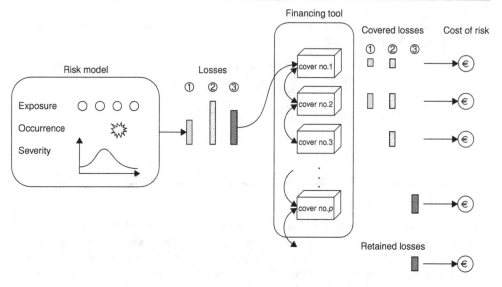

Figure 5.21 A general Monte Carlo simulation framework for risk financing

If we assume that an event meets the cover definition, the process of deciding whether a euro is covered must be done as follows:

1. Check whether this euro is between 0 and 100 000: If the answer is "yes", then stop: this euro is covered by the first line insurance. Otherwise, proceed to the next block.
2. Check whether this euro is between 100 000 and 500 000:
   If the answer is "yes", then stop: this euro is covered by the excess insurance.
   Otherwise, proceed to the next block.
3. This euro is retained by the organization.

In real life, some overlaps may exist between different covers. In order to simplify our discussion, we will assume that elementary covers do not overlap.

For a given financing tool, let us assume that this tool can be described as a combination of interdependent elementary building blocks. Then it is possible for any euro of a given loss to decide whether this euro is covered, and it is possible to identify which building block was activated for this coverage.

This method for dispatching loss euros must be implemented as part of the loss model, in order to be able to compute (1) the distribution of losses covered by each elementary financing block, and (2) the distribution of the losses retained by the organization.

The cost features of the risk financing solution should be integrated in the model as well, if one wishes to calculate the distribution of the total cost of risks.

Figure 5.21 describes this global process for risk financing quantification.

On the left, the organization's risk model quantifies the exposure at peril, the loss occurrence probability, and the loss severity. This model is used to sample one year of losses (or any other period of time).

Each loss is characterized by the object that has been hit, the sequence number of the occurrence from the beginning of the considered period of time, and the loss severity.

For each loss, its amount will be sent through the "dispatching rules" of the financing solution in place. Each elementary cover will keep track of the cumulated covered losses and calculate the cost of risks according to its cost features. When cost features are not defined at the level of an elementary cover, cost is calculated at the level of its parent cover (the cover it is part of).

By applying this process several times, i.e. through Monte Carlo simulation, we sample several years of risks of the considered organization. This allows us to calculate the distributions of cumulated losses, covered losses, retained losses, and risk costs.

The inputs of this process are:

- Exposure, occurrence and severity distributions for each risk being considered.
- Cover features and cost features for the elementary blocks of the chosen financing solution.

The outputs of this process are:

- Distribution of cumulated retained losses.
- Distribution of cumulated transferred losses dispatched over each cover
- Distribution of cost of risks.

Such a process can be summarized by an influence diagram (see Figure 5.22) where:

- Decision nodes are cover features and cost features for the financing tools.
- Input distribution nodes are the exposure, the occurrence, and the loss impact of the considered risks (risk model).
- Output distribution nodes are cumulated retained losses, cumulated transferred losses, and cost of risks.

This influence diagram represents a particular implementation of the general influence diagram introduced in Figure 5.21.

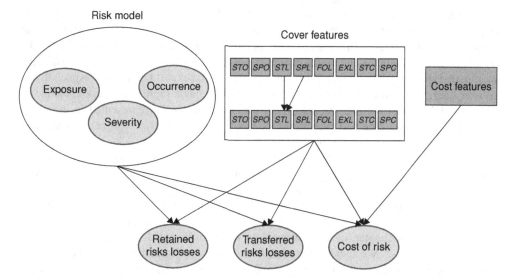

Figure 5.22   The influence diagram for risk financing. This diagram is based on exposure, occurrence, severity risk model(s) and on the decomposition of the financing solution into elementary covers. The cover features have to satisfy some constraints to account for dependency among elementary covers

If we modify the cover features or the cost features of the financing solution, all the output distributions will be impacted.

We can hence compare several financing solutions by playing with decision nodes.

The risk model is based on exposure, occurrence, severity framework which was previously introduced in Chapter 3, but it could be replaced by any available risk model developed by the organization provided that this model works at the level of individual losses and not only at the level of aggregate losses. This constraint on risk model stems from the fact that financing tools generally specify limits on individual event losses, as was shown before.

CONCLUSION

In the two previous chapters, we have studied why risk quantification is useful for risk diagnostic and risk control. These two steps of the risk management process involve an accurate knowledge of the risks an organization has to face and of the levers it could use to control risks. For these steps, although extremely useful, quantification is not always mandatory: under certain circumstances, an organization can still rely on qualitative assessment to identify and control its risks.

For risk financing, qualitative assessment is definitely not adequate to deal with calculating premiums, losses, volatility, etc. An accurate quantification of risks is necessary for a rational risk financing.

Several reasons require the risk manager to address the quantification of its risks.

At first, an organization should know if its financing programme is well suited for the perils it has to face. Financing programme features must be linked to the distribution of potential losses that have to be covered. The questions are: "Is the organization protected against severe losses?" and "Are retained risks mastered so as to reduce their volatility and their maximal level?" Answers to these questions cannot be based on qualitative assessment of risks. Quantitative risk models are the basic tools to run an efficient analysis of this issue.

Second, when an organization has to negotiate with insurers or insurance brokers, it has to be aware of the risks it wants to transfer and more precisely of the distribution of the potential losses that could be transferred. This quantitative assessment of risks should allow the organization to evaluate the theoretical insurance primes. On their side, insurers rely on internal quantitative models generally based on actuary studies or on expert knowledge (especially for disaster scenarios). However, the organization generally has a more accurate knowledge of its own risks, at least for exceptional events which would not be represented in insurance companies' databases. The best situation is found when both insurers and organizations share their knowledge to build an accurate model of risks.

Third, the optimization of an existing financing programme or the design and selection of a new one requires building quantitative models. In the first case, the quantitative model will help to identify the key financing features required to improve the organization's coverage. In the second case, plugging the different financing alternatives with the risk model will give the organization a clear view of the risks it would have to retain and transfer.

As shown in this chapter, modelling the risks is not sufficient if we want to address the objectives listed above. We also have to model the financing programme. We have proposed a general framework where any financing programme can be considered as a set of elementary financing blocks and we have proposed a model for this elementary financing block. This model is suited to a range of classical financing tools – self-insurance and informal retention, first line insurance, excess insurance, retro-tariff insurance, captive insurer, cat bonds – but it might be insufficient or should be adapted to take into account some complex financing set-up. But the more complex the financing programme seems to be, the more the organization should try to catch this complexity inside a model.

But even if an organization did its best and built an accurate model of risks and financing tools, even if it is able to evaluate the theoretical premium it should pay, the market will decide the actual price the organization should pay to transfer its risks. This market may be unbalanced for some special risks. When the insurance offer is unavailable, actual premiums could be very different from theoretical primes calculated by models. Does this argument invalidate the need for accurate quantification of risks? No for at least two reasons: first, even if the final cost of transfer depends on the insurance market, the organization should be aware of that fact and should know the price it has to pay because of the insufficient liquidity on the market. Second, the liquidity of the insurance markets is likely to increase as they get connected to the capital markets. The efficiency of these markets lets us expect that the price to be paid for risk transfer will tend to be the "right" one.

Index

Printed in the United States
By Bookmasters